Effective Strategies for Rural Development

Effective Strategies for Rural Development

Dr. E.D. SETTY

AKANSHA PUBLISHING HOUSE
NEW DELHI-110002 (INDIA)

AKANSHA PUBLISHING HOUSE
4649-B/21, Ansari Road
Darya Ganj, New Delhi - 110 002
Ph.: 23263193 / 9811582579 / 09435116718
Fax: 011-23263193
Email: ektabooks@yahoo.com

Effective Strategies for Rural Development

First Published 2008
ISBN–978–81–8370–150–1

PRINTED IN INDIA

Published by Akansha Publishing House, New Delhi and Printed at Aryan Enterprises, Delhi.

CONTENTS

FOREWORD

Development is a never ending process. It is a long journey and one cannot visualize the end of the development especially in rural communities in view of their backwardness in several dimensions of meaningful and acceptable way of life. The principal objective of Rural Development is to rebuild the villages as self-sufficient units for fulfilling basic wants of life, such as balanced nutritious food to all the members in the family, health and educational facilities, civic amenities as well as dependable transport and communication infrastructure. These may be called as minimal requirements of people for a meaningful and decent life.

It may be emphasized that all aspects of rural life are inextricable, interconnected and individual items cannot be dealt with in isolation. It is only by this ideal of bringing about an appreciable improvement in the standards of rural life and making it fuller and wider ensuring that the energies of the entire development machinery is fully utilized; thus awakening mass enthusiasm and enlisting the active interest and support of millions of rural families.

Some rural development efforts in terms of political overtones, economic objectives, organizational process, plan formulation and programme implementation are a new kind of experience for the people and the development agencies. We are in the process of finding, learning, new and better ways of doing things. There is always a need to look back and take stock of things, so that we can have a clearer perspective of the situation, avoid the pitfalls, overcome the barriers and discover effective approaches and alternatives towards substantial and sustained development in rural areas.

Though there are several publications on rural development during the past 50 years, the contribution of Dr. E.D. Setty is quite timely which looks into the basic psychology of development taking into account the people to be developed and the personnel who are entrusted with the amelioration of conditions in rural communities. With his extensive background over the past five decades as a field level extension functionary, researcher, professor and consultant in the field of rural development, he has brought out his tested and distilled experience in terms of viable and dependable approaches to rural development. He speaks with conviction. I recommend this book to field extension functionaries, administrators, planners and faculty and students in teaching and training institutions. I congratulate Dr. Setty for the efforts he has made in bringing out this volume.

P.V.R.K. PRASAD, IAS
Former Director General,
Dr. MCR HRD Institute of AP &
Ex-Officio Special Chief Secretary
to Govt. of Andhra Pradesh

PREFACE

If one goes around the villages in India he could witness the stages and the conditions in which several segments of the population live today. Owing to historical reasons more especially of the foreign colonial administration and diverse princely states ruling for some centuries, to a greater extent the villages have been neglected entities in terms of minimal humane standards of living. The problems are multifarious and the needs are enormous. With all commitment, sincerity and attention, the state has been attempting to improve the conditions of living in rural communities for the past fifty years in terms of planned and organized development. Since the problem is so vast and the machinery of development is not properly tuned across the entire chain and in spite of good intensions, owing to laxity in terms of realistic assessment of the problems, needs and resources, we have not been able to achieve development as we visualized. One may point out several lapses. In a way, the development efforts have been something like broadcasting of seed without paying detailed attention to certain segments of population and sectors of development. Though there have been ethnic-wise, class-wise programmes, either owing to lack of resources on the part of the government and initiative and response from the people, who are still moving rather slowly with halting paces in the march towards development. Examining the way in which we have been working all these years, one realizes what is needed today is what we may call a clinical approach to rural development. The present volume based on the extensive field experience of the author discusses the clinical approach to rural development. It may be mentioned that some of the aspects discussed in this volume are not new but unfortunately, attention has not been paid to some of the strategies and methods of development. These are some of the missing links in what has gone on so far. As a kind of a remedial measure, the chapters that are contained in this volume focus on and highlight the importance of these missing links and the way to go about making rural development a successful endeavour with tangible results.

We may briefly mention the aspects discussed in different chapters. Chapter - 1 briefly provides the historical background to community/rural development in India beginning with Sriniketan of Dr. Rabindranath Tagore 1921 followed by Royal Commission on Agriculture 1926, Gurgaon of F.L. Brayne 1927, Marthandam of Spencer Hatch 1928, Sevegram of Mahatma Gandhi 1931, The Baroda Plan of Sir V.T. Krishnamachari 1933, Grow more food campaign 1942, Firka development scheme 1946, Mahewa of pilot project 1948, Nilokheri of S.K. Dey 1949, India village service, Fiscal commission under Sir V.T. Krishnamachari in 1949, the constitution of Indian Republic 1950, Grow more food enquiry committee – 1952 and launching of community development programme in 1952. As mentioned above chapter – 1 briefly describes the initiatives taken, attempts made towards village development.

Chapter 2 highlights the lessons to be learnt from the earlier effords towards Rural Development.

We may consider chapter 3 on programme planning as a basic and systematic process in formulating plans in meeting people's needs. It could definitely serve as a guide giving directions to the planners the way they have go to about in formulating plans to meet people's needs.

Chapter 4 speaks of the need to take each village as a unit of rural development. This operationally links to what is emphasized in this volume: a clinical approach.

Chapter 5 covers all the salient areas of development that matter in rural communities. It covers twelve sectors and the problems and needs in each sector and the way to solve these problems and meet the needs and improve the conditions in each sector so that the combined effect of remedies and improvement synchronize in the wholesome overall development of each rural community.

Development envisages introduction of changes, technological or social. There are always problems in making the essential and useful changes accepted by the people. Chapter 6 provides a successful strategy in introducing changes in rural communities. Local institutions at the field level politico, administrative and development in nature have a greater role to play in initiating, managing and accomplishing changes and they may be rightly called as agents of social change at the community level.

Chapter 7 speaks of the role of these local institutions as primary agents of social change.

In the entire gamut of rural development, local leaders are expected to play and do play contributory role. Chapter 8 and 9 speak of the role of local leaders and youth in improving the conditions of living in rural communities.

Chapter 10 focuses on the part that women could play as equal partners of development in rural areas. Almost parallel to the governmental agencies, NGOs, in several fields of development play a significant role and chapter 11 highlights the part played by NGOs in rural development.

Development cannot be mechanical. Social forces influence and operate on any development activity. Caste which is unique in the Indian context for several centuries, though, it is on the decline still plays a significant role both positive and negative in the field of rural development.

Chapter 12 deals with caste dynamics. The life of the Scheduled Castes who are now called Dalits has been a sad story for centuries. They constitute fifteen per cent of the population in India. Though there are several provisions in helping and improving the life of the Dalits, there is a need for special attention to be paid to them.

Chapter 13 provides ethnic-wise, region-wise statistics pertaining to the Dalit population in India.

Compared to several countries, the sanitary conditions in rural areas in India can be described as deplorable. It needs special attention and it is a perennial problem.

Chapter 14 recommends a need for perspective plan on rural sanitation.

Related to rural sanitation, conservation and judicious use of water for all needs is a crucial issue.

Chapter 15 recommends an integrated approach in management of water supply and sanitation.

Chapter 16 lively spells out the Clinical Approach to Rural Development.

Chapter 17 spells out the need for field approach in respect to integrated rural development.

Chapter 18 discusses the indispensable need for securing people's participation in all endeavours of rural development since people's participation is an integral part of development in order to create the sense of accomplishing of projects on the part of the people.

Rural development is a generic concept, subsuming several fields of development that fall under economic development, democratic growth and social justice. There have been several scores of books on this subject. The present volume emphasizing clinical – Field approach spells out the significant factors that the planner, the organizer, the administrator and the field worker has to take care of and be sensitive in understanding people, their needs and problems and working with them for their advancement and welfare. There is no straight highway to rural development. Depending upon the ethnicity and subculture within the fold of Indian ethos, one may have to charter in multiple ways, but may remember and apply the clinical approach irrespective of the programmes focussed upon. The planners, administrators, organizers and field workers, the teaching and the training community concerned with and working in the field of rural development would find this volume interesting and useful.

DR. E.D. SETTY

1

EARLIER ATTEMPTS TOWARDS RURAL DEVELOPMENT

India's Rural Development has an exciting history. This book attempts to give a brief account of several pioneering efforts, experiments in rural development carried on by individuals, voluntary agencies, missionaries and the state and central governments, which have led to the present Integrated Rural Development covering the entire rural India. On reviewing the salient features and limitations of each programme the author presents what he calls the "Clinical and Field Oriented Approach to Rural Development" as a better model to develop Rural Communities all over India*.

GENESIS AND EVOLUTION OF COMMUNITY DEVELOPMENT PROGRAMME IN INDIA

Community Development is not a new idea in our culture and country, but the form in which we now know it is different. It is a synthesis of various elements that have gone into its making in the past. Apparently, it has two elements- the community and its development. By community, we conceptualise a social body which has cohesion, solidarity and a spiritual quality of co-operation, interpersonal respect and

*The terms Rural Development and community development are used carrying the same import.

a certain degree of responsibility. The word development on the other hand implies technology, administration, supplies, services, methods and procedures; programmes, plans, process and progress.

Community Development in India could be discussed in its economic, sociological, cultural, political, historical and psychological settings. But here we shall have a chronological account of the genesis and growth of Community Development as an idea and a programme and how the earlier experiments have contributed to the shaping of the present Community Development programme in India.

In ancient times the primary face-to-face group of communities were knit in a close everyday-relationship of togetherness with one another. The "we" feeling was dominant. In the social structure of the rural communities of ancient times depending on the value systems of those days, the individual sub-served the needs of the communities and the community, in turn gave him services, environmental freedom, and congeniality to grow to his maximum stature. It was out of this concept of mutual interdependence of the community, the individual and the state in ancient India that the welfare of subject was considered as a primary function of the State. Like two halves of an arch the citizens and the state were supported by and supported each other. The concept of welfare state was developed in its full sense so that the state would function in a manner that by its very functioning it would wither away as an entity. The ancient village communities, relatively speaking, had more harmony and community cohesiveness.

By passage of time, the village communities tended to become closed, isolated and limited in functioning, having little interaction among them. In medieval times, the Moghuls developed a system of feudalism, which increased the distance and tended to diminish the closeness of contact between the ruler and the ruled. The intermediaries acquired symbols of authority in their status, roles and applied sanctions according to delegation of authority operating in the system.

In the British regime the emphasis shifted to urban centres of trade and it suited the Britisher to evolve a system of administration which bestowed patronage on certain classes. This naturally ignored the bulk of villagers and the intermediary became the person who reaped the benefit of patronage by ruler and brokerage with the ruled. The legislative and developmental measures taken by the British rulers to ameliorate the conditions of the villagers were negligible.

Famines occurred frequently and the administration became interested in preventing them. The famine Commission Report recommended that development departments such as those of agriculture, public health, public works, etc., be constituted. The impact of these departmental activities was little, remote and feebly felt, if at all it ever existed. The co-operative Societies Acts of 1904, and 1912 were passed to ameliorate the condition of the villager and to provide him with the facility of credit as and when necessary. But, by and large the villager remained as miserably neglected as ever.

Some attempts at rural development were made in the past. The "Community Development and Panchayati Raj" movement is no accident in our history. It has been a continuous process in various shapes and forms since many decades prior to the launching of the official programme. True, that these earlier attempts were not called "Community Development" but in essence their aim was the same, i.e., helping people to help themselves, which is the fundamental principal of Community Development. Though many of these earlier experiments died when the directing hands were withdrawn, still, they have shown us the way and their pitfalls. On the ruins of such earlier experiments the present structure of Community Development in India is being built.

The history of rural regeneration in India (apart from a few isolated experiments) can be divided into three well marked periods. During the first period (1860 – 1920) old feudal India was dissolving and a new India, under the impact of western education and ideas, was gradually emerging. During this period, when the basic ideas of Community development were in a fluid stage, the most active role in the field of rural regeneration was played by the Christian missionaries, who aimed at the all-round development (spiritual and secular) of their Christian converts.

The second period (1920 – 47) marks the adulthood of Indian nationalism and the end of foreign rule. During this period, the Indian patriots, enlightened officials, quasi-missionary societies (Y.M.C.A. and India Village Service) and even some enlightened princes (e.g. in Travancore and Baroda) realised the importance of rural regeneration and made some important contribution in this field. It was at this time that Rabindranth Tagore started his experiments in Sriniketan, Mahatma Gandhi at Sevagram, and Spencer Hatch at Martandam, where they formulated the main principles of rural regeneration.

The third period (1947-onwards) marks the efforts of the Indian Government to find a suitable solution to rural ills and the launching of a country-wide comprehensive scheme of "Community Development and National Extension Service", the conception of which has now broadened into that of Panchayati Raj.

Here we shall deal with earlier attempts of rural reconstruction of the latter two periods mentioned above[1] and in passing we can say that although the Christian peasant settlement failed in many cases to establish a healthy self reliant community there are instances in which they have proved to be a powerful means of uplifting the unprivileged and underprivileged. These settlements were the pioneer attempts in social and economic planning which tested human determination and character and required qualities of organisation and management where men were able to meet these conditions, the settlements have proved to be a source of rural leadership and economic prosperity.

I. SRINIKETAN : DR. RABINDRANTH TAGORE 1921

Tagore is primarily known as a poet-philosopher-but he also a painter, musician, dramatist, actor, educationalist and a rural reformer. In all spheres he had his own style of work and has left the mark of his individuality. It is strange to note that this great poet, who mainly lived in the world of his own ideas, was a pioneer of the village uplift movement in India and the originator of the village worker system according to which rural workers lived in the villages fully sharing the life of the people, while working for their welfare.

Tagore first came in contact with village life in the last part of nineteenth century when the management of the ancestral Jamindari devolved upon him. There he saw at a close range the life, poverty and suffering of the people and came to realize that the real remedy for national regeneration was to be found in uplifting the rural masses.

Tagogre's Ideas of Rural Reconstruction

Tagore had no detailed plans for rural reconstruction. He had a few broad principles. He laid them down and allowed the field workers to fill-in the details. Resources could permit him to work on a modest scale in a few villages and building them up gradually. In these villages he wanted a complete regeneration economic, social, physical, cultural and spiritual. Tagore was very much concerned about the joyless life of villagers. For him the removal of unhappiness was more important than the removal of poverty and in this the poet differed greatly from Gandhiji for whom the elimination of poverty was the first and the foremost problem.

Another aspect of village life which worried the poet was the utter helplessness of the people. Tagore wanted the people to stand on their own feet and cease to look to others for help. To achieve this, he believed in educating the people and not in giving charity. He stressed the principle of self-help in his rural programme. In his opinion an attempt to help the villager from outside was an unnatural procedure and like Gandhiji he believed that ultimately the salvation of the village must come from the village itself. He laid much stress on the training of workers and sent his son, son-in-law and some other Village-workers to Europe, America and Japan for proper training in various rural problems. Thus unlike Gandhiji, he believed that Indian villages could prosper with the help of science and technology. But, at the same time, his approach to rural problems was essentially human. Tagore believed that if work is done intensively within a limited area, its impact radiates outside and spreads widely. It was Tagore who also developed the idea of picking up enthusiastic boys and girls to get interested in rural uplift work. He stressed the principle of picking up agency workers of sound attitude and approach, so that they derived joy from their work, enthused others by their example and by a living touch of sympathy.

Earlier Experiments in Rural Reconstruction

Tagore started his first experiment in rural reconstruction (in 1908) at Silaidaha (Bangladesh), a village in his estate and at Patisar (Rajshahi Dist). In these two earlier experiments the initiative was from the poet and the villagers only obeyed or agreed to his suggestions.

Sriniketan Experiment (1921)

Tagore was not satisfied with his earlier attempts and wanted to make a more intensive and comprehensive experiment in rural reconstruction. Therefore in 1921 he started an Institute of Rural Reconstruction at Sriniketan (Birbhum District) with the help of Mr. & Mrs. L.K. Elmhirst. The Sriniketan area was a decadent region where soil was poor, land scarce, cottage industries declining, climate malarious and people, unenterprising, conservative, poor, suspicious and unhealthy. To reconstruction such a region was difficult task and when considering the success and failure of Sriniketan, we must keep this in mind.

Rural Reconstruction Work by Sriniketan Institute

Tho Sriniketan Institute had four main departments : Village welfare department, Agriculture department, Industries department, and Education department. Of these, the Village welfare department undertook the extension work and acted as a liaison agency between the villages and the institute.

1. Village Welfare Department

The activities of the village welfare department could be divided under three heads : (i) Education, (ii) Sanitation and Health, and (iii) Agriculture and Industries. The educational activities of the department were confined to opening night schools, Brati-Balaks (Boys Scouts) and arranging lectures on general and rural problems.

Health Improvement Measures

Around Sriniketan malaria was a great scourge. Eighty percent of the total deaths were due to it. It was also responsible for the low birth rate and declining population. To fight this disease, at first, a dispensary was set up entirely at the expense of the Institute; but the result was disappointing since the villagers did not try to help the dispensary but demanded medical services as a matter of right. Therefore the above scheme was abandoned and a new scheme of health Co-operatives came into being in 1932. The Health Co-operative was a co-operative society of the villagers for providing medical facilities to its members at a reasonable rate. Each society maintained a dispensary with a qualified doctor and a compounder. The members contributed towards recurring and non-recurring expenditure of the Health Co-operatives. In spite of number of problems and limitation the Health Co-operatives proved their utility.

Economic Activities

For improving agricultural production, better farming methods were shown to the farmers through demonstrations; improved seeds were distributed, and to supplement the villagers' income some cottage industries were introduced. Poultry was developed, co-operative credit societies were organised. The Agriculture, Industries and Education departments helped the extension agency by making experiments and doing research in their respective fields.

2. Agriculture Department

The Agriculture department tried to solve the various agricultural problems of the district on its 25 acre farm as best as it could. Commercial crops were introduced. Storing facilities were created. To improve the fertility of the soil the Agriculture department demonstrated improved methods of farming. Special emphasis was laid on the selection of seeds, rotation of crops, green manuring, preservation of manure, conservation of moisture and the use of improved implements well within the reach of the peasants. Besides attending to land problems the Agriculture department also took in hand the problem of cattle – breeding, poultry keeping, vegetable gardening and fodder growing. Thus it grappled with the burning agricultural problems of the region and tried to do as much as it could under the circumstances.

3. Industries Department

The main objective of the Industries department (called Silpa Bhavan) was to revive decaying cottage industries. With this object in view, Sriniketan experimented with a large number of cottage industries, e.g. weaving, leather works, carpentry, book-binding, embroidery, tailoring, etc. The work of the Industrial department had three aspects- training, production and marketing and extension. Its main aim was to train young men engaged in various vocations so that they might be able to earn their livelihood from their respective crafts. Another aim was to establish workshop for those industries which could be successful under local conditions and run them on business lines and also it aimed to help the local artisans by providing them raw materials and purchasing the finished products in cash by the institute. Thus the institute provided employment to the workers working in the homes and in the workshops and trained new hands and helped them to settle in life.

4. Education Department

Sriniketan made a definite contribution to rural reconstruction by providing a new scheme of village primary education under the name of Siksha-Satra. The aim of this scheme was to give the child that freedom of growth which the young tree demands from its tender shoot, that field for self-expression in which all young life finds both training and happiness. It was an experiment which combined work with play and play with knowledge. There was no examination, no prescribed course, no text books, no time-table and no rod to be used on their tender bodies. It was a modified replica of the old ashram education where children lived with the teacher, cooked their meals, washed their clothes, swept their rooms, tended their gardens, learnt the three R'S and a special craft, played games and went on excursions. They studied nature and lived with nature.

In the girls' school the girls were taught needle work, cooking and gardening besides the three R'S.

The scheme of Siksha-Satra which emphasized the value of indigenous culture and aimed at keeping the boys in the villages deserve praise. The Siksha-Satra boys became the accepted leaders in their villages and showed much foresight and wisdom in their life. Even Gandhiji is reported to have been much impressed by this school and had urged Tagore to loan him the services of the headmaster of Siksha-Satra to help him plan an all India Scheme of Primary education. Siksha-Satra was the forerunner of Basic education. Again Tagore's unique experiment in rural education provided the educationalists with many fruitful ideas for drawing up a scheme for higher rural education for the whole country.

An Assessment

The Sriniketan approach may be characterised by : (1) Holistic view of life and its indivisiblity, (2) Need to culminate the total personality of man and (3) Need to co-ordinate the cultural and material resources to answer the problem of material and intellectual poverty. Tagore emphasised traditional media and methods of communication for disseminating ideas among the village folk. He recognised that change of outlook can be brought about among villagers only through educational process. Tagore emphasised, teaching extension and research are inseparable parts of an integral for sound education. He stressed the principle of self-help. He believed in science and technology and emphasised the need for training and enthusiasm among workers. Tagore has made an integrated approach to solve interrelated problems of the villagers. But the experiment has some limitations and short-comings.

Factors Retarding Progress

The effort was inspired by ideological fervour but suffered for want of scientific, economic and sociological research as well as for lack of co-ordination with existing administrative machinery. The initiative for the effort came from Tagore and not the people. The research and professional support were inadequate to deal with more difficult problems. It had its own limitations in meeting the service and supply needs of the communities around. The government was not prepared to commit itself to a full-fledged programme of rural reconstruction. A single individual or a group working along, could not accomplish the transformation.

The assessment, however, does not imply complete failure of the experiment. There were physical results, notable results : "Economic returns were such that the rising standard of living in the area was very noticeable. New confidence arose among these villagers. They felt able to tackle new things, to defeat pessimism and to achieve results together".

Moreover, according to the poet himself: 'The immense benefit realized by the surrounding villages through constant inspiration, of sympathy and encouragement of Sriniketan must never be belittled in favour of some impersonal abstractions of service, however valuable they may be .... the valuable gift of sympathy is some of our humble workers has worked miracles which must not be contemptuously mentioned because it has neither been measured nor accurately recorded".

II. ROYAL COMMISSION ON AGRICULTURE : 1926

In 1926, the Government of India appointed the "Royal Commission on Agriculture". In their report, the Commission observed that "the welfare and prosperity of rural population will not come by technical advancement alone. If it is true, that better living could be secured only by a combination of better farming and better business, it is equally true, that the will to live better must furnish the driving force that is required at the heart of the problem and development of the desire for a higher standard of living. A vague aspiration now exists and has always existed, but it is rendered ineffective by an inhibition which has to be taken up before larger scale progress in possible" – The observations of the Royal Commission drew attention to the need of arousing people's interest in programmes of their uplift.

GURGAON : F.L. BRAYNE : 1927

Frank Lugard Brayne, son of a country parson and a war veteran, was appointed as the Deputy Commissioner of Gurgaon District (Punjab) in 1920. In that capacity he made an extensive tour of the district and saw at close range the ignorance and poverty of the rural masses – but unlike the other officers, his work did not end by sending a report to the government. He chalked out a detailed scheme of rural reconstruction and put it into practice with all means at his disposal. It took seven years and achieved some definite tangible results. The scheme has since become famous by the name of the "Gurgaon Experiment".

The Gurgaon Experiment

The aim of the experiment in the words of Mr. Brayne, was to "jerk the villager out of his old groove, convince him that improvement was possible, and kill his fatalism by demonstrating that both climate, disease and pests could be successfully fought." Contrary to the policy of the rulers, he engaged himself in changing the attitude of the people but also of the Government which made his task more difficult.

The Programme

The Gurgaon experiment was a four-fold programme. It aimed at (i) improving the farming, (ii) reducing wasteful customs, (iii) improving health and (iv) setting the home right, i.e., educating the women.

Like Tagore, Brayne's aim was not to make people rich but to make them happy. In the programme, stress was laid on agricultural producation by adopting improved methods. Brayne gave attention to improving the prevalent breeds of cattle and particularly emphasised the programme of improving public health and sanitation by taking up schemes of compost making as well as providing ventilators to rural homes. He also devoted attention to women's education and used school teachers for propagating his ideas. The main items of work on which Brayne concentrated attention were : -

(a) Rural Sanitation

(b) Agricultural development

(c) Education

(d) Co-operation

(e) Social reforms

(f) Co-ordination of departmental activities; and

(g) Publicity

The programme covered the entire district of Gurgaon.

Methods

He believed that the Indian villager because of his isolation and illiteracy was more susceptible to intensive propaganda than any other villager in the world. He made use of propaganda and official pressure to push through the programmes. His village guide was a common man for all activities. Brayne thought that the village work could be organised on the following four bases :

1. Knowledge and particularly girls' education, Women's organisation and welfare work.
2. Example

3. Spirit of service
4. Village organisations

Achievements

Brayne was certain that his programme was a success and claimed that a "new India has begun in Gurgaon". The immediate results of the Gurgaon in the fields of agriculture, animal husbandry and co-operation were impressive, but it was a short lived programme. It was the first government sponsored programme which demonstrated that for promoting any programme of change, government assistance is necessary so that the interest of government officials stimulated and enthuses people's interest also. Within a few months of Brayne's departure slackness set in, and after three years, the only remnants of the scheme were a few persian wheels and manure pits. The main reason for the rapid collapse of the experiment was that the reforms came not from within but were imposed from without. Many things were done "by order and through fear". Moreover, the whole programme was far too dominated by the dynamic personality of Mr. Brayne and the District board and the Rural Community council depended excessively on his guidance. It was also found that the remedies suggested were not equally beneficial to all parts of the district (e.g. Hessar bulls-lack of fodder; manure pits unsuitable during rainy season).

The weakness of this programme was that it was not supported by some such permanent organisations as could give it an institutional character and continuity. The village folk were not adequately educated to adopt the programme willingly and they were not convinced about the usefulness of what they were doing. Further, it was a "top-oriented" programme which utterly neglected the poorest people and it was a "top-aided" programme which helped the "haves" against the "have-nots". Moreover, the experiment was ill-timed. It coincided with the period of great political unrest in the country, during which a foreigner or an official was a suspect in the eyes of the people. Thus the experiment failed due to official pressure and impatience, the prescription of unsuitable remedies and its unfavourable timing.

Gurgaon Experiment-an Estimate

Gurgaon experiment was the first scheme which made an allround assault on rural problems simultaneously over such a wide area with the full support of the Deputy Commissioner's authority. It was able to provide many important lessons for the present community development programme. It proved that the East was not so changeless and given proper guidance and instructions, the Eastern villager could make efforts to improve his lot. It also underlined the necessity for a separate and permanent organisation, with its own staff, its own training institutions and its own money to deal with the colossal problem of rural reconstruction. It showed the necessity of an extension worker the village guide (father of the modern village level worker) as a friend to guide the people. By its early collapse, the experiment showed that the task of changing the attitude of the people is necessarily a long drawn process-it can be cone only slowly by education and persuasion. It has also shown that, as for as possible, mass-prescriptions should be avoided as one man's meat may be another man's poison. Thus Brayne's labour was not entirely lost. Both by his successes and failures he set new precedents for later generations and has provided lessons without which the present community development programme would face more obstacles than it does.

III. MARTHANDAM : SPENCER HATCH : 1928

In far South, at Marthandam, formerly in Kerala, now in Tamilnadu, Dr. Spencer Hatch undertook almost at the same time as Brayne, a programme of rural development at and around Marthandam under the auspices of Young Men's

Christian Association. He was particularly interested in the social aspects of rural uplift and later on, the efforts made by him were intensified in collaboration with the Christian Church with special reference to juvenile delinquency among children.

Marthandam village is situated on the Trivandrum Cape Comorin road, thirty eight kms from Trivandrum. The area selected for intensive work was about 175 sq. kms, comprising 46 villages, roughly within a radius of six to eight kms of Marthandam. It had a population of 45, 00 persons out of which 72% were Hindus, 24% Christians and the remaining 4% consisted of Muslims and others. It was a poor area.

Objectives

The main objectives of Rural Reconstruction in Marthandam were five-fold, namely mental, spiritual, physical, economic and social.

Organisation

The machinery of rural programme was simple and inexpensive. Dr. Hatch was in charge of the whole programme. All the experiments were planned and perfected at the "Rural Reconstruction Centre" before being demonstrated to the villagers. The extension work was done by the honorary workers of the Village Y.M.C.As. The whole of Marthandam Rural Reconstruction Centre was confined within an area of one and a half acres of land, which together with one building were rented at Rs. 20/- per month. Part of the building was used for meeting and housing a library. The compound was used for exhibiting the work done at the centre. It had a weaving shed, a poultry shed, bee-hives, a sindhi bull and a few demonstration plots for quick growing fodder grasses. The houses, the library, and the weaving shed, all were made of thatch, bamboo and reeds. This was done not only to keep the costs down but also to make it an ideal village centre, which could be emulated by the people at home. The main reasons for the cheapness of the Marthandam programme were its inexpensive, simple building and a host of honest honorary workers.

Method of Work

The key-note of the work was self-help and intimate expert counsel. Village associations were formed. Each association assisted in the implementation of the various innovations. Above these associations, there was the Regional Development Association which concerned itself with the developmental activities of the entire region. The demonstration centre at Marthandam represented the nucleus of the various village developmental activities and provided information, instruction and guidance. New centers were opened as the area of operation extended. These latter centres were under the charge of rural secretaries. There were also honorary leaders from each village who assisted the rural secretaries. Thus the public had a considerable share in the day-to-day work while the paid personnel provided expert guidance. The chief media of propaganda used by the centre were: Rural dramas, rural exhibitions, intervillage competitions and demonstrations.

Actual field work commenced with a rural survey of the particular locality selected for work. Material gathered in these surveys were studied and findings framed. Action was then chalked out in the light of these findings.

The Programme

The Rural Reconstruction Programme launched in Martandam aimed at a "complete development – a wholly new and happier order" – economic, social, religious, educational and physical. The programme was a comprehensive one and the formula was "self – help with intimate, expert counsel". The villagers were given nothing free except education. Deserving cases were helped through the co-operatives. The extension rule was that no person should be deprived of a chance to progress because of poverty alone. Thus an upward movement was launched.

To supplement the villagers' income and to revive some dying cottage industries, the existing cottage industries were reorganised to make them more remunerative. The main industries thus reorganised were poultry-keeping, bee-keeping, weaving, jaggery-making, cashew-nuts, basket, mat and rope making, etc. Poultry-keeping and bee-keeping were the most successfully organised of the above. Improved breeds of poultry were introduced. To boost up sales and to find reasonable prices for the eggs the Marthandam Y.M.C.A. Poultry Co-operative Society Ltd., was started which took up the selling of eggs at good prices in far and near markets. The poultry industry was a success.

Bee-keeping was encouraged and improved on scientific lines. Bee-keeping and honey-eating were popularised. To make bee-keeping more remunerative, honey was cured scientifically and marketed co-operatively. Marthandam honey became famous and established a reputation and had a good market. Thus bee-keeping became a profitable cottage industry in the Marthandam area.

There were a few other significant economic services rendered to the people such as improving the breed of cattle and introducing quick-growing fodder grasses.

Educational and Social Activities

Night schools were organised in many places for illiterates, young and old. Along with the night schools circulating libraries were oranised and the A.L. Centres and the libraries were managed by the members of the village Y.M.C.A.'s, mostly school teachers. Dramas like Kathakali and Kalakshepam were encouraged. Exhibitions as a means of education and demonstration were periodically organised. Another important feature was the introduction of bore-hole latrines which saved people from hook-worm and bad odour.

Traning of Rural Workers

One of the important features of the Y.M.C.A. rural reconstruction work was the regular training of village workers. The curriculum included many subjects connected with various aspects of rural life, viz., cottage industries, co-operation, cattle-breeding, exhibitions, dramas, rural leadership, demonstration methods, adult education, sanitation, village surveys, women and child welfare, physical education etc. Another peculiar feature of the training school was that it was conducted on a self-supporting basis, i.e. each student had to pay for his food and travel. It attracted students from all over India (the course was for four months) and even from China, Korea, Egypt, Burma and Sri Lanka. By 1948 the Marthandam school has trained 1,700 students.

The Marthandam Influence

The Marthandam spirit proved to be contagious and its influence far exceeded the ten kms limit. Similar centres were started by village people in Oollannore and Paraniyam, where much good work was done. The most remarkable thing in these centres was that the people themselves did everything on their own initiative without any outside help. This spontaneous urge in the hearts of the people for self-development illustrates the success of Marthandam more than anything else. Rural Reconstruction centres on the Marthandam pattern were also started in Pattancheru (Andhra Pradesh, 1931), Kosamba (Gurajat, 1932) and Doddakalapore (Karnataka state) by the state governments, and Y.M.C.A. workers were invited to help in their establishment.

Some Characteristics of the Marthandam Experiment

Apart from being a simple, inexpensive and comprehensive programme, the experiment was sustained by a permanent agency like the Y.M.C.A. The workers except Hatches were all Indians and the agency did not aim at quick results and there was less of a target-minded and statistics-oriented approach. Further, the programme was based on giving nothing free, except advice.

Limitation of the Marthandam Programme

The Y.M.C.A. Programme at Marthandam suffered from the fact that it was mainly confined to male Christians. It did little to arouse and organise women and failed to get the co-operation of non-Christians, who formed seventy two percent of the population. Owing to the then prevailing communal feeling, the co-operation from the non-Christians could not be secured and the village Y.M.C.A. workers, who were generally Christians, did not like the idea of working for other communities. Hence, it remained largely a programme of Christians, for the Christians and by the Christians. Another weakness of the programme was that it entirely neglected the development of agriculture, save, the introduction of quick growing fodder grasses. This neglect of agriculture was due to two reasons: maintaining an expensive demonstration farm, which cannot be (according to Hatch) maintained better than a farmer and secondly most of the people were landless and they could be helped only through cottage industries. Whatever the reason may be, the neglect of agriculture remains a great drawback for the whole programme. Another factor which seems to have limited its influence was the nature of its location.

IV. SRINIKETAN AND MARTHANDAM

It is interesting to compare the two institutions (3,000

kms apart) engaged in rural reconstruction during the last eight decades. Both came into being as a result of the vision of two great Indians (K.T. Paul in the cause of Marthandam who invited Dr. Hatch to India – Marthandam) who wanted to uplift the down-trodden. The establishment of both institutions was made possible through western finance and expertise. Both institutions aimed at an all-round development of the villages by the efforts of villagers themselves and both selected a poor area for making experiments. But in spite of the above similarities there were fundamental differences between the two. Sriniketan was mainly an educational institution with an extension agency. It was also a bigger and more comprehensive institution and financially more sound. In 1932, it had an annual budget of Rs. 72,000 when Marthandam hardly spent Rs. 8,000 a year. It had an agricultural farm, a dairy, a new scheme for primary education, an industrial work-shop with powerlooms, and a department of socio-economic research besides its village welfare department. It carried on both extension and research side by side which no other institution engaged in rural reconstruction had been able to do. On the other hand, Marthandam was a small institution, whose main and only work was extension. It did not adopt projects which required large finances, e.g. an agricultural farm, Socio-economic research, industrial work-shops etc. Martandam specialised in a few activities and worked on them intensively and perfectly. It had not much to show at the centre-its work was in the houses of the villagers. Unlike Sriniketan, whose main job was to make village life more joyful, the Marthandam workers worked for improving the finances of the people. Their greater success lay in organizing the producers' Co-operatives and in arranging for the marketing of the articles produced. In the absence of marketing facilities the Sriniketan artisans could never gain that self – confidence which the Institute wanted them to have, and which was the foundation of rural reconstruction. Thus co-operative marketing was the great advantage which Marthandam possessed over Sriniketan.

Another factor which made a great difference was the provision of expert advice and leadership. In Sriniketan Elmhirst remained for hardly one year and later, for various reasons, Sriniketan could not employ first rate professional experts and as a compromise had to rely on second rate experts. At Marthandam, Hatch remained available for advice and guidance for a very long time and after his departure another man with equal knowledge replaced him. Thus Marthandam was able to get proper guidance throughout its existence.

There was another important difference between the two experiments. Marthandam mostly dealt with a homogenous group (Indian Christias) having a common interest and religion, and as the agency was also Christian, there was a much broader basis of mutual co-operation between the two. Moreover, the background for Hatch's work had to some extent been prepared earlier by the rural Y.M.C.A.'s, started a decade ago, which had members in most of the villages. Much of the Marthandam success had been due to voluntary organisations. Sriniketan had no such advantage. It started from scratch and had to make arrangements for its own reception. It was also dealing with a community divided on religious and caste bases. This heterogeneity also made Srinikatan work more difficult than Marthandam work.

While Marthandam was more successful in the economic field, Srinikethan was atleast as successful in its scheme of Health Co-operatives and training of Brati – Blaks. The Health Co-operatives have greatly added to the physical welfare of the people and have taught the lessons of co-operation and mutual help. Through the Brati-Balak organisation the village boys learnt the lessons of service and unity and rose above caste and religious barriers. The research branch of Sriniketan conducted valuable researches on malaria-control and soil erosion. It also made village surveys, studied the yield of rice-crop over a number of years, and suggested measures for improvement. Moreover, it has been successful in making the area around Sriniketan more literate and in arousing a cultural awakening not found in other parts of the district. Here, we must not forget that Tagore was also the originator of the village worker system in India which has assumed enormous importance under the community development programme, where the role of the village level worker is vital.

In short, both the institutions have made their valuable contributions in different spheres of rural life and both of them can impart useful lessons to the present programme of community development-extension.

V. SEVAGRAM : MAHATMA GANDHI : 1931

The Community Development Programme in India which seeks to initiate a process of transformation of the social and economic life of the village is stated to be, with a few changes, the official version of Mahatma Gandhi's Construtive programme. It was on his birthday October 2, 1952, that the community projects were launched throughout the country. It was Gandhiji who drew the attention of the Indian public to the 7,000,00 (of India and Pakistan) villages and declared as early as 1916 that the salvation of India could only come through the farmer. The objective of Gandhiji's programme of rural reconstruction was to rebuild the villages as self-sufficient units for fulfilling basic wants of human life. It was in consonance with the philosophy of life and cultural background of rural masses and also suited to the economic conditions in which they were living then.

Gandhiji experimented his ideas at Sevagram. The village-uplift activities of the earlier rural reformers, such as Togore, Hatch and Brayne never attracted the attention of the whole country and remained, more or less, localised. The case with Gandhiji was different. His preachings, and practice and his identification with the common masses and his fight for the uplift of the common man had a tremendous and pervasive effect on the people.

Gandhian Experiments in Rural Reconstruction

At Champaran in 1917 he came in intimate contact with the peasants oppressed by the indigo planters. He saw there poverty, ignorance, disease and illiteracy. Champaran villages presented a typical picture of village India. Gandhiji started his rural reconstruction work here in education, health, hygiene etc. but this work, due to lack of local volunteers, could not be carried on for long and declined when Gandhiji and his volunteers left the locality, (Gnadhiji stayed at Champaran for eight months). Champaran was the first laboratory in India where in forged not only his political weapon but also his constructive programme.

SEVAGRAM

Gandhiji, in his multifarious activities never forgot rural India and its appalling poverty. With a view of reducing the chronic unemployment and underemployment in the villages, he started the All India Spinners' Association (1925) and the All India Village Industries Association (1934) whose aim was to propagate Khadi, (a hand spun and hand woven fabric) revive the dying village industries and to work for all-round village development. In order to have first-hand knowledge of village work he settled in Segaon (later named Sevagram), a small village of 600 people near Wardha in April 1936. The village lacked many barest necessities and amenities. Gandhiji at the age of 67, chose to stay in a one-roomed mud and bamboo hut and concentrate on village work. Since sanitation was the first essential in the village uplift, the Gandhian workers began by sweeping the village lanes and urging the people to use a common place for latrines. People were asked to send their children to school and learn to spin. Under the auspices of the All-India Village Industries Association, a few industries were started in the village for providing work to the people in their leisure hours. To give them a practical demonstration in improved agricultural techniques a part of the ashram land was brought under cultivation where new crops such as sugarcane and papaya were grown. A dairy and a small hospital were also started. But the villagers were suspicious in the beginning and they could be won over gradually and the success of the experiment in changing the attitude of the villagers for better and the attempts to do away with some social practices have not been impressive. The main reason for this comparatively unimpressive progress at Sevagram was that Gandhiji in his last sixties being preoccupied with other political problems could not devote more time for the village work.

But the crux of the problem is not what Gandhiji did but what he got done through his various organisations created for public service. All India Spinners' Association, All India Village Industries' Association, Adim Jati Seva Sangh (Aborigines' Service Society), Harijan Sevak Sangh, Go Seva Sangh (Cow protection society), Hindusthani Talimi Sangh, Kasturba Trust, Gandhi Seva Sangh (1922-40) etc., had carried Gandhiji's message of rural uplift into numerous villages of India and did yeoman service for the people, in their respective spheres of work.

Gandhian way of Rural Reconstruction

Gandhiji's blue-print for national reconstruction which has since become famous as his "constructive Programme" was mainly concerned with the regeneration of the 7,00,000 Indian Villages (before partition). For economic development the programme stressed (1) The protection and popularisation of Khadi; (2) Development of village industries: (3)

Improvement of cattle and (4) Socio-economic equality. On the social front it aimed at (5) Communal unity; (6) Removal of untouchability; (7) Prohibition; (8) Equal status for women and (9) Welfare of Adivasis (natives). On the educational side it stressed (10) Adoption of Basic Education; (11) Working for adult education; (12) Development of provincial languages and (13) The adoption of Hindusthani as the national language. To improve General health of the villages it saw the necessity of (14) Improving village sanitation and (15) Imparting health education. In this respect it also exhorted people (16) to take care of lepers. On the Political front it stressed the necessity of organising (17) Peasants and labourers for securing their just rights and (18) Students for doing social work.

For Gandhiji, removal of hunger and poverty was the first and foremost problem. In his attempt to revive Khadi and Village industries, Gandhiji wanted to provide the villagers with honest work and teach them the lessons of self-help and self-reliance. Gandhiji was also aware of the vital need of improving the cattle breed in an agricultural country like India.

By his Social programe Gandhiji wanted to unify India as a nation and raise the social status of women, scheduled castes and tribal population. He did not want Indians to remain divided on religious and caste basis. Therefore, he exhorted the workers to work for Hindu-Muslim unity, removal of untouchability, uplift of tribal people and for providing an honoured place to women in the home and society. As drinking was a common habit with the scheduled-caste and tribes, and was also responsible for the maltreatment of women, he greatly stressed the removal of this curse from the society.

The Gandhian Scheme of Primary Educaton

Convinced that the then existing system of village primary

education was a defective one, Gandhiji drew up a seven-year scheme of primary education for village children, in 1937 which has since then become famous as "Basic Education". It is a craft centred education and life-centred education aiming at developing body, mind and soul. While assigning the central place to crafts in his scheme of education, Gandhiji also kept in view the importance of a liberal education in the full development of the child – therefore he also included drawing, music, social studies, elementary principles of sanitation, hygiene, nutrition etc., in his curriculum. Gandhiji thought that such a system of education would establish jest social order. The scheme had a mixed reception and now mostly it remains as a scheme on paper.

Village Sanitation and Nature Cure

In his view attention to sanitation and hygiene was undoubtedly the first step to village reconstruction. Therefore, he urged the village workers to teach the villagers the lessons of sanitation and hygiene and to become models of cleanliness themselves. He stressed sanitation and hygiene so much because he believed in prevention rather than cure.

Gandhiji also wanted villagers to take to a cheap but nutritious diet, consisting of unpolished rice, hand-ground flour, palm gur, soya-beans, green vegetables and seasonal fruits which would keep people in good health. His main theme was that a balanced diet need not be costly and should be within the means of the poorest. In the treatment of diseases Gandhiji believed more in nature-cure than in doctors and medicines. In his opinion nature was the finest physician as it repaired what man had damaged-therefore the best remedy was to co-operate with nature.

Thus, by his constructive program Gandhiji wanted to build the nation from the bottom upwards and bring about the economic, social, mental, physical and political regeneration of Indian villages. His main contribution was that he tried to look at all issues with the eyes of a peasant and therefore, was able to touch the chords of village India as no one else was able to do.

An important feature of the Sevagram effort was an emphasis on means and process rather than on ends and products. To Gandhiji the achievement of a certain programme was not as important as the methods and means used and this implied his insistence on educational involvement of the people who were expected to stand on their own with as little support from outside as possible.

Gandhiji's Conception of an Ideal Gramsevak

One of the greatest contributions of Gandhian effort was the image of a constructive worker that he developed. His ideal village worker would have the following qualifications:

He should always keep the following eleven vows as a beacon light in front of him. Nown-violence, truth, non-stealing, Brahmacharya (Celebacy), non-possession, body-labour, control of the palate, fearlessness, equal respect for all religions, Swadeshi and spirit of unexclusive brotherhood. He should be a model of industry. His life should be in tune with village life. He should not have a partisan attitude towards villagers. He should not only be a teacher but a learner also. He should not take part in politics and should remain above village factions.

Some of the qualifications prescribed by Gandhiji were relevant to the workers in the constructive programme, but the qualities enumerated above are a must for the village level worker in the C.D. Programme.

Some Defects

The Gandhian way of rural reconstruction has its defects. Firstly, it was not possible to get 7,00,000 Mahatma Grama

Sevaks to be placed in every village. Secondly, as the village worker was to work for his livelihood for eight hours per day and also to look after sanitation, say for two hours, he would get little time to do anything else. Thirdly, the whole conception of the constructive programme was in the nature of philanthropy for the benefit of the pitiable poor and was to some extent surcharged with a partronising attitude which defeated the basic ideology of village reconstruction. Fourthly, as it was planned and sustained on external leadership and inspiration, it failed largely to bring forth local leadership which is the ultimate test of any village-uplift work. It is to be noted here that though the fundamental and basic aim of rural reconstruction programme was to regenerate the villages and make villagers self-confident and self-reliant which implies development of local leadership, the translation of the programme fell short of the desired goal. Gandhiji's prescriptions and programmes must be understood with reference to the context, situation and need of the times. They are to be adapted to the ever changing conditions.

The Gandhian way of Rural Reconstruction and the Community Development Programme

Though the Community Development Programme is proclaimed to be the official version of Gandhiji's constructive programme, on a close study it is revealed that it differs widely with the Gandhian way of rural reconstruction.

1. Gandhiji laid great stress on the principle that as far as possible, village development should be carried out "Within the means of the villagers... without government assistance", so that they may develop the qualities of self-help and self-reliance and cease to look for outside help. But under the development schemes large amounts of money are being spent by the government in the villages, while people's contribution is nominal and generally inflated.

2. The Gandhian concept of progress was a balanced one, and included moral, material and social development of the people. His constructive programme was based on his lifelong principles of truth and non-violence and laid stress on communal unity, eradication of untouchability, advocation of prohibition etc. but the present Community Development Programme in a way ignores these aspects and mainly concentrates on material welfare.

3. Another point of difference is that the Community Development programme mainly stresses agricultural improvement by developing irrigation facilities and distributing seeds, fertilisers. Thus it helps the rich landlords to get richer and thereby increases the economic inequality between the haves and the have-nots. Thus we find, the C.D. Programme differing from the Gandhian constructive programme in several ways. But the situation is remedied to some extent under the present IRD, which focuses on the people below poverty-line.

VI. THE BARODA PLAN

SIR V.T. KRISHNAMACHARI : 1933

Almost at the same time of sevagram experiment, Sir V.T. Krishnamchari was trying an experiment in Baroda. He was then the Dewan of Baroda state and he drew up detailed plans of rural development during his tenure of office. He held that attempts at rural development should be made in a manner that improvement in rural life takes place in all its aspects. He believed that in order to raise the standard of living of villagers, it is a necessary pre-requisite to create in them a desire for aspiring to that level of living. He also believed that any work of rural reconstruction cannot be effective if it is not intensively taken up in a limited area, so that the spread-effect of the effort radiates outward from a focal point. He also emphasised the need for developing village leadership, so that a local organisation exists in each village to continue the effort that is initiated by an agency. The Baroda plan was characterised by an emphasis on a comprehensive programme of improvements in all aspects of rural life. It was woven around the concept that increased agricultural production holds the key to success and that there should be an efficient organisation for supplies, services and credit. The plan recoginsed the role of panchayats, (village councils), co-operatives and schools as centres of activities and local leaders as promoters of change. Sir V.T. Krishnamachari believed that programme of rural reconstruction was part of a broader programme and it was necessary to expand subsidiary activities to promote agricultural production.

VII. GROW MORE FOOD CAMPAIGN : 1942

In the wake of World War II, there was an acute scarcity of food and the Government of India decided to adopt measures for increasing food production. A campaign for 'Grow More Food' was accordingly launched as a result of which some permanent improvements took place in the form of construction of wells or irrigation channels. It also resulted in large scale distribution of seeds and fertilizers and it achieved phenomenal success in Jute and cotton production which captured foreign market also.

But the "Grow More Food Campaign" failed to achieve the desired result because the grants and loans that were sanctioned were used by people for purposes other than the ones they were intended for, or they were used solely for growing cash crops like Jute and cotton. The second shortcoming of this programme was that it was not a sustained effort and there was no organisational support to keep it going. It broke down with the withdrawal of monetary support by the government.

VIII. FIRKA DEVELOPMENT SCHEME MADRAS - 1946

Even prior to the launching of the Firka Development Scheme in the selected firkas and centres, the government had under consideration, the question of rural development in the state. Various measures had been taken from time to time for the improvement of rural conditions. But as the efforts had been restricted in scope and lacked proper co-ordination, the results were neither tangible nor enduring. Lack of direction, support and encouragement from a central authority was responsible for the ineffectiveness of these efforts. It was obvious that the planning of schemes of rural development and supervision their execution should be centralised as also the coordination of the work of the Department of Agriculture, Industries, Irrigation, Veterinary etc., in regard to such schemes.

This was the background with which the Madras Government, under the chief-ministership of Late Tunguturi Prakasam Pantulu (Andhra Kesari – The Lion of Telugu Country) started the Firka Development Scheme. To start with it was the intention of the government to make each selected Firka (ranging from 15 to 20 villages) or centre self-sufficient in the matter of food and clothing and other necessities of life. It was decided to revive or develop, as the case might be, village industries essential for the life of the communities. The government also launched a scheme for production and popularisation of khadi.

Financial Arrangement

In order to give effect to their proposals in this regard, the Government started a special fund and transferred a sum of Rs. 40 million to this fund from the revenue account. Out of this sum ten million was set apart for Harijan uplift and the remaining thirty million to general schemes of Firka Development and other schemes for Khadi production. As and when necessary for rural uplift the sums required were drawn from this fund and the unspent balances were made available for expenditure in subsequent years.

Aims and Objectives

The Firka Development scheme aimed at the attainment of the Gandhian ideal of "Village Swaraj" (Village Self-Rule) by bringing about not only the educational, economic sanitary and other improvements of villages but also by revitalising the spirit of the people and making them self-confident and self-reliant. The object of the scheme was to attack the rural problem as a whole as well as in its several parts. The scheme consisted of definite short-term plans. The short-term plan was the development of rural communications and rural water supply, formation of panchayats, organisation of co-operatives covering every village, implementing a programme of sanitation etc. the long-term plan was designed to further the attainment of self-sufficiency through agricultural, irrigational, livestock – improvements and development of Khadi and Cottage industries.

Launching of the Programme and Extension

The Firka Development programme was first launched in 34 Firkas throughout the state during the last quarter of 1946 and was later extended from 1st April 1950, to 50 additional Firkas at the rate of 2 Firkas for each district and to 24 additional Firkas in April 1952.

The selection of the Firkas was based on considerations of general backwardness of the Firka in regard to communications, sanitation, lighting, water supply, etc., presence of electric installations in or within reach of the Firka or centre and the availability of conditions favourable for intensifying the production of handloom cloth for the development of other cottage industries.

Administrative set up

The provincial Firka Development officer (subsequently redesignated as the Director of Rural Welfare and the Joint Development Commissioner) was put in overall charge of the implementation of the programme at state level.

The District Collector was primarily responsible for the successful working of the scheme in his district. He was assisted by a Rural Welfare Officer of the rank of a Deputy Tahsildar who was in charge of two or three selected firkas, and under him, there were 5 to 10 Grama sevaks of the rank of Revenue Inspector, one for each of the 5 to 10 groups into which the firkas had been divided. Each firka or each group of firkas was also provided with special staff like Agricultural Fieldmen, Demonstration Maistries, P.W.D. Supervisors, Minor Irrigation overseers, a Khadi worker, and a Co-operative Inspector.

Training of Gramasevaks

The Gramasevaks were given adequate training in the fundamental principles of rural development. Two vidyalayas (training centres) were in existence, one at Gopannapalem, Andhra and another at Kallupatti, Madurai District, to train Gramasevaks. The Firka Development Officers were also given training.

Public Participation

Under the Firka Development Scheme, an attempt was made to encourage local leadership and to instil in them the philosophy of self-help. Works under the scheme were generally carried out where the villagers were prepared to contribute towards their cost either in cash or kind or in the form of labour. Emphasis was also laid on the execution of works by the villagers benefited by the works, to the exclusion of profit earning outside agencies.

Association of Non-Officials

The Firka Development Programme Provided a democratic basis for the development of rural areas. The villagers themselves had a share in framing the proposals for their own improvement. Development committees consisting of officials and non-officials were constituted in the firkas to implement the schemes drawn up for the improvement of the villages. There was also a State Rural Welfare Board comprising Heads of Departments and influential constructive workers, which formulated schemes of Firka Development. It was a sub-committee of this Board that drew up in October 1947 a comprehensive plan of Firka Development. The aim of this plan for Firka Development, as Visualised by the authors, was "to organise the villagers for a happier, more prosperous and fuller life in which the individual villager had the opportunity to develop both as an individual and as a unit of a well integrated society.

Outstanding constructive workers were also deputed from time to time to inspect the work done and report to government.

Content of the Programme

For improvements to village communications and rural water supply, the government had sanctioned a sum of Rs. 50,000/- under each head for each of the 34 firkas originally selected and Rs. 25,000/- in respect of each of the firkas selected later. A recurring grant of Rs. 10,000/- per annum was originally placed at the disposal of the collectors in respect of each of the 34 firkas or centres of expenditure on minor and urgent items of work. A sum of Rs. 8,000/- was placed at the disposal of each of the additional firkas subsequently selected. These small allotments attracted huge contributions from the villagers in the form of money, materials and labour and the value of the work done in most cases was far in excess of the money spent on government account.

Wherever specific allotments were not placed at the disposal of the Firka Development Officers, it was ordered that the expenditure on the items concerning rural development should be met from the normal departmental budgets. It was also ordered that first preference should be given to the selected areas in the matter of location of basic training centres and in training teachers.

Sanitation

Emphasis was laid on systematic improvement of sanitary condition in the villages. The goal was a clean and a tidy village. The means was through education and not merely by mechanical activities.

Co-operation

A determined effort was made to bring into existence co-operative societies to cover all the villages in the selected areas through the co-operative department.

Panchayats

Panchayats were also ordered to be constituted in all the villages of the selected areas.

Electrification

A high priority was given for the electrification of the selected areas. The government also undertook to meet the deficits arising out of unremunerative schemes in the selected areas.

Agriculture

Special attention was paid to increasing production of food grains, cotton, etc., by subsidizing the agricultural requirements and offering various facilities to the farmers, viz., land reclamation, compost making, incentives for compost making, sale of fertilisers and plant protection material at half-cost, supply of green manure seeds, supply of improved strains at subsidized rates.

Irrigation

It was also ordered that schemes which would materially contribute for the development of irrigation in the several firkas should be investigated an executed by the regular departments.

Animal Husbandry

The village livestock improvement scheme, which aimed at concentrated livestock improvement in the villages was ordered to be implemented in selected areas.

Entrustment of Rural Development Work to Non-official Agencies

With a view of extending firka development work to additional areas and in order to stimulate and healthy competition between the official and non-official agencies, the Government decided that the firka development work might also be entrusted to non-official agencies engaged in doing constructive work. To start with, five non-official agencies were selected and paid grants for doing firka development work on the following items :

1. Provision of communications
2. Provision of drinking water facilities
3. Improvement of sanitation
4. Improvement of agriculture
5. Development of Khadi and other village industries and
6. Other items of the Constructive programme such as adult education and establishment of multipurpose programme was launched in 1953-54.

The Firka Development Scheme was later merged with the National Extension Service, when this programme was launched in 1953-54.

Contribution of the Scheme

The contribution of this scheme was the idea of concentrated work in a small group of villages and the idea of having an organisation and special staff like a Firka Development or Rural Welfare Officer and a Village worker (Gramsevak). The striking feature of Firka Development Scheme was its emphasis on village industries programme.

Some Shortcomings

The programme, however, suffered from a restriction in scope of its efforts and also for want of direction, policy-support and encouragement from the Central Government. It also suffered for lack of co-ordination with organisations operating at the same level. Though, through these schemes much good work has been done, the schemes stressed social and moral improvements more than economic improvement. They cared more for roads, wells, schools, reading rooms, libraries, sanitation, etc., than for improving agricultural yields. The Gramsevaks lacked technical knowledge for improving agriculture and livestock. Most of them were simply social workers. In all fairness, we must say, that despite these shortcomings a real beginning and an earnest effort has been made for regenerating rural life.

IX. MAHEWA-PILOT PROJECT – 1948

A Pilot Project was tried at Mahewa in Etawah District with American aid and the services of an American architect Albert Mayer were utilised by Uttar Pradesh Government in trying out the experiment. The selection of Mahewa Project was made on the basis that the area selected should be such as can be at par with any other average area in the country implying that facilities available there for work were not extra-ordinary.

The first area to be tackled had its centre in Mahewa, twenty seven km east of Etawah. The scheme in the first year covered 70 villages.

The Central Aim of this Pilot Project

The sponsors of the Pilot Project, Etawah, received inspiration, ideas and guidance from the efforts of the missionaries and other efforts of the various institutions, organisations, and individuals that appeared in the fireld ahead of the Pilot Project and took into consideration their strong and weak points. The central aim of the pilot project, Etawah, was to bring about a synthesis of the good features of the various fragmentary approaches and efforts and to carry out action research experiments to evolve suitable programmes, methods, and institutional and administrative patterns for a balanced physical, economic and social development of the rural communities through the combined and systematically planned efforts of the local people, government and voluntary agencies, on an aided and organised self-help basis with the help of modern scientific and technological aids, in harmony with the cultural traditions and genius of the people.

Objectives

The central aim of the Pilot Project was spelt out in terms of objectives as follows:

1. To see what degree of productive and social improvement, as well as of initiative, self-confidence, and co-operation, can be achieved in the villages of a district not the beneficiary of any set of special circumstances and resources, such as hydroelectric development of large scale industry.

2. To ascertain how quickly those results may be obtainable, consistent with their becoming permanently part of the people's mental, spiritual and technical equipment and outlook after the special pressure is lifted.

3. To see whether these results, if attainable, could be had at a cost in material and personnel which would be within the reach of the state by the existing departments and agencies.

Approach and Methods

Some of the basic principles that guided the approach and methods of work in the Pilot Project are listed below :

1. Emphasis on self – help; (2) Simultaneous improvement on the physical and human plans; (3) Democratic approach and people's participation; (4) Reproducibility (5) The local potential – the local felt-needs and the available local resources, supplemented by outside resources as the basis of programme; (6) comprehensive and integrated approach; (7) Phasing from simple to more complex through selectivity, concentration and time-growth; (8) Economic spear head-focus of activities must be chosen, based on the villager's felt-needs, around which we can later expand his horizon of needs; (9) Rigorous planning and realistic targets; (10) Changes in the attitudes of officials ; (11) Institutional approach; (12) Co-operation of governmental and non-governmental organistions : (13) Full exchange of information between change agencies : (14) Maintenance, follow-up and people's take-over; (15) Economic programmes as key stones of community development; (16) co-ordination between extension services and supplies; and (17) Collaboration by technicians and social scientists. Both the technical as well as the social sciences have their important and complementary roles to play in community development. The provision of a Rural Life Analyst and social education workers is as vital as that of the men qualified in physical sciences. Thus we find right types of methods and approach being made in the Pilot Project.

Organisation

The workers engaged in the programme were re-oriented as people's servants and not as people's masters. It was a team work. A very important member of the team was the "Multipurpose Village Level Worker", who was responsible for many activities at his level. The idea of the village level worker was not new. Brayne had his "Village Guides", and Tagore and Gandhi had their village workers, who served the villges in their own way. But Mayer's Village Level Worker was better trained and better paid.

Another important addition to Mayer's team was a Rural life Analyst-a trained sociologist. The other members of the team were, one District Planning Officer and four Deputy Development Officers (Agriculture, Engineering, Training and Village participation) who worked at the Project-headquarters. They were helped by two Area Assistant Development Officers and five Assistant Development Officers who looked after their own respective areas. In each area there were 12 village level workers, covering about four villagers each, who actually came in greatest contact with the villagers. To keep the workers in touch with the programme and with each other, a regular meeting of the "Team Working Council" was held every fortnight which was attended by all officers and two representatives of the village level workers, selected by rotation. The village level workers used to hold their separate meetings also which were attended by Panchayat secretaries, co-operative supervisors, adult literacy teachers, and women welfare officers of the area. Discussions were free and joint decisions were taken.

Programme of Work

The specific programme of work consisted of increasing agricultural production through the introduction of improved varieties of seeds, chemical fertilisers, green manuring, compost making, improved implements, irrigation, plant protection measures, horticultural development, soil conservation, improved cultural practices etc., improvement of animal husbandry through upgrading of cattle, disease control and management; provision of co-operative services for credit, production, marketing and supply, better sanitation and health services, control and eradication of human epidemics, provision of maternity and child welfare services, improvement of roads, water-supply, drainage and other public utility works, improvement of housing, and last but not the least, a broadbased social education programme by means of adult literacy classes, study tours, field demonstrations, provision of reading room and library service, one-act plays, competitions, farmers' fairs, work with rural institutions and organisations, village leaders' training camps and mass contact programmes.

Results

Significant results have been achieved in numerous fields in the project. Naturally it attracted world-wide attention and numerous visitors from other parts of India as well as many countries of Asia, Europe, America and Africa, visited the Pilot project to study its working with a view of applying the lessons to other parts of the world. The success of the Project paved the way for Indo-US Technical Co-Operation Agreement of 1952 for the expansion of the community Development Programme on a large scale and the first 55 Community Development Projects were launched on October 2, 1952 on Gandhiji's birth day.

In regard to the achievement in several areas of the Project, spectacular results have been achieved in agricultural production. As mentioned in the programme of work, several innovations were successfully introduced in the field of agriculture. Equal has been the success in the field of animal husbandry, in up-grading the liver-stock and in preventing and eradicating diseases and epidemics.

The co-operative movement had gained momentum. Starting with only 30 societies with 608 members and Rs. 3,086/- as share capital, advancing Rs. 10,506/- as loans in 1948-49, the entire project area has been covered with 265 societies (later this number was reduced to 192 on account of merger into large-size societies) with 23,628 members, Rs. 654,580/- share capital advancing Rs. 2,410,822/- as loan in 1961.

In regard to rural industries, co-operative brick-kilns, manufacture of agricultural implements, sericulture and caning and fruit preservation have come into existence as part of the project work. Co-operative brick-kilns have been singularly successful and the growth in this industry has been phenomenal.

Further, significant progress has been achieved in the field of Community works. People's contribution was substantial. Not only a large number of roads, culverts, drains, school buildings and other community works were undertaken in the project area, but the Shramadan (Gift of labour) movement was born in the project area.

In the field of social education, village leaders' training camps and study tours have become popular and adult social education classes in the villages, provision of community centres and, above all youth programmes, have made considerable headway. Further, the general education programme also made big strides.

In the pilot project besides spectacular results, there were mistakes and failures in plenty. What distinguishes the Etawah project is that the mistakes were not repeated very often and the initial failures paved the way for the final success in most cases.

The Etawah Effect

The Etawah experiment proved that (1) Indian farmers,

if convinced, could take to new ways and increase the farm yield considerably, (2) self-generating rural development work need not necessarily take a very long time, (3) planned expenditure on rural development was an investment which paid off in tangible economic terms and (4) the Etawah story could be repeated elsewhere too. Encouraged by the achievements, the Government naturally sought to extend the Etawah Programme to other areas. Between 1949-51 the original project grew to include over 300 villages of the same district and was reproduced in four centres of Uttar Pradesh. It has been claimed that what the Rockdale experiment in England was to the World's co-operation movement and what the Tennessee valley Authority was to the Etawah project had become to the revitalisation of the life of the World's peasantry. We must say that Etawah experiment opened a new chapter in the history of rural reconstruction in India and has provided a pattern on which an all India edifice could be built.

Reasons for Success

Systematic planning and democratic approach to programme implementation were factors that contributed to the success. The able leadership of Mayer was another factor. His technical knowledge helped development in several areas. As an army man he had the necessary executive capacity. He planned minutely, kept the supply line open, drilled his co-workers thoroughly and fixed targets for achievement. Thus his workers knew the "how", "what" and "when" of the whole programme. Another factor was, he was free from any red-tapism. This complete freedom to experiment gave him wide scope for free action and flexibility. Another important factor was, he tackled the problem of agricultural production first. Increased production per acre convinced the farmer about the usefulness of development work. This created the necessary psychological background and economic base for future efforts, and was one of the biggest reasons for Etawah's success.

Thus the personal qualities of Mayer (and his associates), his direct approach to Nehru and Pant, and the success of his agricultural programm were the three main factors responsible for the success of the Etawah experiment. After Mayer's departure the work became slack.

X. NILOKHERI-S. K. DEY-1949

Nilokiheri was another pioneering attempt which drew country wide attention and influenced the C.D. Movement directly through its example and indirectly through the former minister of Community Development and co-Operation, S.K. Dey, who was the moving spirit behind the project.

Partition of the country resulted in the refugee problem and these thousands of unfortunate up-rooted people could not be fed, clothed and sheltered indefinitely any longer by the government. They had to be rehabilitated. A new harmonious society had to be built from an heterogeneous gathering of people. A stupendous task which fell on the able and willing shoulders of S.K. Dey, Kurukshetra, a hundred and fifty kms from Delhi on the main road to Ambala, was receiving the bulk of the refugees. S.K. Dey a foreign trained engineer with administrative experience, was at that time living among the displaced persons at Kurukshetra. He became concerned about the future of thousands of displaced persons. His knowledge and experience of his own village community helped him to blue-print a new society. He made a survey of the camp population, their immediate needs and requirements and the potential of the campers. This potential was harnessed fully and one scheme after another came in, all emphasizing self-help and thus a new town-ship and a new society emerged.

Nilokheri Township was designed to rehabilitate about 7,000 displaced persons on a 1,100 acre plot of marshy land which was transferred to the colony in 1948. The township was afterwards integrated with 100 villages around it. The scheme was called "Mazsoor Manzil", because it was based on the principle of "He who would not work neither shall he eat". Right of living was guaranteed till surplus was available with any member of the colony. Equal rights for education and hospital care for the sick were guaranteed. Religion was declared a private affair.

The objective was to attain self-sufficiency in the essential requirements for the township and the surrounding villages. A vocational training centre was the hub of activities. The colony had its own dairy, poultry, piggery, printing press, engineering workshop, tannery, bone-meal factory, all run on co-operative lines. To man these co-operative enterprises people were trained in the vacation of their choice. About 750 acres of marshy land was cleared and put under the plough. The industrial activities gave employment to about 1,200 adults out of 1,400 able-bodied ones. The colony was not only self-sufficient in its day-to-day needs but it could, in due course, repay the principal with interest.

Panchayat Revitalised

Besides the economic activities, attention was given to social welfare and cultural activities. Most of the economic activities as stated earlier were carried on, on co-operative lines. Side by side with co-operative activities, the activities of the Panchayat were also revitalised. The Panchayat was to look after the political and social aspects of the community life in the colony; it was given the responsibility for law and order, sanitation and community welfare, including assistance to the weaker sections of the community. The panchayat was to act as the forum for the grievances and complaints of the people. There were special sub-committees of the Panchayat to plan and supervise its various activities. Thus were the seeds of functional sub-committees, which adorn the Panchayati-Raj scheme today, sown in the little township of Nilokheri.

Problems Encountered

As the township grew, difficulties began to be encountered. The scale of the organisation of economic activities proved a formidable obstacle. To enjoy competitive advantages more specialisation, increased scale and flexibility in management were needed. Co-operative form of organising and selling production did not suit the industries where skills needs for management, were such a character, that equality or near equality in the distribution of income, could not be maintained. Nor did they suit enterprises where intimate responsiveness to consumer demands and flexible handling of production and sales were the essence of success. The co-operatives had problems of securing consensus and interest, particularly on the part of the personnel responsible for the management of co-operative enterprises. The co-operative sector, therefore, retreated from many of its earlier strongholds, and had to make way for the state or the private sector.

Secondly, unless the economic activities were linked with similar ones in other parts of the country, the growing demand for employment could not be met, particularly in case of workers who became unemployed after the termination of particular construction programmes. The frustration had its effect on the harmony of the institutional fabric, particularly on parnchayats and co-operative organisations, which were severely strained under the seething discontent of unemployed workers.

The villages which were conceived as integral limbs of the Nilokheri vision of society did not grow at the expected rate.

Nilokheri's Contribution

Nilokheri, however, has left an imprint on the face of the Community Development Programme in India. It gave the country its first administrator (Dey) of Community Projects. The idea of agro-industrial township as the nerve-centre of rural development services was recognised in the draft of the First Five Year plan and incorporated in the layout of the financial plan of the first fifty five community projects, even though this idea was put off subsequently and an attempt made to recapture its glimpse in the Second Five year Plan.

Nilokheri Today

The township of Nilokheri was subsequently handed over to the government of East Punjab (now Haryana) with adequate safeguards for the institutions and inhabitants of Nilokheri.

The government undertook to bear the burden of essential liabilities for the period it was considered unavoidable. The administration of the township was fully integrated with the Rehabilitation Department of the State government. The economy of the township has been linked up with the rest of the country. Nilokheri has paid back a substantial part of the investment made on the colony, and is continuing to pay the balance.

Nilokiheri still stands as an objectified dream of agro-industrial township and a constant reminder to the nation of a usefull idea lost in oblivion. It still claims its maturity in its spirit of fellow-feeling and a higher level of employment and income. Nilokheri became a symbol of progress through self-help and mutual aid. It was an outstanding experiment in the practice of secular socialistic living. Despite some problems and drawbacks in the experiment, Nilokheri is still an eminent centre for training various kinds of development personnel and is rightly looked upon as a place of pilgrimage for development workers.

The significance of the Nilokheri experiment has been summed up in these words by Prime Minister Nehru in a message to the anniversary issue of 'Kurukshetra in October 1953.'

"All over India we have centres of human activity which are like lamps spreading their light more and more in the surrounding darkness. This light has to grow till it covers the land. Among these centres, there is Nilokheri which has achieved a good deal of fame in India and outside. That brings a greater responsibility on Nilokheri and on other like centres. They are the examples for others to follow and they must keep up high standards because it is quality that will tell in the end, not the quantity".

XI. INDIA VILLAGE SERVICE (I.V.S.)

Arther T. Mosher of New York, and B.N. Gupta, a big Hindu business man, established it in 1945. B.N. Gupta engaged himself in research work and prepared many a statement in support of his views. When the idea was being contemplated in New York, Dr. William H. Wiser was also thinking on the same lines. Dr. Wiser and his wife came to India and started this rural reconstruction organisation in a model village called Alenganj in Kanpur.

Philosophy and Objectives

Any Organisation, public or private, formulates its own philosophy which guides in the selection and operation of particular programmes. The objectives of this organization were to assist village people to realize the best in their own villages, by developing individuals, voluntary leaders and local agencies, and enable them to be effective in helping themselves and others. That is, in short, to approach man in every aspect of his life. The objectives also included assisting Government in developing villages. Faith in the common man, if taken to its logical conclusion, should lead to the belief that with proper guidance, village people can develop their own local – programmes and generate leadership from among themselves.

Methods of Work

India Village Service adopted some general methods of work which were used in all the specific programmes that have been developed. For realization of the above mentioned objectives, the organisation adopted the techniques like, personal contacts, informal discussion groups, use of volunteers, demonstrations, use and production of visual aids, exhibitions, tours and trips, dramas, books, periodical, etc., In selecting personnel under this organisation, top priority was given to teachers. These teachers were not the type of teachers who felt satisfied with classroom lectures alone.

Teaching begins with the awareness of the need. The village worker is the teacher, who is also a guide who meets the villagers informaly in small natural groups. He discusses with them their specific problems and attempts to bring the discussion to a focus in order to arrive at a procedure with which they would be able to tackle their problems. The procedure, so arrived at, would be within the villagers own realm of action. India Village Service thought that the felt-needs of the community should be the starting point of work. It was deliberately non-institutional in the sense, that it did not have a fixed pattern of work. It maintained flexibility to meet various needs. It also joined hands with other institutions working for village development.

The work should not exceed a limited period. This provision was there to create self-reliance and self-confidence and ultimately local leadership among the village people.

It laid stress on the method of work and was not mainly concerned with measurable results.

Residents of fifteen villages were the beneficiaries of this organization. It has undertaken and completed numerous programmes, viz., health programme, recreation programme, industrial programme, general education programme, etc., These programmes were carried out by the organisation after having gained adequate knowledge of the felt –needs of the people.

I.V.S. also had rendered service in fields like cottage industries, animal husbandry, education, publication and distribution of periodicals, giving visual aids, family – planning etc.,

A very interesting feature of this organization was, it had organized a number of student – work – camps during annual holidays.

From the beginning, this organization had been emphasising the importance of people co-operating with government, because it felt, that government alone could assist in the work of development in the India Village Service area. Government is the only institution which can shoulder big financial commitments and such large scale programmes.

India Village Service was financially supported by donations and contributions. It had branches in Lucknow and Etah (U.P.) and was affiliated to the Presbytarian Church in U.S.A.

From its inception, it had been helping the people in achieving their needs and tackling their problems by its methods as mentioned above. It had widened the horizon of the village people so that they may strive for a better living.

XII. FISCAL COMMISSION – SIR V.T. KRISHNAMACHARI – 1949

While the Etawah and Nilokheri experiments were being tried, the Government of India appointed the Fiscal commission which recommended establishment of an extension service. They observed "In our view, the greatest need at present in India is an Extension Service with the object of bridging the gap between research and the practices of producer, similar to those which have been so valuable in U.K., U.S.A. etc. What we have in mind is an Extension Officer with the necessary staff for a group of forty or fifty villages working on a demonstration farm. The officer will be an agent of all the development departments in the implementation of the schemes of improvement for the villages in the centre and the guide and the friend of the farmers in the area and in close contact with them". The Fiscal Commission had then envisaged an extension agency of the kind we now have.

XIII. THE CONSTITUTION OF INDIAN REPUBLIC – 1950

The cue to fundamental changes in the country's administration was given by the constitution which articulated the revolutionary urge of the freedom struggle. It envisaged a state-order in which "justice social, economic and political shall inform all the situations of national life" 2. It brought into being a system of responsible government. Articles 36 to 51 of the Constitution lay down the fundamental principles which should govern the exercise of legislative and executive authority of the state. These provisions are believed to contain constitutional sanction for C.D. programme, the relevant articles of the constitution may, therefore, be examined more closely.

Article 40 lays down an important obligation upon the State in relation to the Panchayats. It says, "The state shall take steps to organise village panchayats and endow them with such powers and authority as may be necessary to enable them to function as units of self-government".

Article 43 directs the state to ensure all workers a living wage, conditions of work ensuring decent standard of living, and full enjoyment of leisure and social and cultural opportunities. In particular, the state shall endeavour to promote cottage industries on an individual or co-operative basis in rural areas. Article 47 lays down that the raising of the level of nutrition and standard of living of the people and improvement of public health shall be the primary duty of the state. Article 48 requires the state to make endeavour to organise agriculture and animal husbandry on modern scientific lines. A multi-subject-matter-extension service is no doubt in line with the Directive Principles of State Policy. The combination of community development and extension may be interpreted as an attempt to combine the quality of social justice with the endeavour at raising the standard of living. The constitution represents a culmination point of the political and social urge born during the freedom struggle which continues to inspire the current attempts at rural reconstruction. The authors of the Grow More Food Enquiry Committee has these provisions in mind while formulating their proposals for a national extension service which were subsequently adopted by the Government of India. Reference to the Constitution is legitimate as constituting a very important link in the series of development that gave C.D. in India a sense of urgency. It also reinforced the faith of the planners and people alike in devolving functions, powers, and resources upon the institutions of rural local self-government. The constitution thus provided the spring board for action in Community Development Programme.

XIV.GROW MORE FOOD ENQUIRY COMMITTEE SIR. V.T. KRISHNAMACHARI – 1952.

The Government of India has launched the programme for augmenting food production in the form of "Grow More Food Campaign" in 1942 but the reasons for its failure needed investigation. A grow more food enquiry committee was accordingly set up under the chairmanship of Sir. V.T. Krishnamachari. The recommendations of the Committee were endorsed by the Planning Commission and the Government of India. The main recommendations for the Grow More Food Enquiry Committee were that the scope of the campaign should be enlarged to include a wider plan of development of village life in all its aspects. The implication was that, in order to grow more food and increase agricultural production, the purpose can never be achieved by merely concentrating on agriculture. It can be achieved only if an integrated view of life is taken and assistance rendered to the villager in a manner that it takes into account all the inter-related aspects of his existence. The Grow More Food Enquiry Committee also recommended that in order to increase food production, it is necessary to develop and mobilise local leadership. For doing so, institutions like Panchayats and co-operatives should be developed and utilised. The most significant contribution that the Grow More Food Enquiry Committee made was in its proposal to establish an extension organisation for rural development. The committee envisaged and recommended creation of an extension service for permanent farm improvement. The report emphasised categorically that all aspects of rural life are inextricably inter-connected and individual items cannot be dealt with in isolation. By saying so, it was not suggested that particular problems should not be given due prominence, but it was indicated that plan for them should form part of and be integrated with those for achieving the wider aims. The committee emphasised that "It is only by placing this ideal of bringing about an appreciable improvement in the standards of rural life and making it fuller and wider, and ensuring that the energies of the entire administrative machinery of states and the best non-official leadership are directed to plan for its realisation, that we can awaken mass enthusiasm and enlist the active interest and support of the millions of families living in the countryside in the immense task of bettering their own conditions".

Sarvodaya Plan 1952

The Sarovodaya workers also drew up a plan which was Gandhian in principle and also high-lighted scientific development of agriculture. The scheme was worked out by non-officials in the states of Maharashtra and Gujarat. It received guidance from Vinobaji and Sri Jayaprakash Narayan and later on, embodied within it the Bhoodan (gift of land) and the Gandhian movements.

XV. COMMUNITY DEVELOPMENT PROGRAMME - 1952

Community Development Programme is, thus, a blending of all the features of various attempts made in the past. It represents a synthesis of divergent approaches which is so characteristic of Indian Culture. It also represents the aspirations of a young democracy. Some of the important lessons learned from various attempts enumerated before are that

1. An integrated approach to all aspects of village life is absolutely essential for any programme of rural development (Sriniketan, Martandam, Baroda Plan, Grow More Food Enquiry Committee Report, Etawin Pilot Project etc.)
2. The Programme should be initiated by people with proper understanding and conviction. If it is imposed from out side, it does not sustain itself. (India Village Service, Martandam, Gurgaon).
3. Assistance of Government and need for a policy support are necessary to develop a programme of wide coverage in rural areas (Firka Development Scheme, Gurgaon).

4. The programme should be developed around felt-needs of the people so that their interest is sustained on enduring basis (Etawah Pilot Project)
5. Existing institutions should be revitalised and utilised, (Baroda Plan, Grow More Food Enquiry Committee Report).
6. Channels of service should be co-ordinated (Etawah Pilot Project).
7. Development work should be intensified in a compact area for radiation effect (Sriniketan, Baroda Plan, Etawah Pilot Project).
8. Systematic and continuous training of workers is necessary so that they develop a proper approach and attitude to service (Sevagram, Sriniketan, Etawah Pilot Project).
9. An organisational frame cannot serve unless the communities develop a spirit of working together (Nilokheri).

From 1957 onwards, the evolution of the new concept and programme of community development started and it marked an epoch making turn in the annals of India.

XVI. AN ASSESSMENT OF THE EARLIER ATTEMPTS

Tagore being a poet and visionary emphased the development of the total personality of the individual. Gandhiji, being a political agitator and social reformer, offered tools with which he proposed to fight the battle of political and social liberation. Dr. Hatch, being a missionary, could enlist the support of the local members of Y.M.C.A., Brayne, being an administrator, was concerned with the contents of the programme and the administrative architecture to carry it out. The common ground among the attempts was the moral and spiritual meaning which, when linked with the cultural traditions of the country, could fire the deepest emotions of the citizens.

There were short-comings also. The various attempts made by earlier pioneers were isolated. Barring Baroda, which profited from Martandam experiment, and Srinikethan which benefited by a short stay of Mahatma Gandhi, each worked independently without making use of the experiences of others. The principles of approach were almost the same in all the attempts. Their coverage was limited because they could not command the necessary resources for an extensive programme. The attitude of the government of the day was not quite sympathetic and came in the way of providing necessary security to the workers. The technical support was lacking so that more difficult problems had to be left alone. The political climate and the governmental attitude were not favourable.

However, they blazed the trail. Tagore gave the holistic cultural approach to the problem of rural reconstruction. Martandam experience in extension contained the desirable contents. He had already suggested the idea for a multipurpose functionary at village level. The ruling party drew inspiration form Gandhiji's ideology of rural reconstruction after independence and was largely committed to it. The lessons learnt from all these trials formed the bed-rock of the present Integrated Rural Development.

XVII. PROBLEMS OF RURUAL RECONSTRUCTION

It is desirable to discuss the conditions governing the situation in rural India prior to the Introduction of C.D. programme as an official programme before we discuss the features of the programme itself. The rural situation in India was dominated by the following factors (most of them still persist) from which arose the main problems of rural reconstruction and development.

1. A very low level of production largely due to the employment of primitive methods of farming.
2. Lack of resources for investment in development work and a very low rate of capital formation.
3. Considerable unemployment and more underemployment.
4. Limited capacity of the rural people to take advantage of science and technology.
5. A disintegrating community,

These factors, as can easily be seen, are inter-related. Together, they account for the existence of a static and depressed state of economy which has not the capacity to grow on its own impulse and resources. For some time to come, the rural areas will have to depend very largely on, and these are only two, land and man-power.

In a country like India, the society is traditional and predominantly agricultural. A programme of change in it has to be stimulated and guided. New ways of thinking always create psychological insecurities. Change is particularly dreaded in a traditional society because, no one is certain about what may really happen and what can be expected. The old ways and practices upheld by them for generations are likely to be taken for granted as the air they breathe. Thus, there is resistance to change from the people and their leaders who find it advantageous to perpetuate the old way of life. There is also resistance from others whose vested interests in leadership are threatened by change. Introduction of change, therefore, requires careful handling and needs control by skilled workers who have both knowledge and perception to understand how change takes place. They need to possess skills to work with people to induce them to change.

In sociological setting, the Indian society is a "folk society" having limited communication facilities, closed within itself being illiterate and conservative. There are several social, moral and cultural norms which inhibit the villager in India to accept change and to introduce innovations in his way of living. It is widely recognised that for economic development of a traditional society, several non-economic factors have to be tackled to change the thought and behaviour patterns of people. Nothing else than Community Development could be conceived of as an effective way of bringing about social change through educational process. In economic setting, the low per-capita income, the predominance of old traditional modes of agricultural production, the extremely low rate of capital formation, fast growth of population outstripping the productive potential of agricultural output, and the relative absence of capital forming goods – all these combine to point towards the programme of C.D. as the only way of breaking the vicious circle of low productivity, low yields and low vitality of the people. In political setting, the ideals and aspirations of a nascent democracy for achieving a co-operative common wealth and establishing a welfare state pledged to ensure the greatest good to everybody could do nothing better than adopt Community Development as a way of achieving these objective. It would have been far easier to achieve results by fiat, to concentrate on increasing agricultural production through big land holders who have the wherewithal, the technical know-how, the entrepreneurial skills and the capital to invest but the ideals of social justice and democracy could not countenance such programmes as would benefit the "haves" and make the poor poorer still. The concept of people's participation is the crux of Indian Community Development programme. Conceptually and ideologically it is not merely a programme of area development but is essentially a programme which tends to develop communities and which aims to harness the gigantic potential of hundreds of thousands of effectively organised village groups. It aims at harmonising village factions for the greater good of the whole community. The programme combine all elements of an orgainsed activity which are needed to accomplish effective co-operation between local community groups and sources of technical, economic and local assistance which local groups must receive for their growth.

XVIII. COMMUNITY DEVELOPMENT AND NATIONAL EXTENSION SERVICE

In 1952, the government of India started 55 community development projects on a pilot basis each covering about 300 villages. Each project was divided into three administrative units called "blocks", of 100 villages, each with a population of about 60,000 to 70,000 and a total area of 230 to 250 square kms. The expenditure provided for each project was Rs. 65 Lakhs and for finances for running them were provided by the U.S. Government. The then U.S. Ambassador, Mr. Chester Bowels got personally interested in getting the scheme launched. The community Development created a new upsurge in the country-side. The people responded enthusiastically by contributing money and labour. By that time the Grow More Food Enquiry Committee which made an elaborate study of the agricultural problems of India recommended the establishment of the National Extension Organisation for rural work which could reach every farmer, assist in the co-ordinated development of rural life as a whole' covering the entire country. Recommendation and public clamour for opening more blocks led the government of India to start the National Extension Service Scheme. Further, the results achieved in the community Projects were encouraging and its was, therefore, decided that the pattern of C.D. Organisation may be expanded and gradually spread over the entire country. From October 2, 1952 onwards, its coverage of the country by 5,200* national Extension Service blocks was staggered till October, 1963. The community

* As of now there are 5, 0911 Blocks.

projects were launched under the aegis of the Community Projects Administration, Planning Commission. It was thought that the Progarmme would get an impetus if a ministry was formed. In 1965 the Community projects Administration was converted into an independent ministry.

The National Extension Service was introduced in four different phases in the initial stages and each phase was characterised by the kind of work required to be done within specified period and by the provision of fund made available for carrying it out. In the "Pre-extension phase" which was the first in the series of four phases, the staff and the budget were nominal. In the second phase known as the "National Extension Phase", the budget provided was .7.5 lakhs for three years. In the third phases, which was known as "Community Development phase", the period was similar as in the second but the amount was doubled with a view to intensify efforts. The assumption was that communities would have been by then aroused and enlightened enough to participate in a more intensive manner. Budget provision was therefore, made for 15 lakhs instead of 7.5 lakhs in this phases. The fourth and the final phase was known as the "post-intensive phase" in which no special provisions were made and it was assumed that the available departmental funds would suffice to carry on the normal activities that could stabilise themselves as a result of intensive programme of Community Development, which confused the workers and the people alike.

The Programme did not register the kind of response its was expected to stimulate and a committee was therefore set up to evaluate the plan projects. The Committee on plan projects, therefore, suggested that these distinctions should be dropped out and it proposed that the block should be managed in three stages, the first being "pre-extension" stage lasting for one year with a minimum provision of staff consisting of one Block Development officer, one Agricultural

Extension Officer, 5 Village Level Workers, and a budget provision of Rs. 18,000. It emphasised agricultural production as the primary activity and carried on a comprehensive socio-economic survey of the area selected. In the second stage, the schematic budget for 5 years was 12 lakhs whereas in the third stage, it was 5 lakhs for 5 years. The personnel in both the stages were to be the same and the budget of 5 lakhs for 5 years was to be repeated indefinitely. And this pattern was changed subsequently.

XIX. COPP TEAM REPORT-1957AND PANCHAYATI RAJ

After the Community Development programme which was gradually expanding to cover larger areas, was under implementation for about 4 years, in January 1957, a study team under the chairmanship of late Sri Balwnatray Mehta was appointed by the Planning Commission to review the working of community development programme and also the question of reorganising district administration to provide for popular organisations between the village and state levels.

The study team recommended, inter alia, the setting up of elected and organically linked democratic bodies at the village, block and the district levels and the entrustment of all planning and developmental activities to these bodies. This new proposal came to be known as "Democratic Decentralisation", and it is popularly know as Panchayati Raj.

The study Team also proposed that the Ministry of Community Development should take over the management of co-operative. Societies, and all panchayats and it also suggested that is should co-ordinate all activities of rural development in the block and below.

These recommendations were accepted by the Government of India and the result is Panchayati Raj in most of the States of India.

The new statutory institutions Gram Panchayat, Panchayat Samithi and Zilla Parishad* have become the agencies of Community Development – Extension Programmes. In essence this was a further growth in the previous prorgramme, designed to strengthen people's own democratic elected organisations by opening new avenues of opportunities for development. This new device, this institutional approach offers the villages a share in their own direction and self-development which is indeed a new and novel departure in their lives.

Community Development Programme can be considered to have evolved in India through some distinct phases. The first could be called official phase in which the programme was ushered in by the Government endeavoring to secure people's participation. The programme was then being run by the Community projects Administration as an arm of the planning Commission. A Ministry of Community Development was formed in 1956. The programme grew into the second phase which could be called and advisory phase in which the developmental organisations at operational levels were made representative and the "Block Advisory Committees" were designated as "Block Development Committees". This was done after two years of the implementation of the National Extension Service Programme and the idea was crystalised in the Ootacamund Conference of Development Commissioner held in 1954. It was exmphasised that the Block Advisory Committee should be made more representative and really effective. The next phase in which the programme grew could be called a representative phase through which it passed since the Mount Abu conference of Development Commissioners held in 1958. In this phase, an attempt was made to make Community

---

* The nomenclature of the second and third tiers differs in some states, viz., Taluka Development Board, Panchayat Union Council, District Development Council, etc.

Development programme a people's programme with government participation instead of being a Government programme with people's participation .The Mysore conference of Development Commissioners held in1959 emphasised democratic decentralisation as a method of enforcing and giving of practical shape to the growth of local leadership idea.

The genius of Indian Community Development Programme lies in that it combines the elements of extension education and community organistion in the same programme. As Mukerji points out, it is a programme of simultaneously building up democracy, ensuring social justice and promoting economic achievement it from stems for the five articles of faith he points out in his book "Community Development in India"[3].

(a) Faith in the capacity of the rural people

(b) Faith in Democracy

(c) Faith in science and technology

(d) Faith in (of workers) rural development and

(e) Faith in social justice

The Community Development Programme is an integral part of the Five Year plans. These plans aim at promoting an all-round development of the country in a planned and democratic manner. The Community Development Programme is aimed at developing the rural sector.

The same basic objectives and policies govern both the Community Development programme and the Five-Year Plans. These may be very broadly described as economic development, social justice and democratic growth.

Thus far we have briefly looked into the efforts made earlier by several individuals and institutions towards ameliorating the poor living conditions people in the villages. We have also highlighted the positive factors and limitations in respect to the earlier measurers to improve the living standards of the people in the villages. In the chapters that follow we bring out the lessons that emerge from the earlier experiments in rural development and in the ensuing chapters we highlight the strategies and tested methods of working with the people towards their growth and development.

REFERENCES

1. The material on earlier experiments in Community Development is mainly drawn form the two sources cited:

   Setty, E. DESINGU. *Community Development And Extension in India.* Gandhigram, Gandhigram Institute, 1970.

   Pande, V.P. *Village Community projects in India* Bombay, Asia Publishing House, 1976.

   Other related sources on earlier experiments :

   Krishnamachari, V.T. *Community Development in India.* (Revised Ed.) New Delhi, publications Division, Govt. of India, 1962.

   Jain, Sugan Chand. *Community Development And panchayati Raj in India.* Bombay, Allied publishers, 1967.

   Chawadhari, T.P.S. (Ed) *Selected Readings on Community Development.* Hyderabad, National Institute of Rural Development, 1967.

   Ensminger, Douglas. *A Guidet to Community Development.* New Delhi, Ministry of Community Development, Govt. of India, (Revised), 1962.

   Directorate of Extension and Training, Ministry of Food and Agriculture, Govt. of India. *Towards A Welfare State.* New Delhi, 1956.

   Ministry of Food and Agriculture, Govt. of India . Report of the *Grow More Food Enquiry committee.* New Delhi, 1952.

   Planning Commission, Govt. of India. *Report of The Team for The Study of Community projects and National Extension Service:* (Vol. I, II,III) New Delhi, 1957.

Taylor, Carl. et. al. India's Roots of Democracy. Calcutta, Orient Longmans, 1965.

2. The Publications Division, Govt. of India. *The Constitution of India.* New Delhi.
3. Mukerji, B. *Community Development In India.* New Delhi, Orient Longmans, 1961.
4. National Institute of Rural Development. *Trends in public policies, Strategies for Rural Development, and Rural Development Programmes in the Successive Five Year Plans of India* (Mimeo) Hyderabad,1983.
5. Setty, E. Desingu. *A Study of Leadership in Two Valaya Communities in Tamil Nadu.* The Indian Journal of Social Work, Vol. XLII, No. 4, (June 1982) , Bombay, Tata Institute of Social Sciences.
6. Foster, George M. *Traditional societies and Technological Change.* New York, Harper & Row, Publishers, 1973.
7. Setty, E. DESINGU. *Field Approach to Entrepreneurial Development in The Communications of Ideas,* (Ed), New Delhi, Concept Publishing Co., 1980.

2

LESSONS FROM THESE EFFORTS TOWARDS RURAL DEVELOPMENT

Rural development under diverse nomenclatures, during the past five decades in most of the developing countries, has been an adventurous effort with models and theories of development, strategies and methods involving policy makers, planners, administrators, scientists, technologists, academics and ordinary workers. It is a programme of developing rural communities with a network of organizations and institutional linkages from the national level to the village level with several layers of administration in between. It is a multifaceted programme initiated and launched with great hopes and high promises. Some developmental schemes attempted were unchartered explorations. In some respects, it was a trial and error approach. But none can deny the significant contribution of rural development in terms of generation of new schemes, programme planning, programme implementation, organizational set-up, institutional linkages, strategies and methods adopted and the results achieved. Yet, we can draw some lessons from this fascinating journey of rural development.

APPROACHES AND STRATEGIES FOR RURAL DEVELOPMENT THUS FOR INITIATED

With imagination, ideas and new kinds of approaches

with all hopes and expectations of development of various segments of population and sectors during the past five decades we have both at the national and at the state level initiated, instituted and carried on diverse type of developmental programmes which are activity-oriented, segment-oriented and area-oriented which are such as the following:

- Multi-subject-matter extension education
- Aided Self-help programmes
- Development of local organizations
- Comprehensive Regional Development
- Decentralized Development Administration
- Intensive Agricultural District Programme
- High Yielding Varieties Programme
- Land Reforms
- Cooperative Development
- Development of Rural Industries
- Farmers' Training and Education Programme
- Small Farmers Development Programme
- Rural Employment
- Rural Artisan Development
- Food for Work Programme
- Area Oriented Development Programme
- Minimum Needs Programme
- Intensive Cattle Development Programme
- Command Area Development Programme
- Integrated Dry land Agricultural Development Programme
- Drought-Prone Area Development Programme
- Hill Area Development Project

- Integrated Tribal Development Projects
- Desert Area Development Programme
- Applied Nutrition Programme
- Whole Village Development Programme
- Integrated Rural Development

It is not a question of pointing out that they have all failed but each one to do justice has achieved something tangible in terms of what was aimed at. But unfortunately, they were isolated and not functionally linked and integrated in terms of planning and delivery of services.

PLANNING

Planning has come to stay as an integral part of rural development activity. But unfortunately, the very act of planning and the plan document were taken for achievement. We realized that centralized planning without the knowledge and proper understanding of the local conditions, resources, needs, capabilities and the socio-cultural milieu of the people was ineffective and so we came up with decentralized or what you call bottom-up planning. But unfortunately, we have failed to strengthen and improve the planning machinery at the lower level with knowledge, skills, resources and decision-making authority. We have also come to realize that it is not merely top-down or bottom-up planning, and that each approach has certain merits and suffers from certain limitations and so it is wise to adopt a blend of both approaches relevant to the magnitude of development and the sphere of its operation.

PEOPLE'S PARTICIPATION

We came to recognize and realize that people's participation in rural development is a central feature and an unquestionable complement for success and sustainability of any development programme. Despite this recognition, we have largely ignored and failed to facilitate and institutionalize people's participation in developmental activities. We have made a mockery of it. In the name of people's participation, we have exaggerated and inflated the material and labour contributions from the people. We took material and money given by the people as their participation and failed to appreciate and encourage people's participation in terms of ideas, views and moral support.

WEAK GRASSROOTS LINKS

In the organizational structure and hierarchy in rural development, we find in general, a strong top and a weak bottom. Often, we meet with weak links at the grassroots operational level. The crucial part lies at the operational level in terms of understanding people, their problems, needs and motivating and involving them in activities beneficial to individuals and the larger community. Either in respect to expertise, status or recognition accorded, the personnel at the lower rungs of operation are rather weak. We need adequately trained, reasonably paid and highly motivated extension functionaries at the village level.

IGNORED WOMEN'S INVOLVEMENT

In general, we ignored women's involvement in rural development activities. It is not a plea on gender issue, but it is a question of maximal utilization of one half of human resources. In the historical evolution of mankind, woman has been an economic partner to man besides her biological and social roles.

The personnel in the various agencies engaged in socio-economic development programmes, especially the extension functionaries in rural development come in contact with and address themselves to the tasks of menfolk in the client community. Seldom are women contacted, their problems and needs looked into, their opinions and views sought, their participation solicited, appreciated and encouraged either because of traditional social restrictions and prejudices or that women are not reckoned with as important entities vis-à-vis the development programmes. The decision-making is not done by man alone though he is in the forefront of most of the business, commercial and social activities. The woman is there behind many decisions that concern social and economic issues of the family. It is a paradoxical situation that though woman is in the background, her understanding and choices influence the kind of decision a man takes and the course of action he pursues. In many a rural development programme, the women are a missing link. Needless to emphasize that the women are to be accorded the importance they deserve and facilitate their involvement as equal, responsive and potential partners in rural development.

TRAINING

Training of extension personnel and non-officials has been a significant and conspicuous activity as a means and as a necessary prerequisite for effective rural development. Thousands of extension personnel and subject-matter specialists needed a new orientation to work with rural people to improve their conditions of life. It is not just specialization in a subject or expertise in a technical field, but it is the right attitude and the conviction on the part of the development personnel that the people in the rural areas are capable of improving themselves to better standards of life. This orientation to a considerable degree was provided by training. Training of diverse nature offered at different levels and at different stages in the career of extension personnel has come to stay as an integral part of rural development.

THEORIES AND MODELS OF DEVELOPMENT

We were overwhelmed by our own and borrowed theories and models of development. We never bothered to understand and appreciate the indigenous knowledge system and integrate the new elements of development with the existing system. Sometimes, we outright discouraged and voted down the age-old functionally well-integrated and useful customs, practices and technology followed by the people. This was an unwise act on our part. We equated economic poverty of the rural people with intellectual poverty. We failed to listen to the people. Seldom we bothered to know the people's image of rural development, what they need, what they think their resources are, the way they think they should fulfill their needs and the kind of assistance they expect from the development agencies.

POOR FOLLOW-UP

Either compelled by targets or to gain entry into the community or to please some people or to meet some genuine needs of the people, with all initial enthusiasm and exuberance, we have initiated several projects and schemes, small and big, but failed to do the follow-up work. It may be a new idea, practice, method, device, technology or an institutional arrangement that has been initiated and introduced by the development agencies and adopted by the people. In such instances, often we failed to provide what may be called after-sale services. We abandoned the projects and schemes and left the people in the lurch to fend for themselves. It does not mean a continuous prop, but some newly initiated projects, individual or community-oriented warrant follow-up by the development agency.

INCREASE IN PAPER WORK

We increased paper work more than tangible, actual accomplishment in the filed, we increased the number of returns, and reports, a chain of reports from the field workers to higher-ups. At one time in Andhra Pradesh, the Village Level Workers (VLWs) presently designated Village Development Officers (VDOs) were to maintain 26 registers of different sorts. They had to spend a large part of their time in filling up the registers, posting figures of achievement, real and false to save their skin under the pressure of unrealistic and unattainable targets. In many cases, actual field work, over a period of time tended to be neat paper work. The work seriousness was lost.

UNREALISTIC TARGETS

Close to increase in paper work and influencing it, is the over-jealously fixing of targets for several activities. Targets are necessary, but they are to be based on time, resources, manpower, interest of people, their capabilities, physical possibility and sometimes, the relevance of targeted activities or items to the client community. Unfortunately, the target fixing in respect to several activities in agriculture, animal husbandry, health, sanitation and family planning for instance was centralized. The officials sitting at the regional or national level fixed the targets to be achieved. Then the targets as if they were funds, were distributed to the lower levels from one development administrative level to another across the hierarchy. Seldom, the lower levels whose burden it was to achieve the targets, questioned the higher-ups, the wisdom and practicability of the targets assigned to them. Since, more often, targets were not based on field reality and feasibility and since there was the tradition of the lower level administrative unit accepting the orders and instructions coming down from the higher level, the situation led to manipulation of figures of achievement and the statistical data as reported, sometimes, became doubtful of their reliability.

EXPECTED SPONTANEOUS RESPONSE FROM THE PEOPLE

The concept of felt-needs and the felt-needs approach has become popular in the literature of rural development. In some cases we assumed the felt-needs of the people in the rural areas and their priorities too. And so, we came up with our programmes and expected people to respond to them spontaneously, which often did not happen. Either we have not seriously assessed the felt-needs and the people's priorities thereof or we have not prepared and facilitated the people to respond to the programmes.

We expected miracles to take place in a short span of time. Time is an element in growth and development. We became impatient with the pace of people's march towards progress.

Development personnel going to the rural people instead of the other way about was a new and strange experience to the latter. Over a long period of colonial administration and a hard regulatory system of administration, more often, the rural people tended to be silent, passive spectators and receivers. In general, the initiative and action towards development was nipped in them. When development personnel lectured to the villagers on new projects and schemes, either out of sheer respect to the personnel or having not, comprehended the purport of the programmes or finding the programmes irrelevant to them, the villagers remained silent. We misjudged people's silence for their acceptance.

MORE SLOGANS AND PROMISES

Right from the politician and down to the village level extension functionary, we created more noise, came up with more slogans, made more promises to the people, but fell short of actualizing them. Slogans are a part of motivation campaign, a part of movement for development, appealing to the people's emotions, competitive spirit, stirring their unified and concerted action for their betterment. But if the slogans and promises fizzle out as empty sound, the development agency loses its credibility. This has happened in several instances in terms of promised supplies and services to the individuals and to the communities at large.

OVEREMPHASIS ON MATERIAL PHYSICAL DEVELOPMENT

There is no denying the fact that provision and creation of physical and material facilities constitute development, but we took such physical and material things as progress and the end of development. We laid more emphasis on roads, school buildings, toilets, community halls, play equipment, etc., and less on the human side, educating the people, motivating them to higher achievement and facilitating technical and managerial skills among them to increase the production pursuits. We failed to recognize and develop human resources maximally in the rural communities.

More often we thought for the people and acted for the people. In some cases, we made the rural people more dependent on the development agencies, instead of gradually building up and fostering self-confidence and self-reliance at the community level. What is needed is an inner change agency within the community. It comprises the local leadership serving as a positive and leading force for betterment of life in the rural communities. The inner change agency is a stimulant and a human asset.

Wherever we have demonstrated economic gain to the people, such schemes or activities have been successful. More often, short-term gains catch up faster. They serve as motivators to long-term projects. We should appreciate the fact that village people wanted a better way of life; that once the superiority of improved practices and ways of doing things was demonstrated, villagers would accept them; and that once the villagers were assured that the "outsiders" had an unselfish interest in their welfare and advancement, they would accept the outsiders' guidance.

PAMPERED THE RURAL ELITE

There are social and power barriers in the rural

communities. When it comes to reaching the poor and the disadvantaged, we have to pass through, in many instances, the rural elite. They are the nodes of power, authority and influence. The local elite pose as barriers as well as serve as stimulants and supporters to the cause of the rural poor. Some programmes are specifically meant to reach the poor in the community. But the extension personnel at the village level, often cannot reach the benefits and services to the poor directly ignoring the rural elite, since the latter perceive it as a threat to their standing and authority in the community and that their hold and influence over the poor would diminish. And so, as a strategy, the extension functionaries had to work through the rural elite, whether they liked it or not, of course with mixed results. In this process, though very much necessary, we tried to pamper and please and keep the rural elite in good humour. We expected the rural elite to work for, encourage and support the welfare programmes meant for the weaker sections. The results have been mixed. Sometimes, the elite blocked the flow of benefits to the poor. The extension personnel felt helpless and they could not either ignore or antagonize the powerful in the community. The encounter, defiance and challenge to the exploitative stumbling Block-the rural vested interests should come from within the community. Further, inadvertently or deliberately, we have contributed to the creation of cliques, factions and divisive forces in the rural communities.

WRONG CHOICES

We, unjudiciously and unimaginatively mixed up regulatory activities with extension functions. This has distanced the people from the extension functionaries. The latter playing a dual role has affected their primary extension role. We tried to plant new institutions and organizations like farmers' forums, youth clubs and women's clubs in the rural communities but most of them withered away soon, since they appeared superfluous in the context of life in rural communities predominantly of extended families and of a broad kinship system. One major lesson from rural development is that we are far from being effective in coordinating development activities.

CONCLUSION

We may conclude that political will, clear-cut policies, realistic objectives, effective organizational and institutional linkages, a blending of planning from below and above, enlightened involvement of the client system, building up and strengthening of local institutions, training of development personnel and people's leaders, implementing programmes with religious seriousness and continuous evaluation of the programmes would facilitate meaningful and sustained rural development.

3

PROGRAMME PLANNING TO MEET PEOPLE'S NEEDS

Rural development programmes are created and maintained for influencing people to make changes in their way of living and of making a living. The existence of such programmes implies that the present situation of the rural people is not what it should and could be, that something different should prevail, and that it is possible through appropriate action to attain a more desirable status for them. From this assumption another one arises: that it is possible and feasible for a person or group of persons – officials, non-officials or a combination of both – to identify the nature of new conditions that could and should prevail, and devise means for achieving them. Hence, the entire process of planning for rural development implies a need for change. The question then arises: change from *what,* to *what,* by *whom, where* and *by what methods?*

Changes that are important to people are those that help them meet their needs for biological, economic, social, aesthetic and moral well-being. Basically, all programmes for rural development exist to help people meet their needs. If programmes do not do this, people in free-choice societies will not long participate in them. The element of people's needs, therefore, becomes a central concern of planners for rural development. If a society is to find ways to adjust itself so that people meet their needs for an improved economic status, for being more useful citizens and for enjoying a higher degree of social satisfaction, it must identify these conditions and plan realistically to achieve them.

What needs do people have? How can needs be identified? What plan of priority should be set up for meeting people's needs? What resources are necessary to meet people's needs? How should resources be organized and directed to help people meet their needs? These questions give the key orientation and justification for rural programme planning.

THE NATURE AND ROLE OF PLANNING

The controlling objective of India's Rural Development Programmes is to develop in village people the ability to make a better living and to live a more satisfying life as individuals, as family members and as citizens of their community, state and nation. How to attain this objective is the key problem confronting the architects and current leaders of the scheme.

The first step in any systematic attempt to promote rural development is to prepare a useful programme. The term programme indicates focus, priority and design. It assumes the ability among the planners to distinguish important needs from unimportant ones. Such a programme must be based on people's needs to make it significant and on their interests to make it effective. "*If we could but know where we are now, and where we ought to go, we could better judge what to do, and how to do it*". This statement by Abraham Lincoln lies at the heart of the nature and role of planning for rural development. Effective programmes for rural improvement do not just happen; they have to be built. Planning does not go on in a vacuum, or automatically; it has to be made to happen. Good programmes are not developed merely by wishing for them, but by working for them.

The need for planning arises from the complexity and from the importance of the job to be done. Planning is a necessary aspect of any activity that is too involved to be disposed of off-hand. The use of planning is to discover and prepare the way for action that should be taken. Planning gives meaning and system to action. It prepares the basis for a course of future action. Possibly, the most basic fact-giving rise to planning is that effective rural development results from choice, not from chance; it results from design, not from drift; it results from a plan; not by trial and error. Hence, effective work is an intentional effort carefully designed to attain certain specific and predetermined goals assumed to be important.

The use of programme planning stems from a belief in the need for change that results in progress, and from the view that change in certain directions is good for those affected by it. Planning must, therefore, result in programmes that help people find more satisfactory modes of living and of making a living. Planning assumes that the programme, or the lack of one, followed in the past will not do the job in the present and the future.

Designing programmes for rural development is one of the most difficult tasks confronting rural development workers. This is so because planners must avoid programming that has superimposed characteristics and instead assure programmes that have roots among the people. The problem is complex because the components of rural programming are complex. People, their needs, their interests, useful technology, educational process, analysing situations, making decisions about what should be done, determining useful action, projecting the desired shape of things into the future and such other components of rural programming are rarely simple. Programme planning for rural development has but little research support, a wide range of patterns of approach, and consequently requires great imagination and judgement on the part of the planners.

Good programme planning is primarily an intellectual activity, for it usually involves a study and use of facts and principles. It requires knowledge, imagination and reasoning ability. Often it requires a mastery over special skills and techniques of research. It is basically a process of making decisions that will carry into the future. If these decisions are not made wisely, they may not lead to useful attainment. Decisions have to be made about what the present situation is, how it could and ought to be changed and what means can be sued to accomplish the new and more desirable situation. Finally, good planning for rural development requires the ability to synthesize facts and value judgements in a process of sound decision-making about the objectives the programmes should seek to attain and what courses of action are most likely to achieve them. The ability to plan requires:

1. an understanding of the nature and function of planning,
2. skill in formulating planning procedures,
3. skill in identifying problems and needs,
4. ability to decide on significant objectives and goals,
5. skill to formulating means and wise courses of action to attain objectives, and
6. skill in involving key leaders in the planning process.

The first condition of success for any programme to promote rural development is a widespread belief in the usefulness to a large number of people. Good plans are to the professional rural worker what the compass is to the seaman.

SOME GUIDES TO PLANNING

The broad aims set forth for India's Community Development Programme are great and important. They are complex and far-reaching. They are significant and difficult to achieve. But they are assumed to be worthy of effort, since foremost in the order of things they embody are social, economic and human values to which the new India is committed. The process through which these aims were derived was a long and tedious one involving many people, much study, interpretation of facts and careful application of judgement in arriving at final decisions. In short, a massive programme-planning job was done. Plans for rural development are usually made best when a number of propositions are followed in the planning process.

1. *Effective rural development programmes must have clear and significant objectives.* An objective is that which a person, group or agency sets before itself as an object or condition to be attained. Programme objectives designate directions of movement. Since that is so, objectives properly become the focus of primary material and human resources for attaining change. Maximum progress can be made only when the objectives are clear, full commitment of resources is made to achieving them and effective use is made of the resources.

If there is to be progress and not mere evolution in the development of people, the objectives of the programme must be clearly and periodically determined in view of progress and changed conditions. It should be kept in mind that not all people need or desire to move in the same direction or for the same distances. Directions have varying degrees of importance to different people. Extension workers must be prepared to offer opportunity for people to move in various directions. This is what is really meant by the term-balanced programme. Thus, a good programme objective is one that provides possible direction for large numbers of people to move some distance, a direction in which they want and need to move, then provide them assistance in traveling in those directions. This is really the essence of extension work for Community Development.

These facts place great importance on the wise choice of purposes. For, if the choice of purposes is not made well, the resources committed to their attainment will be poorly used. This is a mistake the leaders of India's rural development scheme can ill afford to make, especially at a time like the present when the objectives to be achieved are so numerous and so great and resources for achieving them so few and so small.

2. *To achieve the broad purposes of Community Development requires planning at the top level and also at lower levels including the state, district, Block and village.* Deciding purposes at these lower levels requires a degree of specificity that results in objectives being moved from the level of glittering generality to the level of practical reality. Identifying the most useful purposes, assigning a priority to them and developing effective means of achieving them at the local level is an intricate process which must ebb handled with great skill. If the statement of purposes at higher levels is to be realistic and useful in guiding the programme at lower levels, it must be reformulated at each lower level to align it with varying situations.
3. *There are no unplanned programmes.* Programme development is a relative matter. The quality of a programme is related to the extent to which certain steps are taken that are essential in planning. A number of crucial questions about programming must be asked and their answers taken into account in the planning process. Proper answers to them will improve the preciseness with which programmes are developed. These questions are:

a) To whom and to how many people is the programme important?

b) In what way is the programme significant to people – economically, socially, aesthetically, or morally?

c) What is the relative importance of programme objectives?

d) Who thinks the programme is important – nation, state, district, block, village?

e) Who arrived at the programme objectives?

f) On what amounts and kinds of information is the programme based?

g) Does the programme reflect significant needs and interest of large numbers of people?

h) Who is acquainted with the programme and its purposes?

i) How clearly conceived and understood is the programme by those who are to participate in its execution?

j) What would be the likely consequences in one, five or ten years if work on certain parts of the programme is not carried out?

4. *The most effective rural development programmes result when there is general agreement among village, block, district, state and national officials on three important items.* Village and block workers in order to plan the most effective programmes need to agree on (a) a basic philosophy regarding programme development, (b) a clear policy that reflects the basic philosophy, and (c) a workable procedure that gives general direction but provides ample latitude for

adjustments needed to meet local situations. Questions like the following may serve as a guide for this purpose:

a) What is the relative importance of programme development as a step in the rural development process?

b) Who should participate in programme development and in what way?

c) How much time should be allocated to the task of planning?

d) Should a so-called long-range programme be developed in each village and block?

e) Upon what kinds and amounts of factual information should the programme be based and how should this information be collected?

f) To what extent should procedures provide for participation of people at the village and block level?

g) Should the different phases of a block programme be organized into a single overall unified programme?

h) What is the role of the technical specialist in block and village programme development?

i) To what extent should leaders among the villagers participate and which method is most useful for providing this opportunity?

In relation to these questions there are many different points of view depending on established policy and other factors. But experience and sound principles of good programming suggest that such questions should be considered with care. One point of view suggests that when numerous problems are evident, as in Indian villages, decisions are easily made about what should be done. This argument has validity. But merely making decisions about what should be done is not enough. Also important is how the decisions are made, on what facts are they based, who participates in making them and what priority is to be followed in meeting the needs.

5. *Programmes are most effective when based on adequate and current facts pertaining to local conditions as well as those related to national and regional situations.* No rural development programme or any of its parts can be any better than the facts on which it is based. A programme must be based on adequate and current facts about the situation at all levels and related factors that influence it in order to be most effective. To be useful, these facts must finally be carefully analyzed and interpreted through the joint efforts of the technically trained staff and progressive village leaders. Facts about the local situation and others affecting it form the foundation upon which the Block staff and village leaders, working on various community development problems, build and carry out an effective programme. When properly weighed on the scales of people's values, these facts reflect local needs and the enlightened desires of people. Moreover, they show not only what people think they want, but also what is best for them. To define rural problems it is necessary to consider both scientific and folk knowledge. Thus, the true basis for a programme lies in the needs and problems of the individual, the home, the farm and the community.

The fact cannot be overstressed that local conditions furnish the basic problems with which rural development programmes must deal. People are most concerned about facts relating to their immediate situation as it affects them personally. Community development workers and local leaders use properly interpreted facts about local conditions to show how these facts directly and personally affect the people. In this way interest is aroused and indications found that lead to the solution to problems. Facts about the local situation help to identify problems and needs with which the people are concerned by pointing out the gaps between what is and what should be, by indicating shortages and by drawing attention to undesirable trends. To have adequate facts about a local situation, data that generally fall into these four categories must be obtained.

a) Current trends and outlook.

b) The people themselves – their needs, interests, knowledge, social organization, etc.

c) Physical factors about agriculture, industry, health, sanitation, etc.

d) Community problems – communication, education, etc.

6. *Selection of a relatively small number of the most significant needs singled out for major attention contributes to the effectiveness of rural development programmes.* When the resources for promoting rural development are limited, a programme cannot successfully be at the same time all things to all people. To identify problems or needs that are important is a relatively easy task, but it is not enough. Problems must be found that are not only important but that are most important. Consequently, some careful choice-making must be done. Since it is physically impossible to deal simultaneously with all the needs of people in a block or village, it is necessary to sort out for special attention those needs that are of greatest importance at a given time, thus developing a scheme of priority

for dealing with items in the programme. Programme elements may then be arranged according to relative amounts of time and other resources committed to them. Research quite clearly supports the idea that no single exposure of a person to a recommendation will usually produce much action. Getting the adoption of new practices generally requires that recommendations be brought to people's attention on several occasions spread over a period of time. It is necessary then, in cooperation with village leaders, to ferret out the most significant problems and weave them into the core of a vital and dynamic village and block development programme. The most significant problems can then be attacked with all the resources of the programme which collectively form a powerful force for economic and social change.

7. *Skilful involvement of progressive village leaders is fundamental in planning rural development programmes.* A synthesis of experience in planning rural programmes makes it clear that programmes developed *with*, not *for* or *by* the people, stand the best chance of success. Good programmes result from joint efforts of the technically trained development workers and the progressive members of the villages. The key to successful programme development, therefore, lies in weaving the following information together into decisions about what should be done: facts about local conditions, targets set up at national, state and regional levels, knowledge of block and village staff and that of local and village leaders.

This is a vastly complex task and one of the most important jobs and greatest challenges to better programming and, in turn, to more effective Community Development. There are many reasons that make constant work at this task worthwhile. In the first place, "it is not what the programme does for people but what it does *to* them that counts." Secondly, the assumption is very unsound that either the village leaders alone, or officials at the block, district or national level alone, have all the good ideas about what the programme should be. Good programmes should reflect the best knowledge and insights of *both* village leaders and professionally trained workers.

Furthermore, good planning procedures lead people to see beyond the present felt needs to the basic underlying problems. The ultimate performance must be by the people; for it is what they do that is of transcendent importance. It is clear, therefore, that rural development programmes – if they are to have their roots in the social and economic life of villagers – must be planned in villages and blocks around the needs and interests of the people. Programmes planned in this way become programmes of the people, with all the pride of authorship and satisfaction that comes from joint participation in both their planning and in execution.

All village people, of course, cannot be involved in this process. The problem of people's participation is handled by tuning in the masses through carefully selected village leaders. To attain worthwhile goals there usually must be some compromise between the ideal and the practical – between facts and value judgments. Is there any better way of assuring this than by involving village leaders with the block staff in analyzing situations and in making the decision on what should be done to improve conditions?

8. *Programmes that are planned for longer periods of time than one or two years tend toward greater effectiveness.* Long-time programming, or identifying objectives that aim into the future, is more likely to be effective for a number of reasons. The important needs of people usually cannot be met in the short period of one or two years. Changing what people

believe, what they do, and how they do it, is, at best, a slow process. Long and constant effort is usually needed to accomplish important community development objectives. To assure continued work on the most fundamental needs in a village or block requires provision in the programme for important elements to recur periodically. The formation of long-time objectives is a good technique for assuring continuation of work that focuses on major needs. This point of view suggests that care should be taken in the planning process to provide assurance that the short-term interests of people are also to their long-time advantage.

9. *Procedures in rural programming that assure fairly close integration of problems related to the farm, the home and the community appear to contribute to their soundness and effectiveness.* The word integration implies a smooth and efficient operation of a combination of activities or services in the solution of problems. In view of the wide scope of content in a community development programme and the common objectives of its phases, various aspects of the programme should be blended into one effective force aimed at building better rural communities. The primary way to achieve coordination and integration in programmes is through common understanding among officials as well as between them and non-officials. This can be attained most effectively through joint participation in appropriate phases of the planning process.

10. *Programme planning must take into account cultural values and the social system.* Rural development programmes cannot be most effective unless they are planned and carried out in harmony with the basic

cultural values held by people and the social setting in which they live. Cultural values reflect what people generally think is important. The social system tends to maintain adherence to the scale of established values. In traditional cultures, the social system and prevailing cultural values tend to serve as forces working against social and economic reform. Even in so-called advanced societies these influences are formidable. Programmes, therefore, cannot be most successful when they are too much at odds with innovations the value system will sanction. People's values and their social system must be understood and taken into account by planners of rural development programmes.

11. *Programme content must be determined with care and preciseness.* Predictions with a high degree of accuracy can be made about the probable outcome of programmes to promote change by examining their content. Content specifies the subject areas in which change is expected to be made. Consequently, the content of programmes is the most important index to new ways in which people may be influenced to behave. Programme content represents what actually will be attempted in changing people and the situation in which they live. Methods used for executing programmes are merely means to ends, not the ends themselves. The selection of the content of programmes of change tends, therefore, to be a central or basic concern in rural programme planning.

12. *The interpretation of the programme to officials and non-officials and to the general public is an essential step in successful programming.* It is important that the aims and objectives of programmes become common knowledge among villagers. Interpretation

means translating into familiar language or into terms that are readily understood as well as explanation of the meaning of facts as they apply to local conditions. Interpretation is important, for, unless people know what is available to them they cannot know what kind of help to request for.

PROFESSIONAL ABILITIES NEEDED BY PLANNERS

Planning effective programmes for Community Development requires a number of high-level professional skills. Needed abilities include understanding and skill in at least the following broad areas of competency:

1. Understanding of the nature and role of the Rural Development Services.
2. Knowledge and understanding of technology related to subjects with which the programme is to deal.
3. Ability to clarify the objectives of a programme and to state them so that they are useful in guiding its execution.
4. Ability to organize people and things.
5. Skill at seeing the relationship between principles and practice.
6. Skill at inquiry.
7. Skill in human relations.

In the following pages, a brief characterization is made of each of these areas of competency. If the suggestions made here provide some insight and serve as useful guides to further study, they will serve their purpose.

1. *Understanding of the nature and role of the multi-faceted Rural Development Programme.* Gaining an

understanding of the nature of the services extended in India and its role as a national initiative for promoting rural development, requires a knowledge of the following:

a) Development, present scope, philosophy and objectives of Community Development.

b) Organization and administration of the agency at the national, state, district, block and village levels.

c) The role of various categories of personnel at various levels in the hierarchy.

d) Responsibility and opportunity of the agency in a developing country.

Adequate competency in these areas is fundamental to effectiveness and leadership on the part of officials and non-officials in the entire organization. Each officer is a professional person. Knowing about one's professional affiliation is commonly viewed as a primary tool of the trade in any field of endeavour. Without this knowledge one cannot understand one's job, intelligently defend his profession, or suggest action to improve it. Likewise, he cannot effectively communicate opportunities to those who should participate. Effective professional leadership requires competency in this area on the part of all personnel engaged in the programme.

2. *Knowledge and understanding of technology related to subjects with which the programme is to deal.* Adequate knowledge and understanding of technology appropriate to one's professional job requires the following:

   a) Thoroughness of knowledge.

   b) Acquaintance with current technology.

c) Knowledge of reliable sources of technology.

d) Understanding of how technology relates to specific problems.

e) Continuous study.

Technology related to the various special fields with which Community Development is concerned constitutes the chief commodity the programme has to offer to people. Whether the subject is agricultural production, social education, cooperatives, home science, youth work or any other, a body of useful technology is assumed to be available. Every successful educational effort requires significant technology appropriate to the problems dealt with. Subject-matter or technology is to workers in rural development what food is to human beings; it is life's sustenance. To attempt to teach others something one does not know oneself is to invite failure from the start. Every official in the community development organization, therefore, should have not only adequate knowledge of appropriate technology in his particular field of operation, but also an understanding of it and its relationship to the problems of villagers.

3. *Ability to clarity objectives of a programme and state them so that they are useful in guiding its execution.* The importance and role of programme objectives were mentioned previously. The ability to clarify and state objectives for one's work is also important. This task includes:

    a) An understanding of the nature of purpose and the role of objectives in educational work.

    b) Knowledge of the sources of objectives.

    c) Knowledge of levels and interrelation of objectives.

d) Skill in stating and using objectives to guide educational activity.

It has been said that 'to him who knows not the port to which he is bound, no wind can be favourable.' A frequent criticism of workers in Community Development is related to the fuzziness with which objectives are conceived and stated. Too often statements of objectives at all levels can be characterized as glittering generalities. In this form they are not very helpful in guiding the programme. The importance of clarifying objectives and goals is found in two major truths:

a) Subject-matter and methods necessary to attain educational goals can be wisely selected only when the objectives are specific and clearly stated.

b) Evidence of the effectiveness of community development work can be collected only in the light of specific and clearly defined objectives.

Clear objectives, therefore, improve the preciseness with which educational activity is carried on. One important characteristic of the twenty first century is its requirement of decisiveness in action. Clear objectives give direction to action.

4. *Ability to organize people and things.* This requires an understanding of:

a) The nature and function of organization.

b) Principles of organization.

c) Techniques of organization.

d) The nature and role of coordination and integration in programmes.

The need for organization increases in direct ratio to the growth in the size and complexity of tasks to be performed by an individual or an agency in attaining its purposes. Organization is properly viewed as an arrangement of relationships of persons or functions. It should be looked upon as a means, not as an end. The principle of organization is not limited in its application to people alone, but has a much broader application. People are organized for joint activity. Materials, ideas and facts are organized for common use or for use by one person. Thinking is essentially a process of organizing facts and ideas with a view to taking action. In all cases, the need for organization has its origin in the work to be done. The term organization is properly used when it refers to any collection of persons, materials, procedures, ideas, facts and the like, so arranged and ordered that in each case the parts make a meaningful whole. Good organization then is that which groups activities ideas, facts, materials or persons so as to get the best performance with the least effort. Good organizational ability is shown by definite regularity, predictability and dependability in the everyday performance of persons or groups doing the job expected of them.

The act of organizing requires attention to at least the two following definite and well-established processes:

a) *Coordination.* Coordination means making harmonious adjustment – to give things and actions their proper perspective – to unify designated effort into an integrated whole. Coordination is necessary in carrying out practically any job or assignment. It, therefore, becomes the essence of any effective organization of efforts. There must be coordination in all major community development functions, including administration, supervision, programming, programme execution and appraisal of accomplishments.

b) *Procedure Analysis.* Procedure is a way of arranging sequences of operations necessary for effective action. Certain definite elements must always be considered and employed in both the preparation and evaluation of procedures. Important facts upon which the success of procedures rests must be discovered, selected and clarified. These are the facts which are of such outstanding importance that they must be given consideration in the design of procedures.

Organizational ability is a high level skill and is essential to the effectiveness of extension workers.

5. *Skill in seeing the relationship between principle and practice.* The ability to relate principle and practice involves knowledge and understanding of::

    a) The nature and role of principles related to Community Development.

    b) The nature and role of techniques and procedures for carrying out programmes.

    c) The inseparable interdependence of principle and practice in the extension educational process.

Theory and practice always have a relationship. Principles relate to why, techniques to how. One may understand the structure of theory and be unable to apply it in practice. On the other hand, one may be able to use technique skillfully, but be superficial in one's efforts because one does not understand how the technique relates to the whole process of Community Development, or to the specific aspect of the activity one is performing.

The effective extension worker is neither only an abstract thinker nor only an accomplished user of tricks. He is both. He must understand the principle lying behind his technique in order to make the technique most effective. The importance of principles stems from the fact that they are general rules –

well established truths – that usually have wide application. They serve as useful guides in a wide range of situations. Extension workers equipped with an understanding of principles applicable to their work are more likely to be creative than those who pride themselves on just being practical.

Rural development, workers sometimes appear to misinterpret the term 'practical'. They infer that to be practical, things must be simple, easy to do, primer-like, not complicated. The basic meaning of the term practical really suggests that whatever technique works well in a situation, regardless of its complexity, is practical. Principles give meaning to technique. Techniques give application to principles. One who glorifies techniques without trying to understand the principles related to them is really a captive of technique. One who paramounts principles without an understanding of the technique necessary to apply them is a captive of theory. An understanding of principles related to techniques and skill with techniques is the height of professional competency. The person who only knows how and the person who only knows why are always likely to have a job, but the person who knows both how and why will eventually supervise both of them.

6. *Skill at inquiry*. Ability at inquiry requires the following skills necessary to help individuals:

    a) Identify their problems,

    b) Discover focal points of concern,

    c) Determine alternative solutions, and

    d) Evaluate possible solutions and make decisions about them.

Without this competency, extension workers cannot be effective in helping people analyze their problems. Skill at inquiry is not only basic to planning, but also to guidance. Unless rural development workers are skilful at inquiry they cannot help people discover problems and work out useful solutions to them. It is a relatively easy task to supply answers based on opinion, but a vastly more difficult one to supply leadership that truly helps others analyze their problems and arrive at sound decisions about them. The process of inquiry consists of these four primary steps:

a) *Identifying the difficulty or problem or need.* Inquiry usually begins with a specific problem that causes people to feel that something ought to be done. Whenever a situation cause people – officials or non-officials – to be disturbed, there is need for inquiry, community-wide, family-wide or confined to an individual. Those responsible for planning rural development programmes should be skilful in discovering these feelings of dissatisfaction in order to further analyze the special aspects of the situation in which ***lies*** the specific concern.

b) *Discovering the focal point of trouble.* This step requires facts that will pinpoint the true nature of a problem, its scope and its importance. It usually entails careful scrutiny of attitudes, beliefs, values, habits, prejudices and the like, in addition to the scrutiny of the body of information commonly called facts.

c) *Determining possible ways to solve the problems.* In this step, ideas about plans of action must be developed that offer possible solutions to the difficulty. At this point, community development workers must provide leadership. Often it is easy to supply solutions to problems, but difficult to reach a truly joint decision about how to solve them.

d) *Evaluating alternative plans of actions.* This step requires the ability to project probable consequences of each suggested course of action if it were taken. It involves determining the probable value of each idea, and a decision about which kind of action is most likely to succeed.

Without skill at inquiring, a rural worker's relation with the people is one of the blind leading the blind, or, even the more disastrous one of the blind attempting to lead those with excellent sight.

7. *Skill in human relations.* Ability in human relations is necessary for successful work with people in general, and especially with local leaders, co-workers and those in the administrative organization.

Human relations concern how people get along with one another. Since the job of extension workers is ultimately to bring about educational change in people, they have to discover how to get people act in the ways they want them to. If extension workers cannot do this, they must change their goals to those desired by the people. If rural development workers cannot bring what they want in line with what people want, they may as well give up trying to change people in that particular way. One may know the technical answer, but unless one also knows how to work with people one won't know how to get technical answers translated into better farm, home, and community practices.

Man not having been born a social being, these behaviours have to be learned. Fortunately, they can be developed. Human judgement is fallible and mistakes will always be made. But many errors in relations among people can be avoided if fundamentals of the subject are studied and understood.

A CONCEPT OF "NEEDS"

Efforts to promote change in conditions of free-choice participation are successful only to the extent they are focused on the important needs of people and are effective in helping people meet these needs. Under voluntary conditions of participation, people concern themselves with programmes of change only when they think that the programme is valuable to them in meeting personal, family, group or community needs, therefore, becomes a central concern in rural programming.

Since the people in Indian villages are free to participate in community development activity or not to participate, their participation in effect constitutes casting a vote. When they participate, they vote favourably. When they do not participate, they also vote, but unfavourably. They determine their vote on the basis of their estimate of the probable value to them of the things participation may give them. This judgement is made on the basis of satisfaction, or the lack of it – economic, social, aesthetic or moral – which a villager feels he may obtain from participation. In short, people concern themselves with programmes only on the basis of needs as they see them, not as the officials view them. The central problem, therefore, of successful programming is one of identifying accurately what people want, think they need, and actually do need, and then getting these items woven into a realistic well organized and concerted series of forceful activities. This may properly be called a programme. Effective programmes to promote change are developed through an approach to individuals and groups – by finding people's needs and arranging action that helps meet them. Hence, a clear understanding of the nature and role of people's needs in programmes of change is essential to the leaders of such programmes.

The term need is a simple four-letter word and appears rather innocent at a glance. But it is one of the most important words related to rural development programmes. This is so because the needs of people constitute the core around which successful programmes are built. Needs imply conditions including necessity, requirement, urgency, prerequisite, vacancy, scarcity, lack and indispensability. An understanding of the nature and role of people's needs can be developed by gaining a clear concept of the meaning and implications of a number of widely accepted propositions related to the term need. Some basic aspects of need are indicated as follows:

1. *Man is an independent living system surrounded by an environment with which he constantly interrelates.* Man is constantly influenced by his environment and in turn exerts influence over it. His well-being depends on keeping a balance between the internal forces produced by the energy resulting from the food intake and the external conditions produced by the environment. To keep the human system in equilibrium with the external forces, it is necessary that certain needs be met. In this sense every person is continuously meeting his needs – trying to attain those conditions of living that make for satisfaction. To the extent that the relationship between man and his environment goes out of balance, he has needs. People are constantly attempting to attain, maintain or improve this balance.

The nature and extent of needs depend upon the nature and extent of the imbalance. For example, when a person becomes physically ill, a condition is created in which the affected parts of the body become functionally out of balance with the other parts. Consequently, it is said that the person is sick. To get well, the imbalance must be removed. In a like manner the imbalance between man and his environment in all of its aspects is the source from which people's needs emerge. Man's attempt to attain, and maintain a satisfying equilibrium between internal and external forces represents in a true form his real struggle for survival and economic, social, aesthetic or moral improvement.

2. *People's needs are identified by finding through the programme planning process, the actual, the possible and the valuable.* By the actual is meant *what is;* by the possible is meant *what could be* and by the valuable is meant *what ought to be.* In choosing the things on which to focus programmes, it is necessary to analyze these conditions and possibilities and choose from among them the *most valuable.* Then it should become the objective of programmes to change people and the present conditions in which they live to the most valuable and possible conditions. Making the analyses and decisions necessary in this context is the essence of programme planning to meet people's needs.

3. *People's needs may be defined as the differences between what is, what could be and what ought to be.* Needs always imply a gap between the two conditions as shown in the following diagram:

WHAT OUGHT TO BE

(Desirable situation)

GAP

(Need)

Difference, dearth, vacancy, requirement, urgency

WHAT IS

(Actual situation)

W*hat is* can be determined by a study of the situation. Some of the major kinds of information this study should include are important facts about people, their attitudes, knowledge, and what they think their needs are. It should include facts about physical factors, soils, crops, livestock, home conditions, farm implements, production resources and community services. It should include facts about public problems, programmes, trends and outlook.

What ought to be can be determined on the basis of research findings and value judgements of the people and their official leaders. For example, the results of research may show that the use of recommended practices in rice production will result in a one-third larger yield per acre. The cultivator on the other hand, may not place great value on reaching this level of production, or he may place greater value on spending his available resources on some other goal like better education for his children than on producing extra rice.

It should be recognized that information about *what is* does not make a programme, it only shows the situation. From this point planners have to take another step. This step is that of deciding *what ought to be*- what the desirable situation is. Hence, deciding on *what ought to be* is the process of selecting programme targets, goals or objectives. In setting objectives, care must be taken to assure that the level of *what ought to be* is within the physical, economic, social and mental possibilities of attainment by those who are expected to make the change. Finally, it should be recognized that the nature and extent of the need (the width of the gap)) is an indication of the significance of the problem. The wider the gap, the greater the problem.

4. *People have to recognize the gap between the actual, the possible and the desirable and place value on attaining the desirable condition before they will become motivated to change in desirable directions.*

> This point poses the crux of the problem in programmes of change. Village people being wedded to custom and tradition, often being illiterate and surrounded by many outmoded cultural norms, are slow to make innovations in what they do and how they do it. When people have been schooled by centuries of experience to satisfy their wants by not having wants, it is difficult to conceive them that they should, for example, adopt new practices to increase crop yields or go through the uncertainties of consolidating several tracts of land into one piece.

Reluctance by villagers to change is not due altogether to a natural resistance to change, but to an apparent lack of interest in change. They seem to feel satisfied with their old ways even when new ones are demonstrated side by side with the old. When the actual or *status quo* is seen as the ideal, desirable or satisfactory status of things, no need is recognized on the part of people. Consequently, there is in their minds no need for a programme to promote change because there is no need for change in the first place, as they view the situation. To be successful, therefore, a programme must cause people to recognize the gap between the actual, the desirable and the possible, and place a value on attaining the desirable.

5. *Human behaviour and the status of things can only be judged by some standard and the standard can only be derived from a concept of what is valuable and desirable to attain.* Human behaviour and the status of things usually can be placed on a scale of human values.

The human values are dependant and influenced by geographic, climatic, historical, religious, ethnic, occupational, contact with other cultures, colonization and density or thinness of population. The values are not constant but they are dynamic. They are related and sometimes-unrelated elements lived by the people at a given point of time. Speaking of values, some may remain especially of religious nature constant but food habits, dress and technology may change over a period of time.

From a psychological standpoint, needs may be classified into two groups, viz., felt or consciously recognized needs and *unfelt* or unrecognized needs. In a free society all needs must become felt before they serve as motivating forces. Research in adult education indicates that adults often are not aware of many of their most important needs. To the extent that this is true, adults have needs which are unfelt. Significant needs of which people are not conscious must be ferreted out and met in order to help them advance toward more desirable economic and social conditions.

One of the problems in rural programming, therefore, is to help people identify important needs they do not recognize. Thus it is not enough to base programmes entirely on what people feel their needs are, because these often may not represent some of their most important needs. Leaders of programmes must dig deep and identify needs people have which they do not recognize, then plan educational effort to convert these into felt needs. Without this, rural development programmes will be less significant and may tend to focus on the everyday short-term interests of people rather than on their more basic long-time needs.

6. *Final decision about the selection, or rejection, of needs to be included in a programme should be made with great care.* In the process of programme planning to meet people's needs, many decisions have to be made. These decisions have to be related to the actual, the valuable and the possible. Ultimately they must become decisions about acceptance or rejection of items to be included in the programme. These are crucial

> decisions and are highly significant, not only because the future of the people and their conditions will be influenced, but because extensive physical and human resources will be committed to helping people meet the needs accepted by planners and made a part of the programme. Indeed, these needs become the subject-matter or content of a programme. In turn, they are translated into the objectives or targets which the programme will seek to attain in course of time.

In the process of making final decisions about the needs to be included in a programme, some further points should be kept in mind. All people have needs. Needs vary in nature, scope and significance. Needs are often individual in attachment but they also tend to be common among members of groups. Needs change with time and progress. This tends to be true whether concerted effort is made to meet them or whether nothing is done to meet them. The needs of people change with age, growth and with social, economic and family status situations. People's needs arise from lack of harmony between themselves and their environment. The relative importance of needs is influenced by the physical environment, what is possible in it, and by the cultural factors which form a system of values that people hold to be important.

CRITERIA FOR PRACTICE AND PROCEDURE IN PROGRAMMING

The process of programme planning to meet people's needs includes four major elements or key steps that are generally viewed as of primary importance. It appears that the development staff should give proper attention to these elements in planning programmes that are significant and workable. The elements are:

a) A plan for involving local people in the planning process.

b) Procedure in programming planning.

c) The programme – the product of planning.

d) The annual plan of work.

These elements are described briefly in the following pages and a set of criteria for dealing with each of them is suggested. The criteria are attempts to describe the major steps, procedures or conditions that evidence shows to be good practice, involved in dealing with each element. The criteria are selected and designed to specify conditions, procedures, or practices that are conducive to developing the most effective rural programmes.

ELEMENT - A

A PLAN FOR INVOLVING PEOPLE IN PROGRAMME PLANNING

Rural programme planning, in essence, is a process of making decisions about important objectives to be attained in an area. One of the most significant problems confronting rural development workers is that of deciding on programme objectives which reflect the primary needs and interests of people. How to do this skillfully is a question of major concern to every professional worker. Decisions about programme objectives are usually best when made neither by the officials alone, nor by the people alone, but when made jointly by the officials and the people.

The contributions of the local people to rural programming are obtained most effectively through some form of organized approach. Research indicates that no one type of organization is best for programming in all situations. There are certain criteria, however, which are usually met when the local people contribute to programme development most effectively. These are indicated below:

1. Representative committees of non-officials are organized by the development staff. These function systematically on a continuing basis in developing and maintaining a current programme for development.

2. The people who function as members of the planning committees at the local level represent major interest groups, various economic and social levels of people, major vocations of the locality and other important elements in the area.

3. Each member of the planning groups clearly understands (a) the purpose of the group, (b) how the group can function in attaining its purpose, and (c) his individual role as a member of the group.

4. Members of the planning groups functioning at the local level are selected by appropriate democratic procedures.

5. Policies or rules formed for maintaining continuity of the planning groups include an appropriate plan for terminating the services of the temporary groups, and membership in the permanent groups, and for selecting new members of the permanent groups and new temporary groups.

ELEMENT - B

PROCEDURE IN PROGRAMME PLANNING

Procedure in programme planning means the process, course of action, methods, or major steps taken in an area to develop a suitable programme. A summary of experience of extension workers and conclusions from research pertaining to procedures used in rural programme development supports the following conclusions.

a) There are a number of essential steps in programme development that must be taken to develop a programme of the highest quality.

b) The basic steps are generally applicable with adjustments to meet particular circumstances in local situations.

c) After the steps are properly executed the basic principles of programme development should be applied.

d) The detailed procedures employed for executing each of the basic steps may vary considerably in accomplishing the purpose of each step.

The following is a list of criteria pertaining to the various steps assumed to be essential in procedures for local programme development.

1. The entire development staff has considered and reached agreement on:

   a) The importance to be attached to programming

   b) The amount of time to be devoted to programming

   c) The time when programming is to be done

   d) The phases of the programme to be developed, and

   e) The general approach to be followed in the area.

2. The development staff, with the help of technical specialists and planning groups, has assembled basic facts about the situation for use in developing a programme including such information as the following:

   a) Sources and levels of family income

   b) Health and educational levels of the people

c) Needs and interests of the people

d) Marketing facilities and practices

e) Farming and home-making practices, and

f) Community problems and needs.

3. Basic facts about the local situation have been analyzed jointly by the official staff and the planning groups and decisions made on this basis about major needs and interests of people.

4. A long-term programme has been developed and is used as a guide to all major activity in the area.

5. The technical specialists have assisted in developing the long-term programme by supplying specific basic information and recommendations pertaining to their special field that has been considered by the staff and the planning groups.

6. The development staff, jointly with the planning groups, has defined the problem and taken decisions about the long-term and the short-term objectives of the programme in line with major needs and interests of the people.

7. The development staff, jointly with the planning groups, has arranged a system of priority for work on problems included in the long-term programme.

8. The planning groups along with the official staff, has actively promoted coordination of the long-term programme.

ELEMENT - C

THE PROGRAMME

A rural development programme is a carefully prepared statement written in a form that clearly sets froth the significant changes that are needed in the behaviour of the people and in the conditions in which they live, to be attained over a period of time. Specifically, it is a statement that includes:

a) Primary facts that reveal the situation for each major subject or problem in the area that is to be dealt within the programme.

b) Significant problems or needs.

c) Major means for meeting the problems or needs.

d) Statement of long-term objectives to be attained.

It is of utmost importance that the staff and the people in each area not only develop a basic long-term programme, but also prepare the programme in a written form that is readily understood and is suitable for use as a guide for officials and non-officials. Experience shows that this practice is a valuable guide to the staff and advisory committees and also a very effective means of improving public relations. The criteria listed below represent standards that should be achieved in written statements of a basic long-term programme.

1. The written programme should be suitable for use by the staff, planning groups, and other individuals or groups concerned with the programme.
2. It should state the primary facts that clearly reveal the situation for major subject or problem areas.
3. It should clearly state the important problems or needs identified by the staff and the people in the programming process.
4. It should state both the long-term and short-term objectives for each major subject or problem area that is to be focused on in programme execution over a period of time.

5. It should state the objectives of the programme in a form that:

   a) Clearly reveals the kind of new condition or situation desired

   b) Is meaningful to the staff and the people, and

   c) Will serve as a useful guide to programme execution.

6. It should specify the subject-matter related to each objective that is highly significant to the people, socially or economically, or both.

7. It should include the summary of the long-term programme prepared in a form suitable for public distribution, containing the following items:

   a) Major facts about the over-all area situation.

   b) Brief statement of the organization, statements of major problems, long-term objectives, and major means of achieving them for each of the major subject or problem areas.

   c) Brief descriptions of the situation, statements of major problems, long-term objectives, and major means of achieving them for each of the major subject or problem areas.

   d) The names of members of the planning groups and the official staff, and

   e) Other appropriate information.

8. It should be made available in a summary form to all the members of the planning groups, and the professional staff.

9. It should be circulated by appropriate means so that the general public can understand its nature and objectives.

10. It should be used as the basis for developing annual plans of work.

ELEMENT - D

THE ANNUAL PLAN OF WORK

The annual plan of work commonly consists of a definite outline of procedure for carrying out work related to the different phases of the long-term programme. It should indicate specifically the means to be used and the methods of using them. Its basic function is to provide a guide for use in carrying on development work planned for the year in a systematic manner. The annual plan of work should effectively serve the following functions:

a) A specific guide for carrying out systematically all the major aspects of work planned for the year.

b) A guide to the development of plans and procedures for evaluating accomplishments.

c) A guide to the scheduling of activity related to various aspects of the programme.

The following criteria related to annual plans of work are assumed to be important in their development and use.

1. Annual plans of work should be developed and used as a guide to all major activity during the year.
2. They should be developed from the long-term programme in a way that the content and goals are directly in line with the objectives of the different phases of the long-term programme.
3. They should include facts about the current situation pertaining to major subject or problem areas assembled by the development staff, technical specialists, and planning groups. They should also include facts about accomplishments during the past

year for consideration in developing the annual plan of work.

4. They should include decisions jointly taken by the staff and the planning group on the major problems to be worked on during the year after a careful analysis of the current facts.

5. An annual plan of work in a written form, prepared by the staff, includes the following kinds of information for each project, subject or problem area:

   a) Major subjects or problems to be worked on during the year.

   b) Goals to be attained during the year.

   c) Brief description of work to be done – methods, materials, etc.

   d) Who is to participate in carrying out the plan?

   e) A calendar of work which shows the approximate amount of time to be devoted to each major activity, and seasonal distribution of major activities.

   f) Who is to be reached with the programme?

6. The annual plan of work is used during the year as a basis for:

   a) Coordinating activities of the different aspects of the area programme.

   b) Developing and coordinating teaching plans for different specific activities.

7. The annual plan of work is reproduced in an appropriate form for distribution and copies placed in the hands of (a) local leaders, (b) planning groups, and (c) other groups and individuals whose support is important for advancing the programme.

8. Means are used to acquaint the general public with the major activities to be undertaken during the year that are specified in the annual plan of work.

SUGGESTED GUIDE FOR DEVELOPING AND STARTING A VILLAGE OR BLOCK PROGRAMME

Description of the situation: Include only significant facts necessary to clarify conditions for each subject area. Include facts about (1) the people, (2) physical conditions, (3) farm and home practices followed, (4) trends and outlook	*Significant needs:* Using facts about the situation, list conditions in each subject area that show important gaps between what is and what should be. These gaps represent the needs.	*Objectives to be achieved:* Select from column 2 those needs that are agreed upon by the planning group and state them here in the form of objectives.	*Means for achieving the objectives*: Select and list here the primary means of attaining each objective stated in column 3.	*Calendar of work:* Decide and enter in this column the amount of time to be devoted to each major activity listed in column 4, and the dates on which the activity will be performed.
1	2	3	4	4

(Useful for specialized segments or for more comprehensive programmes)

ORGANIZATION OF PROGRAMMES

Important changes in human behaviour generally are not produced quickly. Usually, no single learning experience has a very profound influence on people who participate in programmes. Changes in the ways of thinking, in fundamental habits, in attitudes, in interests, develop slowly. In free-choice societies, it is only after months and years that workers in rural development are usually able to see major changes resulting from their educational efforts. In some respects, the effect of programmes involving education is cumulative like that of water constantly dripping on a stone and wearing it away. In a day, or a week or a month, there is no appreciable change in the stone, but over a period of years definite erosion is noted.

Correspondingly, by the accumulation of impressions resulting from exposure to recommendations made by rural development workers, profound changes are brought about in the action of rural people. In order that educational effort produces cumulative effect, it must be so organized as to expose village men and women to recommendations periodically over time and in such ways that the programme elements reinforce each other. Programme organization is thus seen as a very important consideration in the process of rural development.

There are two major criteria for effective organization of rural development programmes. The first of these is continuity. Continuity refers to the provision in a programme for important recommendations to recur frequently, thus giving people an opportunity to come into contact with important ideas again and again over a time, and, if possible, at advanced levels. Continuity in programmes is basic to the achievement of cumulative effects. It is often referred to as follow-up.

For example, meetings of village people are often held with a little or no particular follow-up on important ideas or recommendations presented. Under these conditions little actual change in people's behaviour has to be expected. Research related to the adoption rate of new practices by rural people shows quite clearly that as the number of exposures to any idea is increased up to five or six, the number of people making changes increases. Provision for the continuity or recurrence of ideas and recommendations several times and over a period of time is, therefore, a highly important criterion that should guide the organization of programmes.

A second important criterion useful in guiding the organization of rural development programmes is integration. Integration relates to the horizontal relationship of various elements in a programme. It has to do with the relationship of one item with another. Programme organization should be such that it helps rural people increasingly to gain a unified view of major programme elements. To be successful, participants in programmes of rural development must eventually recognize all the elements as a whole, and how each one relates to others and to their problems.

For example, the objective of developing an understanding of the value and need for village latrines should also convey the idea of cleanliness and order throughout the village. The idea of integration implies the concept of transfer of learning. It recognizes that people should eventually see ideas, needs and action in relation to the total task of Community Development. Integration implies the opposite of developing ideas singly as isolated behaviours or activities to be applied only at a single place, in a given time, in certain forms. The total capacity of people for Community Development must eventually be developed. Integration helps the officials and the people to see how one item is related to another and how each one is affected by others. Thus, increased breadth and depth of people's educational development and increased unity in their action in relation to important elements in the programme are made possible.

After considering the two major criteria for organizing programmes, questions arise about an organizing structure. Many structures may be used for organizing programmes. These include specific subjects or projects like animal husbandry, cooperatives, small industry, home science and social education. A second common way of organizing programmes is according to problem areas like health, income, agricultural production, housing, home conveniences and farm equipment. A third used structure for organizing rural development programmes is on the basis of broad fields of content, usually designated as production and marketing, family living, youth development and community services.

A clearly developed structure of programme organization helps to assure proper continuity and integration. It helps one to recognize the kind of activity that fits into a programme and that which seems relatively inappropriate. Those engaged in programme planning to meet people's needs, both officials and non-officials, must think and plan together. It is this kind of action that helps assure programmes that end in unity, rather than in a series of separate sets of knowledge, skills and activity. It is only when each element in programmes reinforce others that they make maximum contribution to Community Development.

Some of the devices for assuring continuity and integration in programmes are carefully stated objectives that are well understood by everyone engaged in programme planning and execution, joint planning between officials and non-officials, especially at the local level, long-term planning, annual plans of work, preparation of programmes in written form, and wide distribution of the written programme among officials and the people who are to participate.

CONCLUSION

The development of programmes that harmonize the local needs as people see them and the national interests with which a country as a whole must be concerned, is a significant responsibility of local non-officials and officials at each level in the hierarchy of publicly sponsored programmes to promote rural development. Any procedure that takes into account the basic concept of needs and meets a set of criteria that will assure that the programme focuses on the significant needs of the people is a good procedure. The measure of success achieved in free-choice societies by public programmes to promote rural development is in direct ratio to the extent to which the programme is built around people's needs and consequently, is an effective influence in helping meet their needs.

To accomplish these desirable ends effectively requires a carefully structured programme at the village and block level that meets the following criteria:

1. It must focus on the felt needs and interests of the people.
2. It must be developed through joint participation of village leaders and block staff, taking into account recommendations from district, state and Central Government personnel.
3. It must be in line with local as well as state and national needs.
4. It must focus on problems that are most important since it cannot be all things to all people at the same time.
5. It must be flexible, but with a 'backbone' that gives it stability and continuity.
6. It must provide for a system of priorities in line with local needs, interests and resources.
7. It must be balanced, that is, contain items of assistance for all major social, economic, age and sex status groups.
8. It must have objectives that are attainable within the economic, social and mental capacities of the people

through education with a minimum of government aid.

9. It must be highly significant economically, socially, aesthetically or morally to a relatively large number of people in each village or block.

10. It must be developed, understood, conducted and judged as an educational instrument for helping people learn how to help themselves.

11. It must provide satisfaction for the people who participate. The central objective of India's National Extension Service programme is to help each individual, each family and each village achieve the highest level of living that is capable of economically, socially, and culturally by means of aided self-help through education. Those responsible for developing a programme to achieve this objective must ferret out and perpetuate only the useful from the past, exercise concern only for the promising in the present and focus skillfully all available resources on the significant elements in the bright future. This is the formula for achieving the new India.

SELECTED REFERENCES

1. *Approach to Community Development*, Editor Phillips Ruopp, W. Van Hoeve Ltd., The Hague, 1953.
2. *Community Development in India,* V.T. Krishnamachari, Publications Division, Govt. of India, New Delhi, 1958.
3. *Cooperative Extension Work,* L.D. Kelsey and C.C. Hearne, Comstock Publishing Associates, Ithaca, New York, 1949.
4. *First Five-Year Plan,* Planning Commission, Govt. of India, New Delhi, 1951.
5. *Guide to Community Development,* Ministry of Community Development and Cooperation, Govt. of India, New Delhi, 1957.
6. *Human Problems in Technological Change,* Editor Edward H. Spicer, Russel Sage Foundation, New York, 1952.

7. *India's Changing Villages,* S.C. Dube, Routledge and Kegan Paul Ltd., London, 1958.

8. *Methods and Programme Planning in Rural Extension,* J.M.A. Penders, H. Veenman and Zenen, Wageningen, The Netherlands, 1956.

9. *Pilot Project in India,* Albert Mayer and associates, University of California Press, 1958.

10. *Rural Social Systems,* Loomis and Allen, Prentice Hall Inc., New York, 1950.

11. *Second Five Year Plan,* Planning Commission, Govt. of India, New Delhi, 1956.

12. *Seminar Papers,* Department of Economics, University of Madras, Madras, 1956-57.

13. *What Man May Be – The Human Side of Science,* George Russell Harrison, William Morrow & Co., New York, 1956.

Source: Adopted with grateful thanks from J. Paul Leagans, Extension Education, Publications Division, New Delhi, 1960.

4

EACH VILLAGE AS A UNIT OF RURAL DEVELOPMENT

The process of organizing rural communities for their participation in development involves working and interacting with the people in the communities. The prerequisite for effective interaction with the people in the rural communities is a knowledge of the characteristics of the rural communities, their way of life, the value systems, traditions and customs, the network or relationships and the kind of changes taking place among them. In the clinical approach, there is a need to consider each village as a unit of development. In order to do this we should have a comprehensive and detailed data pertaining to the village. This will help us in identifying the historical background of the settlement, its natural resources, the kind of avocations people are engaged in, the kind of infrastructure, the topographical details and the human resources the community is endowed with. Further, we may also look into the community common needs and in some cases individual needs also. Treating each village community as a unit of development is a necessity in carrying out gradual sustained development activities in each village. In this context, we may briefly look into the characteristics of the rural communities as a kind of background to understand the general nature of rural communities in India.

Rural communities are not identical in every respect. There is a considerable diversity among them. They could be ranged along a continuum. At one end, we have the sacred-folk societies and at the other end the secular ones, varying in terms of simplicity and complexity. In folk-sacred societies, established practices and ideas are taken for granted. There are few contacts with persons outside of the local geographic areas. Kinship relations are dominant. There is little formalized education; teaching is by means of family training, conversation, preaching and ceremonial. Occupations are learned by apprenticeship. The older men, who have lived longest and whose experiences and memories reach back farthest, are respected and relied upon for advice and guidance. Such societies are relatively changeless; they, in fact, quite generally resist change.

In a highly secular society, means and methods of communication and transportation are ample and ready. Persons are highly mobile both physically and mentally. Formal education is universal occupations and professions are learned as technical sciences. Most social relations are impersonal. Even kinship relations are loose in terms of duties and obligations. Changes of all kinds are prevalent, rapid, and generally welcome. Individuals are members of many groups and live by a number of different value systems.

To be completely bound by folk customs and traditions would mean stagnation. To be completely secular would be inhuman or non-social. No present day society is completely either of them. Those which are nearer the folk end of this continuum are working, some rapidly, toward the secular end of the continuum. The results of too rapid a movement in this direction have been discovered by the study of the most mobile part of the people who live in large cities. The results of little or no movement in this direction are illustrated in a number of countries where a thin layer of wealthy, educated, elite at the top of the social and political structure purposely sabotage change in the large folk segments of their society.

CONCEPT OF COMMUNITIES

Territorial boundary and the sentimental bindings are the essential factors in a community. The group of people that live within a geographic region have the uniformity or similarity in many customs and habits, such as food, clothing, occupation etc. These matters depend upon the availability of material, climatic conditions, nature of soil, etc. The above factors bind the people together.

Another factor, which is the outcome of face-to-face, intensive functional interaction, is the community sentiment. This sentiment, that makes them feel that they are one, or the "we" feeling is the life of the community. The sentiment gives rise to responsibility, makes the members of the communities conscious of their rights and duties. Rights and obligations implicate inter-dependence of the members.

A community then means a group of people living in a given area with common interests, bound by a sense of and common mode of living. A village satisfies the requisite to form a community. It gives the inhabitants a common area of land, common past that brings about a sharing of experience and standard of behaviour and attitudes. They share some degree of common activities or some degree of common life, irrespective of their social and religious differences. It is not confined to any of the various restricted fields of community life on the basis of religion, caste, race, language or profession but one that envelops the whole life of the total community. Whatever affects the villages, affects the whole population. A community may be settled or an unsettled one. It may be migratory having come from another area in search of livelihood or it may belong to the new village where they live for centuries, or they might be newcomers.

Some of the distinguishing features of rural community are:

1. Occupation is mainly agriculture and/ or allied professions.
2. People live closer together and closer to the natural environment. This makes their life and attitude simpler and unaffected.
3. Smallness of the size of the community brings the members closer together in everyday life. This and the common occupational interest make the people know each other better than the urban people do.
4. Lesser density of population is caused by the nature of occupation. People in the rural areas can move more freely.
5. There is greater homogeneity of life than in urban areas; because the people are bound not only by common occupation, but also are bound by common traditions, customs and common heritage.
6. Relatively, there is very little social mobility in the community. They live in the same land generation after generation, by the same occupation, follow the same old customs and habits and maintain the purity of their ethnic identity by avoiding inter-caste and communal marriage or any other type of social intercourse.

Hundreds of local communities in folk societies have been studied by anthropologists. Based on these studies, the characteristics of communities of folk societies can be broadly generalized as follows:

1. Each community is something approximating a complete society in terms of both geography and people.

2. No external forces other than the physical environment enter the community. Few strangers ever come to the community.
3. Each community is composed of families and other kinship groups, the systematic relations between which constitute the social structure of the community.
4. The rights and duties of these groups are passed down from generation to generation and maintained by a value system which consists of the mores of the community. They are accepted by everyone.
5. There are no written constitutions or contracts. Relations between groups are monitored and even enforced by the elders of the group.
6. The community perpetuates itself by teaching each on-coming generations its old way of doing and thinking. Apprenticeship in occupations and initiation into each age group by various types of ceremonial guarantees that each new generation shall know and do as the old generation did.
7. The natural resources with which the people used to sustain their economic life are generally owned by the whole community. Each family sustains itself economically by participating in the development and utilization of these resources, and participates in the economic returns from the resources.
8. The economic relations of the community are the accepted division of labour between groups rather than by trade or even by barter. The economic and social security of all is, therefore, a total community responsibility.
9. There is thus less possibility of change in the status of groups, much less of individuals in the community.

To the degree that simple communities manifest these characteristics, they are whole societies, in terms not only of social, economic and political structures, but in terms of value systems. Each person growing up in one of these communities believes and practices these values, plays his assigned roles without questioning, and as a person is pretty much a complete reflection of the community as a whole.

In the present societies some new types of behaviour develop, but by no means do all the old characteristics of folk society disappear. The total or relative social and cultural isolation of the peasant communities is on the decline. The outside world has moved in on them. Due to multiple factors of influence such as, planned and guided community development efforts on the part of the government, increase in transport and communication, the gradual process of urbanization and industrialization, the emergence of new political and economic institutions, the rural communities in general are in the process of change and the situation in the past few decades may be summarized as follows:

1. The first thing was that trade and commerce entered the village.

2. As contact with trade centers, either with merchants located in the village or with trade towns, developed, at least on the part of a few of the village people there, a knowledge of the outside world in terms of activities about which they had previously known very little. What they learned naturally became matters of gossip within the village and, therefore, some understanding of marketing, prices, and things of that kind developed on the part of all village people.

3. Government had entered all of these villages many years back, but modern government of the type which brings services and assistance to villagers was fairly

new in all of the villages. Agents of the government had come in and promoted development and welfare activities. When this once began there was a new basis for forming new parties, and often new factions developed.

4. Government servants, located in or serving the village were seldom local villagers themselves, therefore, new persons, generally persons with more education and receiving higher incomes than the villagers, introduced a new type of person and, in some ways, tended to introduce new social status among the other statuses of the village.

5. Government made incursions in all cases, sooner or later, in terms of establishing and helping to maintain schools. School teachers were new citizens of the community and in some cases, played quite different roles than any outsider ever played in the village.

6. As some youth of the village received considerable education, they became capable of making contacts and did make contact outside the village and thus became a channel of cultural traffic in and out of the village.

7. In a few cases, persons with a degree of education took up new occupations different from those which they had traditionally followed, and moved away from the village. This has led to occupational and territorial mobility.

8. As the price and market economy entered the village, some persons began making more money. Those who had made more money or had better contacts with outside agencies became money-lenders. Some of them began purchasing land previously owned by peasants who now lost the ownership of their land. Thus a

whole new elite developed in the village, sometimes quite a powerful group.

9. In the case of contacts with the market town or with outside sources of income, some of the villages began to attend picture shows and other recreational events outside the village.

10. A new kind of formal and informal leaders emerged. The youth or the younger generation began influencing the developmental activities in the village. In some cases, government servants began to be looked up to rather than feared.

11. In most villages a degree of individualism developed. Some persons were paid special attention by the development agencies. They gained new importance and they tended to form a group which protected the group against the large owners.

12. In most villages, the lower classes, that is, the lower income people, were paid special attention by the development agencies. They gained new importance and they tended to form a group which protected the group against the large owners.

13. It may be stated here, that the same old reverence for elders, and for the set class structure, and even for the villagers' values, had been considerably diluted.

The rural communities are, however, far from having lost all their old folk characteristics. The following such characteristics, though somewhat modified, are still maintained (Taylor).

(a) The elders, while they no longer constitute the village government, are highly respected and are still counselors in many types of issue.

(b) The village community's organization is perpetuated by each new generation tending to follow the family occupations of previous generations.

(c) There is in all of the villages some division of labour between the families, this division being fixed by the traditions of the community.

(d) Families, generally extended families, are more integral social groups than are the villages as a whole.

(e) Sentiment for the land, pride and tenacity in the ownership of the land, is still very strong.

(f) There is relatively little tolerance for new ways of thinking and doing. If the people were asked to choose between tradition and progress, tradition would perhaps be their instinctive choice although a second choice might induce them to take a few hesitating steps in the direction of change.

REFERENCE

Taylor, Carl (n.d) "Community Mobilization for Group Formulation"

Note:- Please see Appendix for 'Study of Rural Community – Aspects to be covered'.

5

GUIDELINES FOR SECTORAL DEVELOPMENT

For the Panchayat Samithi and the Village Panchayats to be effective in helping the people find solutions to their problems, all programmes taken up by the Block Samithi and the Village Panchayats must be related to solving problems which the people themselves have participated in identifying and have expressed a desire to work together to solve. This being true, there are no alternatives to having the Panchayat Samithi each year assist each village panchayat systematically: (1) identify their village problems; (2) understand what cause the problems; (3) know what steps are required to solve the problems; (4) be concerned and eager to solve the problems; and finally (5) to decide which of the specific problems they wish to tackle for the coming year. For each village panchayat to take all its village people through these steps each year will make it possible for each village panchayat to have before it a realistic village development programme. Only as each village panchayat completes this kind of systematic analysis will it be possible for the Panchayat Samithi to put together a Block programme. Until there is a Block programme which is a composite of these village programmes, the Samithi cannot intelligently allocate staff and financial resources to the village panchayats. It will be absolutely imperative for the panchayat Samithi to have such a realistic programme if the Block staff is to be effective in carrying out an extension educational programme in each village as a sponsored specific panchayat programme.

A prerequisite to the Block staff's effective working relationship with village people through the Panchayat Samithi and the village panchayat, the cooperative and other village institutions and organizations is that they themselves be clear about the village problems. Each member of the Block staff – the gram sevak, the technical specialist and the Block Development Officer – should be able to help village people identify their key problems. While it should be the responsibility of each subject-matter technical specialist to guide the staff in an analysis of the village problems which fall within their respective fields, all members of the Block staff should know the most important things that cause the problem, and the basic action steps each specialist recommends if village people are to solve their problems themselves.

Village life is lived first in integrated families and second in a complex set of village relations. Only as each member of the Block development staff assumes that he is, first, a generalized development and extension officer, and second, a staff member with a specialized function to perform, will he be able to make his maximum contribution to helping the village people in solving their many problems largely through their own efforts, utilizing to the fullest any and all technical help which can be interpreted to them in meaningful and understanding terms. This means, for example, that before the animal husbandry technical specialist can make a significant contribution to improving the cattle, goats, sheep, swine and poultry, he must know the important place each has in the lives of the families. He must know the nature and depth of family and village attitudes and practices with respect to the animals and poultry. He must know which members of the family are responsible for carrying out each individual practice. He must know, in relationship to the many village problems, the relative importance villagers will place on improving their livestock and poultry in contrast to improving their crops. He must know the religious significance the village places on the livestock and what may be involved and implied if he makes specific recommendations about how to improve the livestock and poultry. He must know the place village families assign to livestock in their total village economy. As a basis for finalizing his recommendations he should know why the villagers follow their current practices and what other practices they have followed over the years.

The Block development staff must, as a development team, forever accept the principle that the emphasis for development in each village must be centred on the problems the village panchayats are at that moment ready to recognize and to give a position of prominence in terms of devoting time and effort to their solution. To accept this position does not mean a de-emphasis on educating the village people to the existence of problems which the Block staff may feel to be of urgent importance. What it does mean, however, is that programmes for correction or for the solution of village problems must wait until the staff can, through education, demonstration, and persuasion, bring the village people working, their Panchayat to be concerned enough about the problems to want to accept technical help and guidance in their solution. Any other approach is more-or-less wasted effort, in that it takes up a lot of staff time without enlisting village action.

A wise Block development staff will learn the priorities each village panchayat places on its many problems, and will at first concentrate its own limited resources on helping the village panchayat solve the problems it has concluded to be important at the moment. A wise staff will also know, however, that one of its basic continuing functions is to educate the village panchayat to the existence of problems it may not at the moment consider important.

This chapter devotes lengthy treatment of village problems so as to guide the Block development staff in its working relationships with Panchayat Samithi and the village panchayats within the Block. For each significant village problem listed, there follows first a list of generalized conditions which cause the problem, and second, a list of generalized steps which, if taken, would contribute toward the solution of the problem. Each Block staff will need to prepare a similar list for its respective Block, if it is a wise staff and is to make the maximum contribution toward helping village panchayats identify, become concerned about, and take steps to solve, village problems. This generalized list of problems for the Block should then be broken down and developed for each village. Each village list must be refined with experience and understanding.

A valuable educational experience for each village panchayat would be for the panchayat to develop a large poster on which they would list their problems as they became recognized as significant and meaningful. This would become especially valuable as the panchayats learned to associate with a problem the things which contribute to it, and as they came to know what steps should be taken to solve the problem. The village-by-village definition of problems, the detailing of the things that cause the problems, and step-by-step recommendations should in the first instance be developed jointly by the respective technical specialist, the gram sevak, and the panchayat.

Diagnosing and prescribing for village problems requires three steps. First, the many individual village problems must be identified; second, the thing which causes village problems must be known; third, action steps should be recommended to solve each village problem. This is an essential process of getting the village people through their pañchayats to look searchingly at themselves, and is the only basis on which the village Panchayat can take intelligent decisions as to what they want to do, when they want to do it, how they want to do it, and who is to take the initiative.

This process of village-by-village definition of problems and agreement on action steps is also essential for the Block staff as a team, if it is to have a purposeful working relationship with each village panchayat. With this kind of village-by-village analysis and planning, all members of the Block staff can and should take an interest in all phases of village activity as they visit the villages to work systematically with the gram sevaks there, they were originally called Village Level Workers, later as Village Development Officers and recently they are redesignated as Panchayat Secretaries in Andhra Pradesh

Without this individual problem analysis and later putting together of a village's diagnosis of its many problems and suggested action steps, the gram sevak and extension specialist cannot possibly be effective. The gram sevak must always see the village as a whole, as well as seeing and understanding its many individual problems. Only with this kind of analysis and village planning can the gram sevak make the maximum use of his individual village visits.

One and all should understand that, as the Rural Development staff gains experience and as Village people respond and themselves change with the changes they bring about in the villages, the village problems will be defined and the priorities panchayats give to taking action steps will change. This simply means that the definition of village problems, the detailing of the causes of the problems, and the outlining of action steps should be a more or less continuous process. As a minimum these village-by-village analyses should be updated once a year.

We come now to a detailing of the generalized village problems. For each problem a generalized analysis is given of the things which cause the problem and the recommended action steps to correct the problem.

I. LOW CROP YIELDS IS A VILLAGE PROBLEM

Low crop yields are caused by some or all the following conditions:

1. Following traditional farming methods and using primitive tools.
2. Lack of knowledge about superior yields possible from improved seeds, use of commercial fertilizers, improved agricultural implements and better tillage practices.
3. Lack of understanding about importance of making compost manure and of proper application of compost manure.
4. Lack of enough sure water and improper use of available water.
5. Lack of understanding about the importance of soil testing as a basis for determining the kind and amount of commercial fertilizer to use.
6. Lack of knowledge about the need for growing and ploughing under green manure crops.
7. Fragmented land-holding works against better use of water and use of improved tillage practices.
8. Lack of desirable tenure arrangements, providing security of tenure and appropriate redistribution of land holdings.
9. Lack of credit, at reasonable interest and available as needed, prevents many cultivators from being able to purchase improved seed, improved implements, better bullocks, and fertilizer.

10. Lack of adequate power to quickly prepare the soil, plant the crops, and harvest them.
11. Insufficient plant protection measures against insects, rodents, and other pests.
12. Shortage of pure seed.
13. While increasing number of village cultivators are taking up one or more improved agricultural methods, the need is for more and more of the cultivators to apply as many as possible of the improved practices as a "package".
14. Inadequate supply of electricity for farm operations.
15. Unremunerative prices for agri-produce.
16. Increase in cost of cultivation.

Crop yields can without much extra expense be substantially increased as the Block staff, working through the village panchayats, succeeds in getting village cultivators to recognize that their yields are low; to understand the things which contribute to low yield; to want to increase their yields; to know the specific things they as cultivators can do to increase their yields; and as the cultivators are helped through demonstrations and educational guidance in gaining successful experience with the new practices and methods.

Action Steps for Increasing Agricultural Yields

1. The village extension worker with the advice of the Block extension staff should, working through the panchayat, keep all village cultivators informed about improved agricultural practices for all the major agricultural crops grown in the village.

For each of the major crops, the practices recommended to the village should be a package and cover all phases of the crops life cycle, e.g., cultural practices, improved seeds, fertilizers – kind and application, insecticides – kind and application, agricultural implements, water use, etc.

2. Under village conditions test, through well organized result demonstrations, a package of technical recommendations made by the gram sevaks. Once these improved agricultural practices and methods have been adequately tested under village conditions, then and only then should the recommendations be made on a village and Block-wide basis and intense educational programmes be organized to get widespread acceptance of the proven recommendations.

3. If the village people are to follow through and themselves adopt the improved practices and methods which have through village demonstrations proven to be superior to the traditional practices, the Block staff must then turn to the cooperatives and help the cooperatives become effective in making available the needed supplies (seed, fertilizers, implements, insecticides, etc.). The cooperatives and also the Government must assure that these supplies will be available when they are needed, in sufficient quantity and in close proximity to all villages, and at prices the villagers can afford. If the villagers are to purchase these supplies credit must through the cooperative be readily available on terms and conditions appropriate to all classes of cultivators.

4. Assuming the population base is adequate to organize a cooperative in sufficient size to provide volume and quality service and support competent business management, the Block staff should educate the village people to understand how a well-run cooperative could assist them in at least three important ways:

(a) The cooperative must provide the credit required for villagers to be able to purchase the recommended improved seed, the improved implements, required bullocks, tractors, power tillers needed fertilizer and insecticides.

(b) The cooperative must be the distributing organization for stocking and selling to the cultivators the required and recommended improved seed and implements, fertilizers and insecticides. Private commercial agencies also may do the job.

(c) The cooperative and the Government must assist the villagers in the marketing of their products – essential if the cultivators are to realize the maximum net return on the products sold.

5. While the actual improved agricultural practices can only be carried out by the individual cultivators, the village panchayat can and must take the leadership in assisting the village community to do many things together. It is the combination activity by the individual cultivator and the village community which will be necessary to step up crop yields.

6. There should be adequate supply of power for cultivation.

7. The farmers should be guided and assisted in conserving and judicious use of rainwater both for agricultural and domestic purposes.

II. FRAGMENTIZED LAND HOLDINGS IS A VILLAGE PROBLEM :

Fragmentized land holdings in the villages is primarily associated with population pressure on the land. This along with limited out migration, decay in handicraft economy, and limited employment opportunities in village industries has forced village families to follow the practice of sub-division of land holdings as the only means of providing economic opportunity, though meager, to the oncoming generations.

Since India's immediate need is substantial increased agricultural production, it is imperative for the panchayats and Block staff to give the highest priority to village programmes which will result in increased agricultural production. It is a well-known fact that the present scattered, small and unevenly shaped fragments of land holding prevent cultivators from adopting many of the improved agricultural practices essential for agricultural development. Putting first things first means the panchayats should under the guidance of the Panchayat Samithi develop soon far-reaching programmes to bring the present fragmented land holdings into rectangular consolidated holdings and do so within the shortest possible period of time. To be effective, this programme of consolidation should be taken up and sponsored by the District Zilla Parishad and the Block Panchayat Samithi.

Action Steps for Consolidation

1. Experience with land consolidation in many States clearly indicates that village people are themselves concerned about their fragmentized land holdings and will with the intelligent guidance of the Zilla Parishad and the Panchayat Samithi give full cooperation in working up village consolidation programmes. The Government may come up with a policy on land consolidation.

2. Facts about how other villages have gone about and benefited from consolidating their land holdings should be presented to village people, through the panchayats.

3. Individual villagers – panchayat members and others – who are interested in land consolidation might be taken to villages where land consolidation has been completed so they can make first-hand observations about the programme.

4. As a means of developing villager interest and guiding the village through a land consolidation programme, the village panchayat should be encouraged to establish a land consolidation committee to deal with this specific problem.

5. As a village panchayat's interest is aroused in the problem of fragmentized land holding, steps can and should be taken to prepare an up-to-date map giving precise measurements of all land holdings.

6. When the majority of villagers are ready to cooperate in a village-wide land consolidation programme, a plan should be agreed to for determining the land classification values of each strip of land. These land classification values may be based on any one of the following:

   (a) Valuation on the basis of market value.

   (b) Valuation on the basis of productivity.

   (c) Valuation on the basis of rental value.

The finalized programme for land consolidation should give to each landholder a rectangular piece of land having the total value of his various strips.

7. In finalizing the village land consolidation the panchayat should be encouraged to integrate this programme with all round village development. This means in the final land consolidation plan particular attention should be paid to the following:

(a) Setting aside appropriate land for village roads, drainage, irrigation, etc.

(b) Providing land for such community purposes as pasture lands, fuel plantations, schools, panchayat ghars, play grounds, etc.

(c) Valuation on the basis of rental value of village site or a new piece of land so the entire village lay out may be modernized to permit wide, drained streets, adequate space for houses with latrines, etc.

(d) Setting aside a part of the land for cultivation through the village community, the income from such land being utilized to augment the village panchayat funds.

(e) Development of schemes for more intensive cultivation by improvement of land, adoption of improved techniques and conservation of soil.

III. LIMITED EMPLOYMENT OPPORTUNITIES IS A VILLAGE PROBLEM

Limited employment opportunities are the result of at least the following conditions:

1. The population is increasing faster than production resources and new work opportunities are presently being organized.

2. Lack of planned cottage and village industries keyed to market demand, available raw materials and technical resources.

3. Lack of financial help for small industries –

   (a) to modernize existing industries,

   (b) to procure raw materials,

(c) to market products,

(d) to organize new industries.

4. Lack of adequate technical research and training programmes to help cottage and village industries keep up-to-date on scientific and industrial development.
5. Lack of organized village initiative for improving existing cottage and village industries and establishing new ones.
6. Since many village industry products are of inferior quality and not keyed to market demand, they are not able to successfully compete with similar products produced by larger, more modern industries.
7. Educational institutions are not providing adequate technical training to prepare village boys for useful service in cottage and village industries.
8. Arable land for new workers in agriculture is definitely limited.
9. Too much village emphasis is currently placed on crops which required limited labour – thus definitely limiting the motivations to push up production of commercial crops which may require more labour and investment, but are more profitable.
10. Because of lack of emphasis on water use much land is only partially used and therefore, has limited labour requirements.
11. Until recently little has been done to frame a systematic plan to counteract the growing unemployment in the villages.

As the agricultural segment of the village economy begins to respond, pushing up production and income, and the village people become alert to their new opportunities and express new needs, there will develop in the villages new market demand which can be met through locally produced and marked products. To meet these rising expectations of village people, the Panchayat Samithi should develop as a priority programme the provision of educational guidance and technical assistance to the present and potential cottage and village industries within the Block.

Action Steps for Increasing the Employment Opportunities of Village People

Following are the more important and feasible action steps which, if taken jointly by the cottage and village industrialists and the Panchayat Samithi, should increase employment opportunities in the Rural Development Blocks.

1. Collect data about existing whole-time, part-time and subsidiary occupations.

2. Conduct industrial and marketing surveys of the Block to determine the present and potential market demands and to give guidance about what types of industries have a good chance of succeeding in the area.

3. Through education and demonstrations, help the village artisans and village industrialists realize the need for assistance and recognize that through the Rural Development Block programme, technical service programmes will be organized to assist them in at least the following ways:

   (a) Determine consumer needs, including design and quality preference.

   (b) Establish working contacts with agencies set up for helping the development of rural industries, including the village and small industries technical-research-training-service institute or their branches to help village artisans keep current on processing methods.

(c) Obtain required low-cost financing.

(d) Secure essential good-quality raw materials at a reasonable price.

(e) Move their products into marketing channels.

4. Wherever feasible, modest industrial estates should be organized in selected villages – to provide power, improved working conditions, and better concentration of technical services.

5. Careful study should be made of the slack work seasons to determine the types of cottage and village industries which best lend themselves to spare-time work.

6. The village industries should be actively assisted to reach the minimum strength required for establishment of sound cooperatives and bank financial assistance with full-time competent business management. The organization of such bank facilities and cooperatives should be encouraged to take over a three-fold service:

   (a) Provide the required credit.

   (b) Assist in the procurement of raw materials, machines and tools.

   (c) Assist in marketing products.

7. Programmes for the re-building of villages offer great scope for increased employment. Building materials can be produced by cooperatives which in turn can provide employment.

8. Public works programmes should be organized to take up economic producing programmes such as digging irrigation and drainage channels, leveling of land, contour bunding, planting of trees, and the construction of farm—to-market roads.

Entrepreneurship Development Phases to Promote Entrepreneurship

Identifying, selecting, motivating and training the new entrepreneurs constitute a major task for the entrepreneurial development agency. The promotion or development of entrepreneurship may be undertaken in five phases and we may briefly look into each phase.

PHASE - I

The first phase relates to the basic physico-psycho-socio-cultural and economic study and understanding of the area where the programme is to be implemented as detailed earlier. Industrial potential survey focusing both on material and human resources of the area will be the basis, based on which feasibility studies are to be prepared for each viable candidate industry covering technical, economic, financial, demand and marketing aspects of the enterprise. Such a study will serve the purposes of developing an action – programme for identifying viable enterprises either resource-based, demand-based or footloose and potential entrepreneurs.

Here the emphasis is to be laid on starting small-scale enterprises where the people are living now, cheap enough so that they can be created in large numbers without calling for an unattainable level of capital formation and imports, with relatively simple production methods, so that the demands for high skills are minimized not only in the production process itself but also in matters of organization, raw material supply, financing, marketing, and the production mainly based on local materials and for local use.

With such a purpose, initially to make use of the local resources and the local consumer demands, we are not to look for highly talented, sophisticated entrepreneurs, but people with some interest, with some investment capacity, who are partially unemployed or totally unemployed, people who are looking for some avenues to increase their income, people who are likely to take certain amount of risk in venturing into some entrepreneurial activity. Highly achievement-oriented individuals seek opportunities, create conditions, need less propping and venture into industrial activity. Such people can take care of themselves with minimal support from the development agencies. But our task is to gradually shape the common man into an entrepreneur. Against this objective, potential entrepreneurs in the client community may be drawn from the following segments: (a) artisan groups, (b) high school dropouts, (c) educated unemployed, (d) merchant-trading groups, (e) farmers who are in the process of or likely to partly shift to some enterprise, (f) farm-labourers who are likely to take some small business or enterprise and (g) woman entrepreneurs.

In the first phase as a constructive approach and strategy, the entire client community is to be exposed to the idea of entrepreneurship development. No segment in the community should feel it is isolated or ignored and the programmes are meant only for certain sections. The general exposure of the entire client community to the idea and prospects of entrepreneurship will create awareness, interest among them which will gradually motivate the potential entrepreneurs to move into action.

The creating of awareness, preparing the community, motivating and facilitating some individuals in the community to take decisions, secure the sanction of their families and opinion leaders, that is cutting through the socio-cultural barriers may be done through entrepreneurship-extension education through individual and group methods and through the mass media, always reinforced by personal contacts and counselling. One of the foremost things in the process is raising the aspiration level of the people. They have to be told convincingly of the social and economic advantage inherent in industrial activity. The rise in their standard of living as a result of successfully running an enterprise has to be projected and brought home to them. These ends can be achieved through what is called 'intensive campaign' technique. It is a package of activities comprising an industrial potential survey, publication of the survey findings, holding of small group meetings explaining to people in the community, the kind of enterprises that are feasible in the area, the requirements for starting the recommended enterprises, who can undertake them, the kind of assistance they can expect from the various industrial development agencies and in such a type of campaign, the industrial development personnel and the selected local and political leaders will be involved. The inclusion of influential local and district leadership would build and reinforce confidence and morale on the part of the potential entrepreneurs in the local community.

It may be in order to mention here the steps that may be taken in identifying the viable enterprises and potential entrepreneurs in the client community.

The Steps:-

1. Identification of the natural resources the community is endowed with.
2. Listing out the ongoing economic and industrial activities carried on by the community based on the resources at its command.
3. Listing out the associated skills available with the members of the community (or the target population).

4. Listing out the kind of new enterprises technically feasible and economically viable that could be promoted based on the available resources and skills.
5. Listing out the existing and required infrastructural facilities in view of the new enterprises suggested.
6. Appraising the client system of:
   - the kind of new enterprises they could take to;
   - the financial, managerial, technical and marketing requirements in respect to each enterprise;
   - the kind of people who can take up the suggested enterprises;
   - specifying in general the qualifications, personal aptitude and abilities and investment capacity on the part of the prospective entrepreneurs.
7. Appraising the client system of:
   - the kind of help the multiplicity of agencies connected with entrepreneurial development can extend to the prospective entrepreneurs, which may cover questions like What? When? To what extent? How often? To what purpose? etc.
8. Final identification of potential entrepreneurs and matching their interest with the enterprises.

A word on identification of potential entrepreneurs. Depending on the extent of response, the level of candidates, the potential and the capabilities that are sought among the candidates, the optimum number that the resources and schemes could support and sustain, one may go in for psychological tests such as: (a) Achievement Motivation, (b) Risk Taking, (c) Value Orientation, (d) Adoption Propensity, (e) Level of Aspiration, etc. These projective or psychological instruments are rather complementary to the information provided on the application that the candidate fills in, concerning his family background, his educational attainment, work experience, his choice of enterprise, his experience if any in entrepreneurial activity, his investment capacity and his socio-cultural affiliations.

Importantly, the means employed for identification are the application, interview and if need be, the tests mentioned above. One invaluable resource for identifying potential entrepreneurs is the client community itself.

When it comes to identification and selection of potential entrepreneurs, more often, we ignore the local community. The people in the local community may not be conversant with attributes or traits that are contributive to successful entrepreneurship, may not have any idea and understanding of some of the projective techniques used sometimes to measure the strength of need for achievement, value orientation, risk taking and adoption propensity on the part of the prospective entrepreneurs, but they will have a fairly good understanding of the people in the community as to who would do what and to what extent one would fair well and who is innovative and who would manage an activity effectively. This kind of knowledge of individuals is based on the day-to-day observations irrespective of an individual's profession or occupation. And so, one can, to a large extent depend upon and make use of the local community, the small groups in the community for identifying and selecting potential entrepreneurs. As we have pointed out earlier, once the viable enterprises have been identified based on industrial potential survey, one may list out the personal requirements that one is looking for or in other words the kind of people who can answer these requirements in order to respond to the recommended enterprises. Once this information is communicated to the community through individual contact and small group meetings, it is possible for the local community to indicate the names of individuals who are likely to be successful as small entrepreneurs. This could be in addition to individuals themselves coming forward to take to some entrepreneurial activity. The stress here is that the local community could well serve as a source and guide in selecting potential entrepreneurs.

PHASE II

It consists of training various categories of personnel who will be involved in locating and developing entrepreneurship in the area under question. A general but comprehensive course of three to four weeks is to be prepared keeping in view the earlier work-experience of the personnel. The participants will be familiarized with the prospects and problems of entrepreneurial development in the area of operation. Further, the programme will include inputs on feasibility studies, techno-economic surveys, preparation of industrial profiles, entrepreneurial development, marketing, etc. Representatives of financial institutions in the area may be associated with the training programmes. By the end of the second phase, the agency will be in readiness with the knowledge of the area of operation, and also trained personnel to select and train entrepreneurs.

PHASE III

It consists of selection and training of potential entrepreneurs in the client community by the agency. The training of the entrepreneurs will be arranged at district or sub-district headquarters. The personnel of the development agency who have already undergone training will conduct the training programme. The duration of this training may range from two to six weeks. It depends on funds and the category of candidates trained. In some cases, inclusive of in-plant studies, the courses are run for 14-20 weeks. The training inputs will include elements that would enable the entrepreneur-trainees acquire basic knowledge, skills and motivation to establish their units and manage them successfully. The training will be both theoretical and practical. Towards the end of their training, the candidates will go back to their villages and make a mini-market survey concerning their enterprises, or prepare project reports. They bring back the field data, and work these into project proposals for securing funds from financial institutions.

PHASE IV

It consists of the agency collaborating with other functionally associated agencies to guide and help the trained entrepreneurs in establishing their enterprises, either individually, in small groups or through industrial cooperatives.

PHASE V

In the final phase, which will be taken up after a lapse of six months after the training of entrepreneurs, the training programme will be evaluated. The objective of the evaluation is to find out as to how many of the trained entrepreneurs were able to establish their enterprises and the problems they faced in setting up their ventures. In the light of this experience the training programme for other batches of entrepreneurs will be restructured if necessary.

Support for Marketing of Products

More often, the entire success of small enterprise promotion in rural-tribal communities hinges on marketing of products of the neo-entrepreneurs. In the initial stages and also, in some cases on the sustained basis, the promotional agencies should help in marketing of the products. The induced and emerging entrepreneurs may be too weak to organize the marketing of their products on their own. The promotional agencies may go in for internal or external export of the indigenous handicrafts and products through a network of marketing channels. Such a support would sustain the ongoing entrepreneurs and also motivate the potential entrepreneurs to ventures into the field.

In sum, we may say that the women constitute a significant segment in the population. Till now, they have not been the focus of entrepreneurial development. The need today to develop entrepreneurship among them is imperative, the development of entrepreneurship among men and women being simultaneous. The question of EDP among women is a question of choice, priority and organization.

IV. LACK OF VILLAGE SCHOOLS,

Poorly trained and inadequately paid teachers, a school programme unrelated to village life and development, and high illiteracy among teen-age youth and adults, constitute major educational problems for the villages of India.

Some of the more important things which have contributed, and still do contribute, to the educational problems of the villages are listed as follows:

1. Because of the economic pressures on the village families to earn and produce the base essentials for survival, some of the children have of necessity had to remain out of school and go to work.
2. Much as they value education for their children, the villagers look at their past experience and conclude, with some at least of the actual facts on their side, that the youth who have gone to school have become dissatisfied with village life and have moved on to the larger towns and cities.
3. The village school, the village teacher, and the school programme are not effectively related to village within the village and to earn an effective living either as a cultivator, artisan, or village industrialist.
4. Many villages are without schools.

5. Many villages are without teachers.
6. Because, the villages of India pay such low salaries to teachers and have such limited facilities for their effective living, including meager recreation and health services, the better trained teachers who have other opportunities avoid going to the villages where they are so sorely needed.
7. Until we gained independence and new opportunities arose for all to contribute to the nation's development and to their own personal economic and social advancement, being literate held no particular attraction for the masses of village people, for it could not convincingly demonstrate that to be literate would result in their advancement.
8. Now that it can be demonstrated that being literate is essential if all are to fully profit from independence and are to make their maximum contribution to the building of New India, there are limited facilities and too few teachers trained in the modern techniques of literacy education.
9. There is a great scarcity, of good reading material, readily available at a reasonable price for the neo-literate.

One has only to exercise his mind to understand that, in the building of New India through the process of re-building each of our 558,000 villages as significant cultural units, effective education for all is essential. The study of world history and of the rise and fall of great civilizations supports the conclusion that a nation's greatness is dependent upon the importance the nation places on education, and upon the effectiveness of the educational institutions in training people with creative, reflective minds capable of guiding the nation's growth and sustaining a great and significant culture. It is, therefore, of great importance that the Panchayat Samithi and village panchayats accept the challenge which is theirs to help all villages in the process of rural development tackle the village educational problems, bringing to this task the forthright leadership the people deserve and must receive if India is to again grow into a great nation.

Action Steps for Improving the Status, Services and Facilities of Education in the Villages

1. Through various educational media, demonstrate to the people the importance of all being literate in order to take advantage of the benefits of science and technology and all children having an opportunity to attend a school taught by a competent, well-trained teacher adequately paid.

2. As the village grows in its interest in having a village school, help the village organize itself to contribute its labor and as much material as possible toward the construction of a school.

3. Assist the village in organizing literacy classes. Whenever literate local people are available, they should be trained and assisted in conducting the literacy classes. When local literacy instructors are not available plans should be worked out for outside instructors systematically to visit the village to conduct the literacy classes.

4. To assist in the socio-economic upgrading of the village teacher and thus in enabling the village to secure and keep a competent teacher, the panchayats should be encouraged to see the importance of the village providing the teacher with a house and an adequate vegetable garden. Panchayats should also be encouraged to develop plans for self-taxation to

contribute towards increasing the salary of the village teacher.

5. So that the village school can increasingly become an effective village institution and the teacher can play a more prominent role in village development, the Panchayat Samithi should in the first instance organize a ten-day training camp for all the village teachers in the Block. The purpose of this training should be to train the village teacher to serve as a village leader, assisting in stimulating the entire village to be interested in all-round development. Following the first camp, yearly refresher camps of a week should be organized.

6. Continue to emphasize to the village people that, while in the past they have survived with limited or no education, in the future education will become more and more important for success as a cultivator, artisan or industrialist, and for participation in village and state affairs. Point out that, whereas in the past survival was based on familiarity with traditional methods, the future will require familiarity with and understanding of the application of science.

SCHOOL AND THE COMMUNITY - DRAWING STRENGTH FROM EACH OTHER

School availing facilities in the neighbourhood communities and the community making use of the facilities at the school, playground, library, etc. The school periodically organizing some extension lectures for the farmers. These lectures will relate to any useful information, namely health and sanitation, importance of adult literacy, augmenting the creation of awareness on important local and national issues. School will play as a forum for dissemination of information relevant to the community. The kind of relation between the school and the communities depends on the location of the school, whether it is of rural setting, urban setting or in a metropolitan area. Because, the environment such as farming, industry, service, do matter in respect to the children learning from their environment and the communities making use of the facilities at the school. Interaction between the teachers and the community members especially the teachers interacting with newly emerging rural leadership such as self-help groups (SHGs). The schools inviting people who are known for their expertise in certain fields to address the pupils at the school. The children also may be placed in the rural communities to learn something as to what goes on in terms of activities that are carried on in the rural areas related to farming, and sometimes the children may also benefit from the way in which the segments in the community and the community mobilize the resources to resolve their disputes. It is bringing the school closer to the community and drawing the community closer to the school. That will enthuse both the parents and their children. The teachers may also become part of the community. The result of such an interaction between the school and the community will create healthy relationship and establish emotional bonds which would enthuse both the school and the community. And when we come down to the elementary school, for example, we find the teachers having intimate to moderate contact with the community where the school is located. The children apart from their learning through the stipulated curricula would learn more about the dynamics of the community life. You may call this as extra curricular education. The school children will also at their earliest age may come to know the newly instituted Village Panchayats, mandals/development blocks and so on. Some times, the school may also invite some of the functionaries of several departments operating at the village and mandal/development block level to address the student community sharing the kind of programmes/activities they do in rural communities. Depending on the resources of the school, they may have a mini or a modest extension centre wherein they may organize seminars, workshops, extension lectures, and permanent exhibits. Sometimes, depending on the interest, with the capability on the part of the schoolteachers, they may take-up some of the issues, problems and needs confronting the community and carry on research on those aspects which would be a kind of further education. The Community-School approach to rural development was initiated as a model in the Philippines. A toilet, kitchen garden and planting of trees and sanitation may first be introduced at the school, so that the children get used to such facilities and they will be the promotional agents of such things in their families and the communities. Involvement of the children in environmental sanitation. The school may interact with the newly emerging community level associations such as DWCRA, Vana Samraksha Samithis, and Neeru-Meeru Programme.

V. POOR HEALTH IS A MAJOR VILLAGE PROBLEM

Some of the more important things which contribute to poor health in the villages are listed as follows:

1. The villages have all too few medical services and facilities.
2. Lack of family planning, spacing of children, contributes to poor health of the mother and children and intensifies the problem of inadequate food.
3. Village people have deep-seated religious and traditional attitudes and biases in favour of traditional remedies and health practices.
4. The following types of poor environmental sanitation contribute to poor health:
   (a) contaminated drinking water,
   (b) pollution of tanks, soil and surroundings with night soil and animal dung,

(c) smoke-filled and poorly ventilated houses,

(d) inadequately cleaned and drained village streets.

5. Insect and rodent are carriers of diseases – flies, mosquitoes, flees, rats, etc. – contribute directly to poor village health.

6. Lack of adequate and nutritious diet contributes to poor health.

7. Lack of protection from certain preventable disease through immunization causes poor health.

Regardless of what programmes the Panchayat Samithi may feel demand priority attention, developmental experience all over the world supports the conclusion that the response of village people and their participation in sustained development is closely related to their physical and mental health. Because this is so, it does not follow that the Block staff should be expected to impose a health programme on the people before they are ready to accept such a programme and to provide the required leadership to make good health a village goal. The implication and strong recommendation, however, is that the Block staff should early and continuously use all effective media for educating and guiding the Panchayat Samithi and the village panchayats toward improvement of all phases of village health.

Action Steps for Improving Village Health

Following are some of the more important action steps involving both the Panchayat Samithi and the village panchayats in improving village health –

1. Because village people have for so many years learned to live with poor health, the Block staff should devote its best efforts to a village-by-village health education programme that will awaken the village

people to want better health, and will aid them in understanding

2. Minimum adequate health service and facilities should be provided for each Block, and continuous health education programmes should be carried on to guide the village people to make appropriate use of the newly provided services and facilities.

3. Each village panchayat should be encouraged to want and should be helped to provide and protect a safe drinking water supply for the village. Arrangements should be made for maintaining the pump and keeping the area near the well drained and clean.

4. Special attention should be concentrated on educating the people to construct and use suitable latrines. Villagers should be told that the diarrhoea and dysenteries which kill about twenty lakhs of persons every year in India and make about five crore ill are due to improper disposal of human excreta.

5. Educate the villagers to see the relationship between many of the common diseases and insects and rodents, and then assist the village panchayats in organizing programmes to eliminate these disease-carrying insects and rodents.

6. Through education, assist the village people to understand the relation between the food they eat and their health, and then assist them in raising more varieties of vegetables and fruits to broaden their diet, and in following methods of food preparation which will give them a more nutritious diet.

7. Educate villagers to see that many of the deaths in the village could have been prevented if all were protected by immunization against certain diseases common to the village such as smallpox, cholera,

typhoid, tetanus, and diphtheria. Encourage those who want protection from these diseases to get their inoculations regularly at the health centre.

8. As the village health programme takes shape, the panchayat should be encouraged to involve the village school in order to assure that all phases of the village health programme are taught and practiced in the school programme.

9. Educate villagers to understand that a village house which is fully protected against rain and cold, and which permits entrance of sunlight and fresh air, is a healthier house for the family. As village people express interest in ventilation, guide them in installing protective windows and smokeless chulhas.

10. Through education, continue to impress on the village people that is much easier to prevent disease by following protective health programmes than it is to cure disease.

11. The Block staff should know the religious and traditional village attitudes toward present and recommended health practices. The staff should seek guidance as to appropriate approaches directed toward changing these religious and traditional attitudes.

12. Get the village panchayat to understand that a village with clean, well-drained, paved streets will also be a healthier village.

13. Through educational programmes, village panchayats should awaken the village people to the importance of family planning in relation to the health of the mother and the children and the social and economic well-being of the family. The Block health centre should be the distribution point for information

on the recommended family planning methods and their application.

14. The village extension workers and the entire Block staff should set an example by their own housing, sanitary facilities and health practices.

(Note:- Please see Chapters 14 & 15 for more details.)

VI. POOR FAMILY LIVING IS A UNIVERSAL PROBLEM OF ALL VILLAGES.

Poor family living is caused by some or all of the following conditions:

1. Until Independence and the organization of the Community Development Programme, village families had generally neither the means nor the incentives to live better, thus producing attitudes of indifference toward all aspects of family living conditions.

2. Throughout the villages most families do not always fully appreciate the full importance of –

   (a) Personal body cleanliness and clean clothing;

   (b) Clean food;

   (c) Clean, attractive, ventilated homes;

   (d) Clean, drained streets;

   (e) Clean courtyards;

   (f) Destruction of pests;

   (g) Beauty in their surroundings;

   (h) Using a sanitary latrine;

   (i) Having pure water to drink;

   (j) Sheltering cattle away from the house;

(k) All members of the family knowing how to read and write.

3. Village people live as they do partly because they lack knowledge of the following things:

   (a) The importance of growing and eating fruit and vegetables essential for a nutritionally healthy diet;

   (b) How to make such simple improvements in their homes as building smokeless chulha;

   (c) How to care for children;

   (d) How to get family planning information about appropriate methods of spacing the children born in the family;

   (e) How to make and mend clothing;

   (f) How to preserve fruits and vegetables;

   (g) How to store and care for clothing and bedding;

   (h) How to provide more recreation.

The building of New India must start by kindling within the families of village India a desire for a better way of life. Through the Rural Development Blocks, programmes will be organized to make possible a gradual and sustained rise in the level of family and village living. If the programmes which the Block emphasizes and the various services available are to make their maximum contribution, *it is essential for all having a responsibility for the programme to understand that the manner in which the services will be used, and the ultimate success of the entire programme, will rest upon the rising expectations of the families for a higher standard of living and upon the motivations from within these families to achieve and sustain such a higher standard.*

Those who plan administer and serve the Rural Development Block programmes must understand that broadly defined village problems and needs take on significance only as they find expression within the family. As a problem takes on significance to the family the motivation for its solution also takes new shape. To illustrate – as the family builds up a desire for better family living expressed in a desire for better housing, clothing, health, education, food and recreation, the motivation for increasing agricultural production becomes a family motivation and therefore, a purposeful one commanding sustained family effort.

In using the terms levels and standards of living the reader should understand that *level of living* is used to mean the things village people now have and the way now live and *standard of living* is used to mean the things the people express as new wants and the way they wish they could live, and are willing to strive to attain.

Following are Some Suggested Action Steps for Improving Family Living:

1. The first essential step in improving family living is, through education, to create an earnest desire on the part of the families for attaining a standard of living, i.e., more and better food, clothing, shelter, health, education, recreation – which is higher than their present level of living – i.e., the things they now have and the way they now live.

2. Three new values which should, through education, become important family and village values are orderliness, cleanliness and beauty. These can best be developed by the Block staff taking an active interest in encouraging village after village in the Block to plan new village, providing for straight, wide,

drained and paved streets, space between houses, sanitary latrines, a village park, flower-beds, a school, a community-cum-panchayat hall, and attractive well-ventilated village houses.

3. As the interest of village women is developed, they should be given training and guidance in the following activities and programmes -

   (a) Sewing, knitting, embroidery and care of clothing and bedding;

   (b) Women taking to mini-entrepreneurial activities, small business;

   (c) Learning the nutritional importance of different foods;

   (d) Learning how to prepare, cook and serve food in ways that will preserve the maximum nutritional value and ensure clean handling of the food;

   (e) Understanding the importance of more milk in the family diet;

   (f) Learning how to plan, plant and care for a family vegetable garden;

   (g) Learning how to preserve fruits and vegetables;

   (h) Learning how to store food.

4. Encourage interest in and use of recommended family planning methods.

5. Using carefully selected, influential families demonstrate how to build and use the smokeless chulha, showing how it saves fuel and removes smoke from the house. Then encourage all families to construct and learn the proper use of a smokeless chulha.

6. Demonstrate the importance of providing appropriate storage space for utensils, and the simple construction necessary for this.

7. Demonstrate the desirability of each family having a sanitary place to wash dishes and utensils, and aid in developing simple plans for this.

8. Create interest in and organize group programme to train women in better care of children.

9. Develop family plans for construction of a sanitary latrine adapted to the village, and demonstrate in family group meetings how to build a latrine. Through education, build up village social pressure for each family to have and use a sanitary latrine.

10. Develop village plans for housing the animals away from the family living quarters. These plans may be either for housing the animals in a separate shed in the compound, or for the villagers working together to construct a village cattle shed near the edge of the village, in which each villager would have his unit of stalls.

11. Encourage families who would be expected to have a good following in the village to clean up their courtyards and keep them clean, and to plant shrubs, trees, and flowers. Encourage the entire village to adopt "clean attractive courtyards" as a village programme.

12. Demonstrate plans for getting more sunlight and fresh air into the homes.

13. Create an interest in and get the village panchayats to organize campaigns for continuous destruction of flies, mosquitoes, rodents, etc.

14. Create an interest in the family having and using pure water for all household purposes.

15. Provide and demonstrate improved plans for family grain storage.

16. Demonstrate and create an interest in washing clothes often and properly and in storing them properly.

17. Create a desire on the part of all members of the family to learn to read and write – pointing out through case illustrations how families have profited and been aided in their business transactions by being literate. Great emphasis should be placed on the fact that the Community programmes are family and village programmes, and on the fact that those who are literate can both participate and contribute to the maximum.

VII. DIRTY, CLUTTERED VILLAGES AND POOR HOUSING ARE VILLAGE PROBLEMS

Dirty, cluttered villages and poor housing are the results of some or all of the following conditions:

1. Poorly planned villages with narrow, crooked, and inadequately drained streets.
2. Lack of appreciation of importance of cleanliness or orderliness.
3. Acceptance of present conditions.
4. Failure to see the need for better houses.
5. Designs for better homes using indigenous materials not available.
6. Lack of community planning.
7. Simple, inexpensive improvements in homes have not been demonstrated.

8. Local readily available building materials have not been used effectively.

9. Better construction methods have not been demonstrated.

10. Needed rural credit for home improvement is not available.

11. There are too many houses on too little land.

12. Animals are housed under the same roof with the family.

13. Grain is stored in the same space the family lives in.

14. Space for family and village latrines is lacking.

In the building of New India village people must be educated to have a new outlook and assisted in achieving a higher level of living. They must see themselves as self-respecting citizens, capable of planning for their future, and must learn through experience that they possess within themselves the resources to solve most of their problems. They must, through education and extension education programmes, develop new values and new attitudes which motivate them to want a better standard of living. They must through experience learn that only as they apply themselves and take full advantage of science and technology in improving their agriculture, industries and cooperatives can they achieve their new desires for better living, expressed in improved house, improved water supply, improved sanitation, better schools, and recreational facilities.

Today village people live in crowded, dirty villages which in and of themselves produce a "cow-dung psychology".

What is needed is a Panchayat Samithi programme, underpinned by village panchayat plans to rebuild the villages. Such a programme will go a long way towards creating the "New –village" outlook that is so essential in making village development a continuous dynamic force. In this new outlook which can flow from the physical rebuilding of our villages, two new values – *Orderliness and Cleanliness* – can be expected to emerge.

Furthermore, village families will become concerned about wanting to live better. As they move into new and improved houses in new villages with wide, paved streets; with drains; with houses spaced to permit sanitary latrines and planting of flowers and shrubs; with playgrounds, village schools and community buildings; and with pure water – as they learn to want to live better – they will be motivated to exert greater effort toward learning how to improve their agricultural and industrial production, which will provide them the additional resources required to meet their growing demands for better living. As the villagers' desires and needs multiply, the basis for an expanding village industries programme can be fostered through the creation of community workshops.

Such an approach would stimulate at one end and at the same time an increasing demand for goods and an increasing capacity to produce the wanted goods. The growing village market for bricks, tiles, simple home furnishings, locks, hinges, window-frames, and soon would make it much more feasible than otherwise to foster new village industries.

A Block programme for the planning and physical rebuilding of our villages need not be approached as requiring large expenditure of funds. The immediate need is for an educational approach to the village panchayats to awaken in them the desire to rebuild their village, either by expanding the present site or on an adjoining piece of land. Once the interest is created the village panchayats will require help in laying out a new village, including land allocation for each type of building, location of wells, playgrounds, community hall, latrines, schools and a modest village community workshop. There will also be a need for help in learning about improved building plans.

Perhaps the greater need will be to help the village panchayat develop a village plan for the building of new houses or the rebuilding of existing ones, development of streets, wells, schools, and community halls and community workshops. It is here that village cooperatives can play a significant part. A cooperative brick kiln may be appropriate, likewise cooperatives to provide other building materials, such as a carpenter shop to produce doors and windows and a pottery to provide tiles for the roofs. A cooperative to manage a community workshop should have a prominent place. By working together the villagers can on a five to ten-year programme basis build for themselves new villages – without requiring much outside capital.

Once new village plans have been laid out in Rural Development Blocks, under the sponsorship of the panchayat Samithis, the resources allocated for wells, paving of streets, and building of schools, should be applied to the new village as an added incentive for the villagers to take up the building of new houses.

In arousing the villagers' interest in moving the village to a nearby site, a search should first be made to find a piece of land. Wherever possible an effort should be made to have the new site contributed through Bhoodan. Where a land gift is not possible then plans for the panchayat to purchase a new site should be worked out. In some cases government grants will be required for the purchase of a new village site.

Action Steps for Planning and Rebuilding our Villages

1. Stimulate the panchayats to take up the rebuilding of their village, either by expanding acreage of present site or moving to a new site.

2. Create panchayat interest in wanting the village to be clean and orderly.

3. Develop panchayat interest in desirable sanitary practices essential for better health.
4. Take influential villagers to adjoining areas to see how villagers have worked together in rebuilding or improving their village.
5. Demonstrate:
    - the advantages of improved housing design;
    - the better use of local and inexpensive building material;
    - improved construction methods;
    - various types of latrines.
6. Emphasize simple improvements:
    - smokeless chulha;
    - sanitary place for washing utensils;
    - adequate, well-ventilated space for family members;
    - storage for clothing, bedding and cooking utensils.
7. Recommended:
    - village and family latrine areas;
    - animal shelters away from family living area;
    - safe storage space;
    - courtyards with gardens;
    - planting of trees, flowers and shrubs;
    - paving of village streets;
    - drains for village streets;
    - sanitary bathing areas;

windows for home to permit sunlight and fresh air.

VIII. TOO MANY POOR CATTLE IS VILLAGE PROBLEM.

Some of the causes of too many poor cattle are the following:

1. Limited area for grazing.
2. Limited fodder for feeding.
3. Poor breeding practices.
4. Restraints against killing useless cattle.
5. Diseased cattle left unattended.
6. Scrub bulls allowed to run free in the villages.
7. Prejudice against artificial insemination.
8. Limited veterinary services.

Common sense dictates that village people cannot and must not continue their current practice of keeping a large number of unproductive and useless cattle which compete heavily with village people for the all-too limited food and fibre.

Action Steps for Improving Village Cattle

1. Through soil and water conservation practices increase grass yields from grazing area.
2. Encourage practice of tying cattle and cutting and feeding forage and fodder.
3. Intensify education and services of artificial insemination centers.
4. Encourage panchayats to sponsor programmes for castration of all bull calves not planned for later use in artificial insemination centre.

5. Discourage practice of allowing stray cattle free movement in village area.
6. Educate people to the importance of fewer but better cattle for both milk and work.

IX. POOR ROADS IS VILLAGE PROBLEM.

Poor village roads are caused by the following:

1. Failure to see that village panchayats have a responsibility for constructing and maintaining good roads.
2. Roads are frequently made without information on proper construction and drainage methods.
3. Monsoons are heavy destroyers of roads.
4. Failure to appreciate the need for multi-purpose roads.
5. Failure to see the importance of clean, well-drained village streets.

If our village people are to remove themselves from their traditional isolation and participate effectively in purchasing essential supplies and in marketing their products they must have approach roads which are kept in good repair all year round.

Action Steps for Improving Village Roads

Following are some of the important things which can be done to assist panchayats to provide for and maintain improved roads.

1. Demonstrate the importance of good roads:
   - easier and faster procurement of supplies and marketing goods;
   - easier and faster communication with other areas.

2. Showing well constructed and maintained roads:
   - well drained;
   - usable in all seasons;
   - adequate for village-to-market use.
3. Encourage the panchayat to organize a "better road" committee that will:
   - help village people understand the importance of good roads;
   - obtain the advice of a good road engineer;
   - stimulate the village people to build roads with their own labour;
   - encourage village people to work together to maintain roads.
4. Impress on the village people the importance of clean, well-drained village streets.
5. As a means of providing employment for those either partially or entirely unemployed and to assure the construction and maintenance of needed good farm-to-market roads, the panchayat Samithi should organize and have each village panchayat participate in carrying out a public works programmes for the construction of roads.

X. LACK OF RECREATION PROGRAMMES AND FACILITIES IS A VILLAGE PROBLEM

Following are some of the more important reasons why our village people have little recreation life: *(Please see chapter: Role of Youth in Rural Development for more details)*

1. Failure to understand the importance of recreation.
2. Limited experience in assuming initiative for organizing recreational programmes.

3. Training on recreational leadership is lacking.
4. Facilities for recreation are lacking.
5. Youth's energy and enthusiasm are not channeled into healthy and constructive activities.
6. Cultural folk art is being forgotten.

The villagers must through the Panchayat's leadership be awakened from their slumber and put to work making village life attractive and stimulating. A full recreation programme for all age groups, both men and women, and all classes of village life will do much to bring new satisfaction and create a healthy atmosphere for village cooperation in all phases of development.

Action Steps for Improving Recreational Programmes and Facilities

1. Creating a desire for a well-planned village recreation programme.
2. Encouraging the panchayat to organize a village committee responsible for a recreation programme, and assisting villagers in:
   - planning for recreational activities;
   - finding and training recreational leaders and recreational talent;
   - establishing places for recreational activities;
   - obtaining recreational equipment.
3. Encouraging village people to keep alive the best of their folk art in:
   - dramas;
   - songs;

- poetry;
- puppet shows;
- dances;
- bhajans.

4. Encouraging the panchayat to take the leadership in organizing youth clubs for both boys and girls.

XI. Lack of Youth Participation in all Phases of Village Life is a village problem

Some of the explanations for limited youth participation are the following:

1. Village traditions have in the past ruled out consideration of youth's:
   - ideas,
   - enthusiasm and energy;
   - cooperative spirit;
   - sincerity and readiness to participate in development programmes.
2. Lack of Youth Organizations

It is as certain as night follows day that the youth of today will be the men and women of tomorrow. The surest way to guarantee that the village of tomorrow will be better than the village of today is to start today working with and training the youth in effective citizenship by providing them with a variety of opportunities to participate in youth programmes and activities.

Action Steps for Improve Youth's Participation in Village Life

Following are some of the action steps for improving youth's participation in village life:

1. Through education change traditional village attitudes to make it possible for youth to assist in decisions in regard to family, village, and national problems. This can best be done by having the panchayats sponsor youth clubs.
2. Helping panchayats secure better teachers and provide schools for girls and boys.
3. Helping all village youth become literate.
4. Promoting better health.
5. Providing wholesome recreation programmes and activities.
6. Demonstrating home improvements to make the home more livable and attractive.
7. Encourage village panchayats to early bring young people into village panchayats.
8. Through youth clubs encourage youth to take the lead in demonstrating new agricultural practices.
9. Training youth leaders.
10. Encourage village elders to give youth greater leadership responsibilities. *(Please see Chapter 8 for further details)*

XII. Lack of Voluntary Village Organizations is a village problem :

Some of the more important factors which contribute to the lack of voluntary village organizations are the following:

1. Traditional dependency on outside agencies for both aid and decisions.
2. Organizations for self-help village work only recently encouraged.

3. Cooperative organizations have in the past tended to be operated organizations and not people's cooperatives which have come up from the people's understanding, interest and leadership.

4. Few people trained in-group organization to guide and encourage village people in setting up their own organizations.

5. Caste prejudice divides people.

6. Group factions tend to be interested in the welfare of limited groups only.

7. Village people tend to shy away from formal organizations.

8. Conflicts persist between present elected panchayats and village-organized informal panchayats of the past.

To assure the full, effective and sustained participation of village people in making the community programme a people's programme, intense effort must be given to encouraging a wide variety of voluntary non-government organizations and institutions.

Following are some suggested action steps for encouraging and nurturing the growth of voluntary village organizations:

1. Panchayats must play an effective role in all round village development.

2. Encourage the organization of people's cooperatives which have their roots deep in the villages.

3. Encourage present leaders to expand their scope and help new leaders develop.

4. Develop self-help activities for the entire community.

5. Encourage panchayats to sponsor the organization of :

- farmers' forums and associations;
- women's clubs;
- youth clubs;
- boys' clubs;
- girls' clubs;
- recreation clubs.

6. Train leaders in-group methods.

Once the village panchayats have, with the active assistance of the Block staff, completed the village by village diagnosis of their problems, and decided on the programmes they wish to emphasize, the next step will be for the panchayat Samithi to consolidate these village plans into a Panchayat Samithi programme. When this is completed, the sarpanches and the village extension workers will have common objectives in stimulating village panchayat activities and the Block technical staff will have clearly defined objectives and work assignments as they move into the villages.

Note:- Partly adopted from Dr. Douglas Ensminger's " A Guide to Community Development" (Revised) 1962, Ministry of Community Development & Cooperation, Government of India.

6

APPLICATION OF TECHNOLOGIES APPROPRIATE TO RURAL AREAS

When new ideas, procedures, systems and technology are introduced in a community, normally the responses will be either acceptance or rejection. When people are used to a particular way of life the tendency is to continue with the same. People at the time of introducing a change may not be in the need of or aware of the benefits of new things that are being introduced. In order to make people accept the benefit of the changes they are to be guided, educated and motivated, so that they will accept and become familiar with the new elements of change and adopt them for better in their life. You cannot think of blindly introducing any technology in a traditional type of community. As it is obvious to everybody, one is to be wary in introducing changes and preparing the people to accept changes. In this context, we may briefly refer to introducing new technologies in a rural community.

One of the objectives of rural development is to develop, transfer and popularize technologies in the rural areas in the fields of agriculture, small and agro based enterprises. Such a scheme for rural development necessitates a plan of action to take into account:

a. An understanding of existing technologies in the specific areas of development.

b. Identification of appropriate technologies available within the country and elsewhere for a specific process or operation in farm and non-farm activities.

c. Identification of gaps in technology and

d. Prioritizing, selecting and concentrating on a few technologies for dissemination to begin with.

The above background information, the state of the situation, the gaps in technology, the technological problems faced by the farmers in their several farm operations and the small-scale entrepreneurs in terms of increasing production and productivity, reducing cost of input and labour, saving time and the overall enhancement of their earnings is necessary. Such knowledge on the part of the project personnel would facilitate the development, adoption, modification and extension of technology to the users.

CONCENTRATION ON SELECT ITEMS

It is suggested that a list of priorities with a broad time frame may be made and work on a few selected items which may meet the following criteria:

a. The immediate problem it would alleviate

b. The drudgery it would reduce

c. The time it would save

d. The economic gains it would provide

e. The potential population it would be relevant and useful to

f. The cost of the technology

g. How soon could it be made available to the clients.

PERSONNEL AND EXPERTISE

In order to develop, strengthen, motivate, familiarize and

keep abreast of the technology development in the targeted fields, the technical / research staff may visit or keep in touch with technology research and dissemination institutions in the country. This would facilitate coordination of efforts and reduce or eliminate duplication and overlapping of work.

ESTABLISHING FUNCTIONAL - OPERATIONAL LINKAGES

Development and transfer of appropriate technology towards rural development cannot be a sporadic and scattered effort. As a technological input towards rural economic and social transformation, it is of utmost national importance. There is a need to mobilize, integrate and channel the efforts of institutions engaged in some or several aspects of development and transfer of appropriate technology for rural development. The project may establish informal and formal functional and operational linkages with development, academic and research institutions in the country such as:

a) Relevant government institutions / organizations.
b) Technical universities / institutions
c) Farmers associations
d) Small Industrialists
e) Manufacturers
f) Traders
g) Non-Government Organizations (NGOs)

For instance, when a prototype technology has been tested at the lab and the field and found to be useful, the concerned department may invite some small-scale industrialists or manufacturers to appraise the technology recommended and encourage or support them or support them to produce the machine or the tool on a commercial basis. The manufacturers and traders are the effective and quick means of technology transfer.

Further, technologies at different stages of development, testing and application may be grouped under different development heads, viz., agriculture, small-scale / cottage industries, handicrafts, domestic appliances, etc., and establish linkages with the relevant agencies for popularizing these technologies through their on-going extension machinery.

PROFILES OF TECHNOLOGY

There is a need for preparing a detailed profile of each technology on hand. These profiles will be useful for publicity and help the extension personnel a great deal. The profiles may also be sent to some of the prospective entrepreneur-manufacturers, and other agencies of publicity.

The profiles may cover the following aspects:

1. Name of technology
2. Whether original, innovative, prototype (adopted or modified)
3. Its technical components, design and physical properties
4. The stage at which its development is.
5. Its uses.
6. Its advantages
7. Its limitations if any.
8. Its production capacity, efficiency.
9. Does it replace any existing technology?
10. Is it a substitution?
11. As a substitute, how better it is?
12. The cost of production of a unit

13. Cost of a unit when mass produced
14. Energy used
15. Who will be the potential users?
16. The attempts made thus far to disseminate the technology
17. The response to the technology transfer
18. The channels and methods employed in technology transfer
19. The organizations engaged in similar development and transfer of technology in question.
20. The government's functional linkages with such organizations.

Transfer of technology or any new method, practice or innovation amounts to introducing of change in the client system. Here, we look into the effective ways and process in introducing change.

INTRODUCING CHANGE

The major problem in introducing social change is to secure enough local initiative and participation so that the enterprise will not be vulnerable as a foreign importation. The major questions we have to remember in this process of introducing changes are:

Who brings the change? What kind of change succeeds? And

How is it best done by what procedures and in what climate?

A. Who brings the change?

- Resistance will be less if administrators, change agents and community leaders feel that the project is their own-not one devised and operated by outsiders.

- Resistance will be less if the project clearly has wholehearted support from top officials of the system.

B. What kind of change?

- Resistance will be less if participants see the change as reducing rather than increasing their present burdens.
- Resistance will be less if the project accords with values and ideals which have long been acknowledged by participants.
- Resistance will be less if the programme offers the kind of new experience which interests participants.
- Resistance will be less if participants feel that their autonomy and their security is not threatened.

C. Procedures in instituting change

- Resistance will be less if participants have joined in diagnostic efforts leading them to agree on the basic problems and to feel its importance.
- Resistance will be less if the project has been adopted by consensual group decision.
- Resistance will be reduced if proponents are able to empathize with opponents and to take steps to relieve unnecessary fears.
- Resistance will be reduced if it is recognized that innovations are likely to be misunderstood and misinterpreted and if provision is made for feedback of perceptions of the project and for further clarification as needed.
- Resistance will be reduced if participants experience acceptance, support, trust and confidence in their relations with one another.

- Resistance will be reduced if the project is kept open to revision and reconsideration if experience indicates that changes would be desirable.

D. Climate for Change

- Readiness for change gradually becomes a characteristic of certain individuals, groups, and organizations. They no longer look nostalgically at a golden age in the past but anticipate their utopia in days to come. The spontaneity of youth is cherished and innovations are protected until they have had a chance to establish their worth. The ideal is more and more seen as possible.

It is relevant to mention some illustrious factors that affect our day-to-day life:

1. Necessity leads to change
2. Understanding leads to change
3. Appreciation leads to change
4. Scarcity leads to change
5. Abundance leads to change
6. Innovation leads to change
7. Deprivation leads to change
8. Affluence leads to change
9. Love leads to change
10. Motivation leads to change
11. Competition leads to change
12. Discovery leads to change
13. Force leads to change (may be for a short period)

14. Concern leads to change
15. Status leads to change
16. Jealousy leads to change
17. Situation leads to change
18. Change in Ideology leads to change

7

LOCAL INSTITUTIONS AS PRIMARY AGENTS OF SOCIAL CHANGE

People's participation in the sense of sharing their ideas, interests, needs and views with the development agencies could be direct and indirect. Direct people's participation in any development activity is constrained, besides other community factors like its size, its geographical spread, and in other words the population in the community and its social composition. One logical, practical and simple mechanism for people's participation is institutional representative participation wherein people's elected, selected, nominated representatives, of diverse people's bodies (organizations/ institutions) from the village to national level participate on behalf of people and for expressing their views. These are formal statutory bodies like village panchayats (India, Nepal), Tambon Committees, Mandals, Samithis, Unions (Thailand and India) and Upazillas in Bangladesh (suspended after General Ershad's exit) and Zilla Parishads in India. Apart from the above statutory bodies which are the administrative and institutional products of decentralization we may also cite voluntary and feeder organizations such as Youth Clubs, Women's Clubs, Farmer's Forums and all forms of cooperative societies facilitating institutional representative participation of the people in the promotional and developmental activities.

Decentralization at the district and sub-district level in terms of policy formulation, planning, resource mobilization, allocation of resources and implementing development programmes is a measure and a means to bring down development administration close to the people for their active involvement. Democratic decentralization is a facilitating factor in representative people's participation and this takes us to look into the various facets and dimensions of decentralization.

DECENTALIZATION: ISSUES, EXPERIENCE AND POLICIES

Decentralization means decreasing the role of central government, and augmenting the authority of responsive local institutions. It is concerned with increasing accountability between people who provide local services, and the people who use these services. Above all, it is about the improved management of some of the development activities in the rural area. There are many forms that decentralization can take, including transfer of authority from central to local government, from provincial government to community and non-governmental organizations, and to the private sector. It is a tool for better rural management, by changing the institutional framework to include a significantly greater role for local and community institutions. Decentralization is official policy in many countries of the region. It is no longer an issue whether local governments will assume greater responsibility, but how they will perform the functions statutorily devolved and entrusted to them.

Whether the formal or constitutional structure of the state is federal or unitary, governmental functions are performed in most countries at several levels. While responsibilities for some of the crucial functions such as defence, external relations and macro-management of the economy rests with the national government, several other functional and technical services in agriculture, education, health care and social welfare are usually the responsibility of the administration at the sub-national or local levels. In some Asian countries, the administrative structure is made up of more than two tiers, with the second tier looking after subjects like law and order and justice, and the planning and execution of development programmes at the regional or provincial level, while government bodies below them are entrusted with the responsibility for providing basic civic services. In developing countries, although forces favouring centralization have usually been strong, a common tenet of policy has been to decentralize governmental functions and foster the growth of local government.

It is universally acknowledged that certain functions of the state are best performed at the local level for the simple reason that decentralizing the provision of basic civic services (eg. Sanitation, public health, primary education and social welfare activities) maximizes welfare by responding efficiently to public needs. Local governments responsible to the people from the locality are in a better position to respond to the preferences and needs of the people than governments functioning at a distance. To a developmentalist the decentralization of the powers and functions of the government among different levels, which essentially underlies the rationale for federalism, helps to reconcile the aims of achieving unity in the midst of diversity. From the economic point, optimal provision of public goods calls for both centralized and decentralized decision-making in the appropriation and allocation of resources in the public enterprises.

In the developmental context, decentralization acquires special significance in view of the fact, given the requisite authority, local bodies can generate activities suited to the resource endowment and needs of the local people. Local government units can undertake more effectively activities like improving local infrastructure, such as roads, transport and communication facilities, water supply, electricity and energy, apart from delivering social services in the area of health, nutrition, sanitation, housing, and so on. Local governments can also make valuable contributions to irrigation and land utilization, the protection of the environment, animal husbandry, household industry, public works and the supply of inputs for agriculture and cottage industries. Excessive centralization in planning and implementation of development programmes often causes needless delays and wastage while stifling local initiative. It is increasingly recognized that real grassroots development can take place only with the active participation of local government bodies in these activities.

Local units are also perceived to be in a position to tap resources, which centrally administered revenue, instruments cannot reach. Participation of the people in the government at the local levels makes it possible to tap resources in ways which may not be acceptable if imposed from above.

The healthy growth of local government units together with the representation of the people also helps inculcate participatory government and development. The units can serve as a training ground for the people and their representatives in responsible decision-making and meaningful participation in national life. Above all, it helps to impart a sense of fulfillment among the people as citizens and thereby strengthens the foundations of a democratic polity. These considerations, as well as the widening resource gap of the public sector in many developing countries, which underscores the urgency of developing more resources and ensuring their efficient use, have impelled many governments to look to decentralization as a partial answer to their problems.

Despite recognition of its merits, however, and the resolve to decentralize governmental functions in planning and management, the process of decentralization is yet to strike roots in most developing countries. Planning has to be decentralized if idle resources are to be utilized optimally and local needs and aspirations are to be met efficiently. Diseconomies and other costs of over-centralization coupled with advances in technologies, particularly in the field of information and telecommunications, have made decentralization both imperative and feasible.

The term "decentralization" in the context of governmental organization is generally taken to mean the transfer of authority from the national or central government to its field offices, local authorities or other local bodies. Decentralization in the economic sense implies the transfer of responsibility for planning, management, resource raising and allocation of resources in the public sector. Such resource transfers can be effected through the devolution of powers and functions of government to lower-level bodies with a degree of autonomy, by the deconcentration of central government offices, and by deregulation, and with the setting up of public enterprises.

If the benefits of local participation and involvement in deciding the use of national resources for public purposes according to local preference are to be derived, decentralization has to aim at what is implied by "devolution". Such devolution should proceed to the lowest possible level where the people can effectively participate in development and have direct access to the benefits of growth as well as civic and social services that governments provide to their citizens. It follows that to be meaningful, devolution carries with it the need for introducing an element of self-governance or some representative character in the lower-level government bodies to whom responsibility for specified functions, along with requisite powers and autonomy, is transferred. Fiscal decentralization, which essentially implies a greater access to national resources with increased powers to mobilize and use them for meeting local wants, provides the real content of functional decentralization.

While decentralization has been attempted in developing countries in all the forms distinguished above, the picture that emerges from the close scrutiny of the countries shows that progress in devolution has been rather slow and halting. Seldom was the intention to devolve matched by necessary action, and even where action was taken in the form of legislation or creation of necessary institutions, other conditions for devolution to be effective were not met with. While there are more than two tiers of government in all the countries, few have succeeded in devising local government institutions which could involve the people in the function of government and in its various activities. At this point, we may at length look into, in a larger sense, a revolutionary change in India – democratic decentralization and Panchayati Raj.

PANCHAYATI RAJ

The institution of Village Panchayat is as old as Indian history and is part of Indian tradition. The ancient Panchayats discharged most of the functions affecting the life of village communities and were effective units of administration until the eighteenth century. With the advent of the British, however, they got relegated to subservient place in the colonial administrative set-up. Even during the British rule, particularly after Ripon Resolution of 1892, attempts were made to revive these village institutions. Accordingly, Panchayats and Local Boards were set up in the Provinces of British India.

THE NEED FOR PANCHAYATI RAJ:- THE CONSTITUTIONAL SANCTION BEHIND IT

The Panchayats, the Taluk and District Boards and the

Municipalities established after Ripon, were either purely nominated or containing some members elected by narrow electorates. Under Montague-Chelmsford Reforms, Local Self-government was made a transferred subject and the State Ministries concerned attempted to broaden the foundations of these local bodies.

In some States, Village Panchayats were sought to be established on a wider scale. But all these efforts were half-hearted and the establishment of Village Panchayats and reconstruction of other local bodies on a truly democratic basis figured prominently on the platform of the Indian national Congress.

After Independence, the importance of revitalizing the Village Panchayats and assigning them a specific role in administration was recognized and it was laid in the Indian Constitution as a Directive Principle of State Policy that "the State shall take steps to organize village Panchayats and to endow them with such powers and authority as may be necessary to enable them to function as units of Local Self-Government" (Article 40).

ITS RELEVANCE TO COMMUNITY DEVELOPMENT IN INDIA

The first organized effort to tackle the problems of rural India was through the Community Development Programme, which was launched in fifty-five selected projects on October 2, 1952. The programme, based on an integrated approach to the various aspects of rural development, emphasized from the beginning the importance of working through the people's institutions like Village Panchayats, Cooperatives etc. to ensure their involvement in the planning and implementation of development programmes and to secure the fullest possible public participation. A great deal of consultation and development work was done under the National Extension Service Schemes. The Planning and

Development Committee set up in each Block was merely advisory.

After the Community Development Programme, which was gradually expanding to cover larger areas, was under implementation for about four years, in January 1957, a Study Team under the Chairmanship of Balwantray Mehta was appointed by the Planning Commission to review the working of the Community Development Programme and also to examine the question of reorganization of district administration to provide for popular organizations between the Village and State levels.

The Study Team recommended, *inter alia,* the setting up of elected and organically linked democratic bodies at the village, block and the district levels and the entrustment of all planning and developmental activities to these bodies. This recommendation was accepted by the National Development Council in 1958. The Central Council of Local Self-Government in its fifth meeting at Hyderabad in 1959, took stock of the action taken by the States to implement the decision of the National Development Council and recommended that "while the broad pattern and the fundamentals may be uniform, there should not be any rigidity in the pattern. In fact, the country is so large and Panchayati Raj (democratic decentralization) is so complex a subject with a far reaching consequences, that there is the fullest scope of trying out various patterns and alternatives. What is most important is the genuine transfer of power to the people. If this is ensured, form and pattern may necessarily vary according to conditions prevailing in different States".

All States have accordingly undertaken to establish Panchayati Raj. Thus we find the ideology and the objectives of Community Development and the concept of Democratic Decentralization-building or extending democracy to the grassroots are fused together, and christened as "Panchayati Raj". The new statutory institutions have become the agencies of Community Development Extension Programmes. In essence, this was further growth in the previous programme designed to strengthen the people's own democratic, elected organization by opening new avenues of opportunities for their development. This new device offers the villagers a share in their own direction and self-development which is indeed a new and a novel departure in their lives. In this programme the people under their own organizations at the Village, Mandal, Block and District level were given equal share and status in the working of the whole community development block. Village Panchayats are constituted through elections and given democratic powers and responsibilities. The Sarpanchs or the Presidents of all the Panchayats formed a Panchayat Samithi, the Panchayats formed a Samithi at the block level and Samithis constituted the Zilla Parishad at the district level. The functions of the Rural Development Agency and the people's organizations at all levels up to the district are to further strengthen and make the rural development programme more dynamic and its structure more complex.

"The Community Development approach has to be an essentially democratic approach as this will draw large masses of the people as active partners in the tasks of developing the vast country. For, only thus can this gigantic task be accomplished. The Community Development approach, while it will depend on the democratic process, will at the same time also help to strengthen it. There is, therefore, complete inter-relationship between Community Development and the progress of democracy; they are two sides of the same coin. Both are processes of human development. It is for this reason that the Community Development Programme came to focus attention on the importance and urgency of democratic decentralization. Democratic Decentralization must not be understood as merely the creation of Local Self-Governing Institutions of the people at different levels or as transfer of real power to the people. Its object is to give vitality to the whole democratic process and to provide to a new born democracy a wider and firmer base" (Mukerji, 1961).

BASIC ELEMENTS OF PANCHAYATI RAJ

The term "Panchayati Raj", which is popularly used in the country includes the two words Panchayati and Raj. Panchayati means "of the Panchayat", which consists of a group of "Panchas" who are representative leaders of people at the village level. What is emphasized is the representativeness of Panch, irrespective of how this element of representativeness is determined. The word "Raj" in this context means Government. The term "Panchayati Raj" therefore, literally means "Government of People's representative leaders". In this sense it is an expression of the essence of democracy as internationally understood. The Balwantray Mehta Committee Report expresses this categorically in these words: "in the ultimate analysis, the establishment of the Panchayat Samithis with a wide devolution of powers by the State Government has to be an act of faith-faith in democracy".

The fundamental or basic principles of Panchayati Raj emphasized in the COPP Report are:

(a) It should be a three-tier structure of Local Self-Governing bodies from the village to the district, the bodies being organically linked up.

(b) There should be genuine transfer of power and responsibility to them.

(c) Adequate resources should be transferred to the new bodies to enable them to discharge these responsibilities.

(d) All development programmes at these levels should be channeled through these bodies.

(e) The system evolved should be such as will facilitate further devolution and dispersal of power and responsibilities in the future.

The primary objective of Panchayati Raj is to establish an integrated structure of local democratic or self-governing bodies linking the village within the district and to make the Village Panchayat as a unit of planning and execution of all schemes of rural development. Secondly, Panchayati Raj aims at developing the initiative of the local people and create conditions for maximum popular participation. Thirdly, it seeks to develop sound leadership at all levels in the district necessary for the success of democratic institutions. And finally, it seeks to provide at the instance of Panchayati Raj bodies, a development-oriented and efficient administration.

In terms of organization or structure, the programme of Panchayati Raj, as mentioned earlier, envisages three tiers of the Government from the village up to the district level. These three tiers are:

1. Panchayat at the village level consisting of elected representatives of the people with provision for the co-option of two women members and one member each from the Scheduled Castes and Scheduled Tribes.
2. At the Mandal or block level, an elected Self-Governing Institution to be called Mandal Parishad Panchayat or Samithi. Membership in this to be by indirect elections from the Village Panchayats. Its jurisdiction to be coextensive with a Mandal or Community Development Block.
3. At the district level there is a body called Zilla Parishad. In order to ensure necessary co-ordination between the Mandal Parishad or Panchayat Samithis,

Zilla Parishad was constituted which consists of the presidents of the Mandal Parishads or Samithis, and elected political representatives of the area namely MLAs, MPs and district level government officials.

In recent years there has been changes in the size, nomenclature and mode of election to the above bodies one example is Andhra Pradesh.

Three tiers viz., Village Panchayat, Panchayat Samithi and Zilla Parishad when constituted and operated simultaneously make up the structure of Panchayati Raj in a district. Functionally, Panchayati Raj is assumed to be operative to the degree that it results in the community understanding its problem, realizing its responsibility, exercising the necessary powers through its chosen representatives and maintaining a constant and intelligent vigilance on local administration.

PROGRESS OF PANCHAYATI RAJ

Panchayati Raj, as mentioned earlier, is an institutional arrangement for decentralized planning and plan implementation. It was brought in to enhance and facilitate people's participation, even though it was representative type of participation. Panchayati Raj was first introduced in Rajasthan and Andhra Pradesh in 1959. This was on the recommendations of Balwantray Mehta Committee on Committee on Plan Projects (COPP) appointed in 1957. This was followed by the Ashok Mehta Committee in 1978 which made vital suggestions for restructuring the Panchayati Raj bodies. It recommended three-tier system of Panchayati Raj institutions and direct elections to Chairpersons of all the three tiers. It also recommended election of women to Zilla Parishads and the Mandal Panchayats, and in case no women were elected to these bodies, they are to be co-opted. Ashok Mehta was followed by three Committees i.e., G.V.K. Rao (1985), L.M. Singhvi (1986) and Bommai (1989). Amongst other recommendations of these Committees was reservation of seats for women in these bodies to a tune of around one-third.

Though the spirit and objectives of democratic decentralization are the same in all the States in India, there are a few variations in terms of number of tiers, their structure, nomenclatures, levels of their operations and provision in them for women representation. The lowest tier is called Gram Panchayat, the middle tier is variously known as Panchayat Samithi, Panchayat union and Mandal Parishad, and the tier at the district level predominantly goes as Zilla Parishad and in a couple of cases as District Council. The idea here is only to indicate the institutional structure and not to go into the details of their constitution and mode of elections, co-options and ex-officio membership at the middle and the upper tiers.

As of December 1992, the following States have a three-tier structure of the Panchayati Raj system: Andhra Pradesh, Bihar, Gujarat, Himachal Pradesh, Karnataka, Madhya Pradesh, Maharashtra, Orissa, Punjab and West Bengal. In case of Haryana, Kerala and Tamil Nadu, it is of two-tier structure at the village panchayat levels and block levels which were earlier community development blocks.

TOWARDS FUNCTIONAL DEMOCRACY

Panchayati Raj is in our making. Statutory changes alone do not bring in the desired changes and transform the human elements. Slowly, patiently, and methodically the statute must be translated into action. For a planned social change towards a richer and meaningful life for the masses in the countryside, an inter-disciplinary approach is the means. A scientific approach to the problem is the answer. Hit and miss methods may not pay higher dividends in the long run. Panchayati Raj must become more a way of life of the rural people.

In a democracy the individual is no more than a spectator; he is actually one of the spectators. He cannot play his part unless he is properly informed as to the processes of democratic government at all levels. Planned public relations are essential to inculcate civic spirit, civic pride and civic unity in villages, as the percentage of literacy is low, a judicious selection of the media of public relations will have to be made. The radio, the film, civic exhibitions, civic weeks and civic *melas* are some of the useful tools of public relations in rural area. Civics with due emphasis on rural self-governments should be made a subject in the curriculum of schools, colleges and universities.

In a greater measure, the people's representatives are to deliver the goods. On them depend the development of the local community the strengthening of the democratic institutions and largely the success of the Panchayati Raj. This development of local leadership and responsible and responsive citizenry could be achieved only through Social Education Programmes apart from economic measures. The community must be mobilized, interest groups identified and organized into responsive and dynamic groups. This mobilization of the community into institutions, interest groups and associate agencies will create the conditions necessary for the emergence of leadership at the local level.

It is only by educating the general public, could we expect awareness, leadership and initiative among the elected members of the Panchayat or of higher tiers, we cannot neglect the general mass and merely concentrate on the elected representatives. A massive adult education movement is desirable to educate the general mass. Literacy Programmes should find a predominant place in the adult education movement. All illiterates below 40 years must be made functional literates within reasonable time. Further, radio-forums and reading rooms-cum-libraries could be organized for dissemination of knowledge.

It is needless to emphasize that the elected representatives should be trained and educated in all aspects of Panchayati Raj. In the course of the Panchayat term, the Panches (or the sarpanches and up-sarpanches as the case may be) should be trained at least twice-once soon after their election to the office and for the second time, in the middle of the term. The stress must be on utilizing the institutional facilities available and not on merely creating institutions.

In educating the sarpanches and the panches the Extension Personnel in the Community Development and more especially the Extension Officers, panchayats could play an effective role. At least once in a quarter or six months, the Executive Officer of the Panchayats may convene a meeting of all the sarpaches and panches of one or two gram sevaks circles at a convenient place and arrange for talks by special invitees – officials and non-officials on Panchayati Raj. This may help understanding and motivating initiative on the part of the elected representatives.

There is no element of force or coercion in making people do things. The means are constant persuasion and education.

Multitudinal problems arise in the working of the Panchayati Raj Institutions. These problems need scientific treatment and solutions arrived at on empirical studies. Action research with an interdisciplinary approach to the problems is a must in the field of planned social change. Under such a built-in action research programme the social scientists and the administrators have to devise ways and means to ensure effective and active participation of the elected representatives in the working of the Panchayati Raj.

An attentive study of the process of decentralization in various countries suggests a few impeding factors in decentralization.

ABSENCE OF LEGAL FRAMEWORK

The disappointing progress of efforts to decentralize can be attributed to a lack of adequate constitutional and legal backing and a weak fiscal base that is fundamental to such a process. We may say that India is an exception in this kind of lacunae. In many instances, local bodies have failed to come up with legal support provided through constitutional recognition or separate legislation. This is true irrespective of whether the country in question is federal or unitary. In Pakistan, a federation, several attempts were made in the last forty years at the initiative of the central government to set up local governments throughout but none has been of much avail. In Thailand, a unitary country, the local level bodies with elected assemblies have been created through specific legislation laying down the structure as well as the powers and functions of the local bodies at different levels. Local governments are, however, not in a position to perform more than a few functions assigned to them by the laws which brought them into being (Cohen and Uphoff, 1977).

LACK OF FISCAL AUTONOMY

A more serious impediment to the functioning of local autonomy is the financial dependence of the local bodies on the central and provincial governments. Almost invariably, the bulk of the financial needs of local governments are met out of the share of the national taxes, and / or subsidies from the center or grants, and the dependence seems to be increasing.

The domination and control of local bodies by the central and provincial governments, which is partly attributable to their financial dependence, has also been responsible for stifling local autonomy and blocking decentralization. In most cases the central government is unitary type and the central and provincial governments in federal structures exercise control over the local bodies in various ways, direct and indirect. In Thailand, while the degree of control varies between different local bodies, all are subject to close control by the central government. Central control is maintained in Thailand through a system that allows the Ministry of Interior directly to control the administration of all local bodies in the kingdom. Supervisory powers over local bodies are delegated to the provincial governors, who are also assigned responsibilities to monitor the activities of local governments. The statutory authority of the local bodies to raise certain taxes and incur expenditure is subject to the rules and regulations of the central government.

China is perhaps the only country to have seen substantial decentralization. Although a country with "unified leadership and government", China has in practice allowed considerable latitude to the local government entities, the provinces and the municipalities, in their function. Even though the country has a unified national budget, the provinces and municipalities have their own separate budgets and run enterprises often on a large scale. Decentralization gathered momentum in the 1980s and in fact the pace appears to have been too rapid for the country to adjust. It may, however, be fair to say that much of the freedom which the local governments enjoy in China despite a monolithic political structure stems from their relatively strong financial base (Cohen and Uphoff, 1977).

FISCAL MISMANAGEMENT

In country after country what has prompted higher level interference is financial mismanagement. In Thailand, the financial weakness of the local bodies is attributable partly to the inefficiencies of the local governments themselves and their inability (or unwillingness) to make full use of whatever tax powers they have under the law. The poor yield of the house and building tax which constitutes the most important component of local taxation in Thailand is due both to deficiencies in the structure of the tax as well as inefficiencies in its administration. While liberal exemptions undermine its base, administrative inefficiencies have also stood in the way of its effective implementation and tackling evasion practiced in various ways by landlords. Tax rolls and maps are not updated and cadastral maps of even resourceful local authorities like the Bangkok Metropolitan Administration are 40 to 60 years old. The system of billing and maintaining tax rolls is outdated. According to a recent estimate, computerization and regularization of the tax-payers would alone double the yield of the tax. While with urbanization one would expect a rise in the revenue from this tax, its contribution to local revenue has gone down (Jurgen, *et.al;* 1989).

ADMINISTRATIVE WEAKNESS

In many countries, especially at the district and municipal or village levels, there is lack of trained manpower to levy taxes efficiently and mange their affairs. The elected officials or representatives furthermore do not always display the sense of responsibility or dedication required for fulfilling the objectives of the local government and often engage in intrigues for power, seeking personal gain to the detriment of public interest. Super-session of local bodies in several countries has also often followed from their mismanagement and the failure of the democratic system to work at the local level (Cohen and Uphoff, 1977; Jurgen, *et. al;* 1989).

STRATEGY OF PLANNING FOR DEVELOPMENT AND EFFICIENCY ARGUMENTS

An important factor impeding the process of decentralization in the developing countries is the adoption of planning as a strategy of development with considerable involvement of the public sector. A degree of centralization is inherent in a strategy of planning, with the government taking a lead role and laying down the basic programmes and priorities at the national level to ensure consistency and efficiency although decentralization might lead to faster development of better-endowed but less developed areas, central intervention and allocation of resources were often thought necessary to bring about the balanced development and provision of public services at a minimum level in all parts of a country. Modern technology with the vast economies of scale spilling across regions in areas like power and communications also have reinforced the trend towards centralization. A lack of expertise in and familiarity with modern techniques of harnessing and managing natural resources also have strengthened the case for a certain degree of centralization. In addition, there are the gaps in technology, resources and skills at the local levels which cannot be made up without help from above. The creation of specialized agencies or authorities to undertake specific tasks like metropolitan planning and development is often motivated by considerations like these.

Considerations of efficiency also argue for centralizing certain important functions, as do the centralized collection of the major taxes like the income tax, which unavoidably created a vertical fiscal imbalance in the system and so the dependence of the local bodies on higher level governments. This is compounded by their lack of managerial and technical skills. Denuding the central government of its command over resources also undermines its capacity to even out regional imbalance, as is now being witnessed in China.

RECENT TRENDS

Experience of the last three decades has, however, cast doubt on the efficacy of centralized planning in promoting growth and spreading the benefits to all sections. Moreover, disenchantment with over-centralization has led to a search for other ways of decentralization apart from devolution. Given the will, it is argued, solutions can be found for the problems and dilemmas or at least these can be rendered manageable. Although decentralization often gets stalled because of a lack of managerial skills, there are examples of good results achieved by associating the people in governmental activities at the lower levels. The involvement of the local population in some of the States in India where elections to panchayats were held in recent years seems to have activated hitherto untapped energies and resources and made tangible contributions to improving public services and activities in those regions. There have been several instances of positive gains from the association of local people and organizations like village cooperatives in the past in Thailand, Pakistan, India and Malaysia. Besides, not all the weaknesses of the local bodies of their own making. As already mentioned, their fiscal powers are often constrained by central control exercised in various forms.

As is to be expected, decentralization, even when acknowledged as desirable, encounters resistance from those for whom it implies a loss of governmental power and authority. A striking example of how the central authorities tend to shackle the autonomy and initiative of local bodies, even when the involvement of local government is sought, is provided by the guidelines issued to district councils in India to implement an employment programme in the rural areas in the late 1980s. Rodinelli and others conclude their discussion on what impedes decentralization with the following observations:

"Untimely however, decentralization is an ideological principle, associated with objectives of self-reliance, democratic decision-making, popular participation in government, and accountability of public officials to citizens. It is a political decision, and its implementation is a reflection of a country's political process and maturity". (Rondinelli *et.al.,* 1983).

These observations are equally valid even after a decade and a half. The recent experiences and trend show that there is now greater political awareness of the need for decentralization than before. Hence the search for solutions to the problems encountered in its implementation and the urge to draw lessons from the past.

Decentralization with its full complements of vertical geographic devolution of powers, administrative control, financial and resource raising authority, freedom of allocation of resources and mandate and responsibility to development planning and plan implementation at local levels, by itself is a great leap forward in the governance of public interest and welfare. People's and people's representative leaders' participation in all the above functions will strengthen the roots of democracy and ensure enduring people-oriented development.

REFERENCES

1. Cohen, J M and Uphoff N.T, (1977). Rural Development Programmes: Concepts and Measure for Project Designing: Implementation and Evaluation. *Rural Development Monograph Series No.2*; Cornell University, USA.
2. Jurgen, Ronald (1989). *Local Governments in South East Asia*. HSD Working Paper, Asian Institute of Technology, Bangkok (Thailand).
3. Mukherji, B. (1961). *Community Development in India*, Orient-Longmans, New Delhi.
4. Rondinelli, D., *et.al.*, (1983). *Decentralization and Development*, UNCRD Regional Development Series, Japan.

8

LOCAL LEADERS AND THEIR PARTICIPATION IN RURAL DEVELOPMENT

There is a close relationship between the leadership in a rural community and the nature and degree of their participation in rural development activities. The local leaders may be instrumental in mobilizing and motivating people to participate in development activities or they may sometimes be barriers inhibiting and subtly or deliberately discouraging participation for their selfish ends and or do so out of ignorance, misinformation, avarice, or trying to keep their followers as marginal and occasional beneficiaries of development programmes and not as active participants in decision-making or authors of any policy issues.

Participation in development programmes as a product or function depends on the structure and type of leadership and the ethnic, social and class composition of the rural community. Sometimes, the numerical strength of the ethnic, occupational and professional groups are factors to be reckoned with when we speak of local leaders as stimulants or barriers to people's participation in development programmes.

We may have a brief look at the rural leadership and some instances wherein local leadership was a deciding factor for any initiative for promotional or developmental programme or the local people accepting a project, innovation or participating in a communal activity.

The village community world over, despite its social, ethnic, religious and lingual composition, is a social entity. It has its structure and traditions. The diverse activities of the community, both individual and communal are carried on and regulated by some individuals from within and outside the community. The individuals who guide, who are sought after to guide and shoulder the affairs of the people in the village may be called leaders. Sometimes, the pattern of leadership and its functions vary from community to community. It is interesting to look into the principles that control human relations and how a social group organizes and lives its life. More often, the burden of village responsibility rests on the leaders just as family responsibility rests on the head of the household.

AREAS OF LEADERSHIP

Leaders emerge and function in diverse fields. The areas of leadership and the number of leadership and the number of leaders functioning in each area and one leader functioning in several areas depend on the size and social structure of the rural community and, as mentioned earlier, on the occupations and profession of the population, their literacy and intellectual levels, and also on the degree of their interaction with the outside world.

In a broad sense, when we think of rural-traditional communities, the following activities may be considered as areas wherein the question of guidance and consulting arise and the local leadership centre around these functions.

1. Coordination of village communal undertakings.
2. Liaison between the people and governmental personnel.

3. Guidance in times of epidemics.
4. Guidance in religious magical matters.
5. Financial problems – monetary matters.
6. Political matters.
7. Guidance in legal matters.
8. Financial help for marriage and death ceremonies.
9. Settling quarrels-disputes outside the village.
10. Settling quarrels-disputes inside the village.
11. Agricultural matters.
12. Guidance in educational matters.
13. Guidance in warding off the effects of witchery and sorcery.
14. Guidance in employment opportunities.

As communities progress, with the increase in skills and literacy rate and change in the value system the nature of needs, degree of dependency and also leadership change. Leadership is a social phenomenon and it is subject to change and will in some measure, in some areas persist forever.

LEADERS AS FACILITATORS AND BLOCKERS

One comes across innumerable instances in rural communities and equally in urban settlements too wherein local leaders function as motivators and facilitators encouraging and enthusing people to participate in development activities concerning their community and as blockers discouraging the people in participation. The local leaders have been instrumental in accomplishing several projects for their communities. Participation by significant individuals in the community secures the projects as a sanctity, approval and acceptance by the generality of the community. We may look into a few cases wherein the weight and significance of local leaders manifest itself.

PARTICIPATION FOR A NATIONAL CAUSE

During the Indo-China War in the last quarter of 1962, over the border dispute which lasted for a short period, the Government of India had to mobilize its resources and a fund raising campaign was started all over the country. It was called "War Fund". The State Governments were asked to raise funds from the people and they acted through several of their line and development agencies. During this period what were then called Community Development Blocks were given each a certain target of amount to be raised from People's Contributions towards the War Fund. As usual (we mean the target distribution downward in the hierarchy) the Block Development Officer (BDO) assigned each Village Level Worker (VLW) a certain target of amount to be raised in his circle comprising households ranging from 1,500 to 1,800.

During this period the author happened to be a VLW and the target of raising money for the War Fund fell on him. Inclusive of hamlets he had around twenty villages under his jurisdiction. Indo-China war was a distant cry for the people in the area. Many of the villagers had no idea of China, its geographic location and its borders with India and the disputed borders. It became a big problem to explain the situation to the simple but intelligent villagers. We had to approach the local leaders for help in raising the amount. Through the initiative taken by the local leaders, we were able to raise small amounts of money ranging from one to twenty rupees or so, from each household.

In this context the author would like to cite one instance pertaining to a community of shepherds in one village, most of them poor and landless, mainly thriving on rearing sheep and goats. We told them that the millionaire-farmer and politically influential leader of a higher caste community from the neighbouring village was visiting their village on such and such a day and he expected them to contribute their mite for the War Fund.

The day the leader visited the shepherd community, one could see the spontaneous and enthusiastic presenting of old silver bangles, rings, waist-strings made of silver, the only valuable ornaments some of the families possessed. Most of them had no money to give. Some of the silver ornaments given by them can be considered antics, for they were of old-fashioned and some may be called of tribal-wear. Later, we sold the silver ornaments to some well-to-do families and passed on the proceeds to the BDO. The participation of the people in this instance was overwhelming and largely it was to be attributed to the respect the villagers had for the leader and his very visit to them seeking their humble contribution. As mentioned earlier, to a large measure, the people's response and their contribution, as a symbol of their participation for a national cause was not a response to Government nor to those skirmishes taking places at the international border between India and China, but for the influence and initiative of the local, small leaders and the big wealthy leader from the neighbouring village.

The following two cases reflect the spirit of healthy competition amongst the rural communities and the significant and appreciable role-played by both, by the formal and small informal leaders in effecting popular participation in mobilizing resources to start a high school and forming of approach roads to the villages.

SMALL INFORMAL LEADERS COLLECTING CONTRIBUTIONS FROM THE VILLAGERS FOR A LARGE EDUCATIONAL PROJECT

Rampur* is a fairly big village with a population of around three thousand at the time of this incidence and is located in Chittoor district, Andhra Pradesh, South India. It is a multi-

*The real name of the village is changed

caste community. It is a market center for the main villages and hamlets within a radius of 15 km. The population of the cluster of villages around Rampur in 1960s was around 30,000, but there was no high school in the whole area. The majority of the population comprised small farmers, landless labourers, artisans and petty traders. Since there was no high school within the walkable distance and many families could not afford sending their children to distantly located high schools and keep them in hostels, many children had no chance of going beyond primary education.

As a contrast to the conditions of the commonality of the communities under reference, one family of the dominant caste-Hindus in Rampur was rich. This family and its clanfolk and kin in the neighbouring couple of villages and other districts were traditionally affluent. The head of the rich family in Rampur is a graduate, well-informed, with high connections, wielding influence with the administration at the district and at the State level too. He is a big farmer, moneylender and most of the farmers in the neighbouring villages were to borrow money from him and so they were captive sellers of their groundnut produce to him only. He was politically powerful and whether the people like it or not he had a sway over them and there was no opposition to him. He could send his children to expensive public schools and colleges and so he had no felt-need for a high school in the village. The neighbouring villagers felt an acute need for a high school in their area. It was reported that some of the important people in the area approached this rich man and raised the question of a high school for the area. His response was evasive, with excuses and explanations of impractibility of opening a high school in the village to serve the village and the neighbouring communities. A high school was a long felt-need. The neighbouring villagers sensed and realized that the big man was not interested in a high school in his area, may be thinking that if the children of poor families received higher education, his importance and his family status will go down, when poor get educated and become rich it is a threat to the already rich.

A few leaders in the neighbouring villages took initiative, went around the villages, discussed with local leaders the prospect of raising money from each family after the harvest of paddy and groundnut, the principal crops in the area. This silent campaign for raising contributions was done without the knowledge and approval of the big man of Rampur. It was a successful fund raising campaign. Obviously, the message of popular concerted efforts, mobilization of small resources in cash and kind and the community's solid social action reached the big man as a shock and threat to his eminent position. He realized that he could not stall the starting of a high school for the area, for the people were determined, have raised considerable amount from the people to approach the government for sanctioning for opening a high school in their area. They were to offer their collections as a matching contribution to government's grant. The big man realized that it was already too late and even if he opposed subtlety or diplomatically the opening of the educational institution, it would come with the popular force. And so, not to be left behind and sidetracked he sent invitation for a grand feast to all-important leaders in the neighbouring villages. Some of the invitees knew that it was a face saving mechanism. A large group gathered on his spacious mango garden and after treating them with a rich feast, he gave a small speech, how, for a long time, he had been pondering over the need for a high school for their area and that he was glad that some initiative was taken by the local leaders and the people in the area and announced with a flourish that he was donating three acres of prime land close to the main road in his village for the high school and certain amount in thousands and wished that the high school may be named after his late father.

After a few months the high school was sanctioned by the government. From then on the big man assumed the lead position. The buildings came up. The high school was opened and for the past forty years now the children of this area have access to higher education. It is the small informal and formal leaders in the rural communities, who initiated the movement and secured popular participation. We should acknowledge the help rendered and boost given by the big man in Rampur whatever might have been his initial attitude and intentions for a high school to serve the needs of the common people in the area.

PARTICIPATION IS CONTAGIOUS

When an occasion arises, when proper climate is created, when people's competitive spirit is kindled, when people perceive the tangible benefit for them and when properly guided by the local leaders people's participation in promotional and development activities becomes contagious. The term "contagious" is used here in the sense of exciting enthusiasm from one to the other for a positive course of action.

It was Andhra Pradesh in India which was the first State to introduce Panchayati Raj system in September 1958, in the Community Development Blocks that were in operation during this period. In order to celebrate the first anniversary of the Panchayati Raj system in the State, a grand programme of multiple development activities viz., kitchen gardens, soak pits, drainage, mass environmental sanitation and formation of earthen approach roads to the villages where they did not exist then was initiated. Of all the above programmes, the formation of cartable and suitable approach roads to villages was given the place of primacy.

The present case refers to the former Chowdepalle Community Development Block in Chittoor district, Andhra Pradesh. The approach road campaign in particular was carried on for a couple of weeks by the Community Development Workers and local leaders. Prizes were established for the best people's participation in terms of their labour contribution in forming the roads. For a few weeks it looked like a massive festive activity in dozens of villages, people engaged in cutting, digging, forming and aligning the earthen approach roads to their villages. One could see the spontaneity and enthusiasm among the people. It was really contagious. Later, the VLW circles which had the best performance were selected and the concerned Village Level Workers were awarded the prizes by the Block Agency. Here the credit goes to the people and their leaders.

WHAT HAPPENS WHEN A LEADER IS IGNORED

As mentioned earlier in this chapter, participation by significant individuals in the community secures the projects a sanctity, approval and a legitimacy. The local leaders are the gate keepers and one can visualize the role of these gate keepers in rural communities. We may look into the case wherein an educational institute as a development agency failed to contact a local leader and solicit his involvement in a housing project for the cobbler community, a constituent of the village. The failure to contact the leader by the development agency was not deliberate or negligence, but it was out of ignorance of the personnel of the development agency, and local communal dynamics and the leader's influence over the cobblers. The non-involvement of the local leaders of different caste and religion acted as a stalemate to the project in the beginning.

SERVAIPURAM

Servaipuram is one of the villages in what is called Achampatti complex of villages, close to Dindigal town in Tamil Nadu. The complex comprises around ten villages which used to be the service area of Gandhigram Rural Institute. The institute had several extension and service activities such as pre-school education, women's clubs, agricultural societies (for access to credit), leather tanning and housing for the weaker sections. The institute was receiving funds from a German voluntary agency and this was the only source of funds for the institute for its extension service activities. These activities served as a field orientation to the students of the institute.

Servaipuram is fairly a large village with a population of 2,500 persons. The majority comprised of Servai Christians and there is a church in the village with a priest who was an outsider and a local leader as the manager of the church. Obviously, the manager of the church was a Christian and was religious and secular leader in the village. Nothing in the village should happen outside his knowledge. He had a grip over the Hindu minority groups in the village.

THE COBBLERS

One such minority group was cobblers, the leather workers comprising 45 households. All these families were living in hovel like huts, crowded in a small area outside the main settlement of Servaipuram. The most immediate need for the cobbler community was housing. The institute's faculty (the author was one of the faculty) on deliberations with the cobbler community arrived at this priority of housing for them. The housing project required acquiring of land for house sites and building the houses for the 45 families. The leaders in the cobbler community were asked to choose some land around the village (private or government land) so that preparations may be made for formal acquisition of land for housing.

The faculty from the institute used to meet the cobblers periodically in order to know the progress in their selection of land. Thus, the faculty spent ten months without getting any indication from the cobblers. Whenever the faculty assembled the cobbler leaders and discussed the question of their choice of house-site, the response was silence or some vague and evasive answers. The faculty were at a loss as to why the cobblers were not coming forward with any indication of their choice of land for their new houses. After ten months of futile meetings with this clientele group, the faculty at one point asked them as to what was holding them in making a decision. The leader of the cobblers came out in an hesitant way and in a faltered tone informed the faculty that they better consult the manager of the local church. Later, it surfaced that the manager of the church felt that he was not consulted by the institute's faculty and he was ignored though he was also a secular leader of all segments in Servaipuram. He had kept vigilance on what was going on between the cobblers and the service agency. It came to be known that he mildly and indirectly warned the cobblers that he was not happy about what was going on between the cobblers and the service agency. The cobbler leader threw a hint at the faculty that better they discussed the house site affair with the manager. The faculty realized the lapse on their part that they have failed and did not bother to know the nexus of relationship between the cobblers and the majority Servai Christian community and more importantly the influence of the church manager. He blocked the activity, since he felt that his importance was not recognized and the programme did not go through him.

After a few days this lapse was remedied. The faculty went to the manager, apologized for having been ignorant of his status and his importance as a local leader and arranged a big meeting of the community including the cobblers and the manager was requested to preside over the meeting wherein the housing for the cobblers and other programmes (a community hall, loans for draught bullocks, a kindergarten) were discussed. Later on, the housing project for the cobblers was routed through the manager. We cite this case in order to emphasize as to what happens to development programmes in rural communities, when individuals do not participate in the development activities.

Further, it is not only a question of enthusing, motivating the existing local leaders to encourage and induce participation among the people, but it is also cultivating new leadership in the local communities to generate and institutionalize more and more of people's participation in development activities. Activities or programmes are the means to build new leadership and strengthen the existing leadership. Local leadership is an invaluable human resource and energy to build up healthy rural communities on the plank of participation.

9

ROLE OF YOUTH IN RURAL DEVELOPMENT

Youth constitute a potential and a rich human resource in any community. The youth with the vigour of their age, most often bubbling with enthusiasm for change for better ways of life look for opportunities to fulfill their psychic, social and economic needs. It depends on how the youth is motivated, mobilized, organized, facilitated and utilized in building newer and progressive communities. The programmes should satisfy them and should also be contributory to community development.

When we speak of the rural youth, we meet with a diversity in their case, literate, illiterate, people with some social and technical skills, rich and poor, employed and unemployed. And so the rural development programmes are to be satisfying and challenging to them so that we can secure and ensure their participation. The youth are involved in development programmes as adults in general and there are special schemes like the National Service Scheme (NSS) in India wherein the students of colleges and universities, volunteer and contribute their labour in forming approach roads, digging irrigation canals, and other kinds of manual work beneficial to rural communities.

Youth development or involvement of the youth in development forms a department in the ministry of Education, Human Resources Development in some countries (e.g., India) or a separate ministry as in the case of Bangladesh. We may focus on twin objectives in this chapter-developing the youth and the youth developing the family and the community which may be called "Family-based Integrated Youth Development".

FAMILY-BASED INTEGRATED YOUTH DEVELOPMENT

Developing the youth is of prime importance in all societies. Ministries of Youth Development and in some cases the Departments of Youth Development have been attempting the development of youth in creative, constructive and productive activities. But it has been realized that by focusing on youth alone, the desired kind of development changes among the youth are not encouraging and commensurate with the efforts made. It is found necessary that youth development should be an integral part of family and community development. At least in the initial stages, there is a need for an intensive coordinated approach and effort in developing the youth and their families simultaneously- the youth contributing to the parents and the family and the parents and the larger community guiding, helping and giving moral and socio-economic support to the youth and involving them in constructive and productive activities.

Such a desirable youth-family development could be achieved only through a systematic approach which may be termed as "Family-based Integrated Youth Development".

OBJECTIVES

The main objective of family-based integrated youth development is to take each family as a unit of development, study its material and human resources and help the members in the family in their developmental pursuits and assist them in utilizing their physical, material and human resources for increased productive activities. In other words, in the programme, we look at each family, take stock of what its resources are, how the resources are utilized today, how best they could be utilized, the kind of support they need, develop initiative and motivation among the youth and the adults in the family in order that they mobilize their own resources. In addition, technical and managerial guidance and marginal monetary assistance is extended to them so that each family attempts a maximum level of resource utilization, physical as well as human.

PROGRAMME CONTENT

In the proposed scheme, the activities will comprise moral, spiritual, social and economic programmes for the youth for their own progress and for the betterment of their families and their communities. The on-going programmes in the Ministry or Department of Youth Development will be carried out intensively involving each family as a unit of development.

Basically the scheme will comprise social and economic components. The emphasis in the scheme is maximal utilization of the internal resources of the family and the community, mobilizing the youth as instruments of change.

The programme may comprise:

1. Collection and processing of family-community data.
2. Identification of small enterprises, self-employment avenues which may be taken up by the youth ad their families.
3. Preparation of feasibility studies on small enterprises.
4. Training of the youth to take to small entrepreneurial activities.

5. Organizing the youth into viable associations.
6. Involvement of the youth in community development activities.

COVERAGE OF THE PILOT SCHEME

In view of the clinical-family community-intensive integrated youth development, initially as a pilot measure two units each comprising 5-8 villages may be taken up under the pilot scheme. Preferably one pilot project may be selected in a better off area and another in a backward region. The two pilot project schemes will lend themselves for comparison and future replication of the programme. The criteria for selecting the pilot project areas may comprise:

(a) The cluster of villages or the blocks/unions selected for the pilot project are neither too close to an urban center nor too isolated.

(b) The units selected currently carry on satisfactory youth development activities and have the response and immediate potential for intensive development; and

(c) The units enjoy minimum transport and communication facilities and some infrastructure for small enterprise development.

INSTITUTIONAL ARRANGEMENTS

The existing organizational set-up of the Ministry or Department of Youth Development at the district level may be utilized for planning and implementing the programme in the pilot area with a small staff to keep in touch with and monitor the youth and a small staff to keep in touch with and monitor the youth and family development activities. A small information-monitoring center in each village of the pilot area may be established which will have in its office the family resource and development cards pertaining to all the families in the communities. In addition to the youth development agency, the other promotional agencies may be involved in planning and implementing the activities. The data and information system will be maintained at the pilot project headquarters concerning all the villages in the area. It can be envisaged that each family will have a "Family-Resource and Development Card". This card will contain basic data about the family; its members, their age, educational attainment, how they are occupied, means of livelihood, how their present assets are utilized, their income and expenditure, their needs, the way they would like to improve their conditions and potential and scope for further development with external guidance and assistance. The data from the family cards will be aggregated both at the community level and pilot project level. The data could be classified in different ways both at the village and the project levels for purposes of planning and implementation of programme.

ORGANIZATIONAL SET-UP

The overall functioning and administration of the pilot project will be under a "pilot project committee" comprising elected or nominated youth representatives from each village in the pilot project area. There may be one or two representatives from each village and wherever there is response, women also may serve on the committee. The committee will elect a chairman from amongst themselves to head the committee.

The committee will be entrusted with powers to decide, formulate, implement and monitor all activities under the "Family-based Integrated Youth Development". The committee will be assisted by an executive wing consisting of an executive officer and field and secretarial staff. The executive officer may be the Assistant Director of Department of Youth Development or any officer with a different title but with a similar function. He will guide and assist the committee in its deliberations and decision-making. It is envisaged that the pilot project committee and the executive wing are complementary to each other and they are to work in unison.

STAFF OF THE PILOT PROJECT

1. *Project Executive Officer:* He will be in overall charge of the project.
2. *Rural Social Analyst:* A qualified person in social sciences with experience in social surveys and human resource development. He will be responsible in assisting data collection, processing of data etc.
3. *Field Investigators (two):* They will assist the Rural Social Analyst and most importantly the youth volunteer investigators who will collect data pertaining to families and the community.
4. *A Secretarial Assistant: A steno-typist-cum-cashier.*
5. *An Office Attendant.*

It is envisaged that the secretarial and transport assistance will be provided by the Department of Youth Development.

APPROACH TO THE IMPLEMENTATION OF PILOT PROJECT

To begin with, detailed data as mentioned above, in respect of each family will be collected by the youth in the community as volunteers with the assistance of the project officials. The *Family resource and Development Card* will be so designed that it will contain basic data about the family and also will have provision to record subsequent development activities etc. A copy of this *Family Resource and Development Card* as mentioned earlier will be with each family and one at the village center and another at the project headquarters. At any given time it is possible for the family, community and project to know the present position and what is happening and what should be done at three levels; family, community and project. A monitoring system of to and from informal dissemination will be developed, sometimes using computer facilities where necessary. The *Family Resource and Development Card* will serve as a reminder and as a progress card of the youth and family developmental activities. It involves initial information gathering and recording of the data and coding the families, the activities and the communities in the project area. In the monitoring system, there will be regular and periodical feed-back and evaluation in respect of each family and community. In the total process of planning, implementing and evaluating the activities, the youth will be the principal participants.

TIME FRAME

The first cycle of the two pilot projects will have a two-year period. During this period the basic data of the families and the community will be prepared and aggregated at the community and project levels. Programmes of action will be formulated. Youth organization and other institutional arrangements will be made. Programmes of immediate and long-range activities will be planned and scheduled for implementation.

The pilot scheme suggested above could be extended to all the rural areas depending on the success gained in the pilot schemes and with improvements too. The youth involved in the programme could be those educated, high school dropouts looking for employment or self-employment and those who are still doing their studies in secondary schools and colleges. The objective is to benefit the youth and at the same time make them active participants in rural development.

10

WOMEN AS PARTNERS IN DEVELOPMENT

There are two issues of global nature or call them problems or challenges, one currently facing the entire mankind and the other a few societies or distinct cultures; environment and gender development. Environment encompasses what man has done to nature, the way he has exploited, fouled and abused it resulting in threats to the health and survival of future generations of mankind and other species – plants and animals which have been a source of man's survival thus far. The gender question revolves around what man has done or doing to woman, the other half of the mankind. The environment problem is physical, economic, industrial, technological, avarice and senseless short-sightedness on the part of the modern man whereas the gender question is complex steeped deep in history influenced by prejudices, discriminatory religious and social codes of behaviour imposed on women, and man's audacity in arrogating to himself a superior status and treating the woman his subordinate. The status, freedom and respectability accorded to and enjoyed by women in society is a mark of wisdom and civilization of that particular society. We can conceive of a continuum wherein at one end of the continuum women enjoy equal rights, respectability and are equal partners in economic pursuits and social positions and at the other end, one finds women treated inferior to man, deprived of freedom as enjoyed by man. The gender question is a perennial question. The world body may declare equal opportunities and rights for women and men but it is the nation states and the religious and ethnic groups that have to translate such a principle into reality. One is forced to come up with a statement that so long a man does not treat a woman his equal, he is not civilized. Looked at from any angle, political, economic, social, religious, spiritual or moral, woman is an equal partner and should be an equal partner in all pursuits of life.

The purpose here is not to carry on the debate over feminine rights but to look into women's participation in development activities. Their participation, the variety, extent, and mode of participation and the activities in which they participate is influenced by religious sanctions (mostly mistaken and misinterpreted by ignorant and selfish men), economic conditions, ethnicity, occupations, professions, social status and personal endowments like literacy, knowledge and skills. Of all the forces that keep women off the economic and social activities as equal partners is religion. Unfortunately and lamentably sanctions and tenets of some religions are unquestionable. That is, you cannot question the logical inconsistency and irrationality in those sanctions and tenets. It is highly sensitive and explosive.

The women in such religious groups, in most of the cases are confined to their homes just to carry their housekeeping, child-bearing and child rearing roles. Quite lamentable, what forces, what authority, what revolution would emancipate the women in these groups so that they contribute economically, benefit socially, grow individually and advance spiritually?

In order to make women as equal participants in all development activities, it is not enough that you bring in constitutional and legislative measures ensuring equal rights

which are not profitable enough to attract or support larger modern businesses, yet are necessary to serve the local consumption needs of the population at large, particularly lower income groups. It is significant that women are frequently the only members of the indigenous population who can compete with minority immigrant groups in such activities.

Thus women's employment or self-employment in market production makes an important direct contribution to economic growth, and particularly to the development of certain "modern sectors" and industries which could not survive without them and have proved especially important to the balance of payments. But women's non-market activities also play an important though largely unrecognized and unrewarded role.

Women's subsistence agricultural production, for example, subsidizes many rural workers' families and thus lowers the real wage that employers have to pay them, increasing the surplus available for reinvestment and growth. It includes not only the cultivation of staple grains, but also poultry rearing, vegetable farming, collection of forest products and other supplementary activities. Women's craft production for the household use has the same effect. And in many areas, the time-consuming and backbreaking tasks of fetching and carrying water, and gathering firewood, are assigned to women, as is household marketing and the transport of goods often for considerable distances on foot. Child rearing, including the teaching of household and farm production tasks, which largely devolves on women, daily housekeeping and cooking, and general household management, including budgeting and financial management, complete the wide range of activities which comprise women's reproductive duties.

It has become common to describe women as invisible to depict a situation in which planners of development strategies have failed to pay serious attention to the differential roles and functions of women. The differentiation between men and women's role and work may be classified as follows (ESCAP, 1989).

(a) *In agricultural process:* A sexual division of labour assigns to women specific tasks. For instance, in rice cultivation, women are involved to a greater extent than men in transplanting, weeding, harvesting and in some post-harvesting process.

(b) *In industry:* Women have provided the bulk of the labour force in light industries which in many developing countries have spearheaded industrialization programmes, eg., industries such as electronics, textiles and garments, food processing and pharmaceutical. Within this industry there is an uneven distribution of sexes within employment hierarchies, women dominating the lower wage, unskilled or semi-skilled production process. This means that women are vulnerable to particular occupational hazards in the operations in which they are concentrated.

(c) *In domestic roles:* In addition to the unsubstitutable function of child bearing, women are the main providers of basic family needs: food, water, clothing, domestic energy and maintenance of family shelters. They bear the major responsibility of child-care, thus functioning as the principal transmitters to future generations of attitudes and values. In their hands is the burden of the health and well-being of present, past and future generations of the enumerated labour force. The performance of these tasks, particularly in rural areas, is inefficient in the use of resources of time, labour and energy. It is these talks which account for much of women's labour, resulting in an imbalance in which women's work-hours exceed those of men.

In maintaining and nurturing the family, women frequently find ways to add to household income. Their entry or exist from market activities are sometimes flexible, dependent on contingency. This activity occurs mostly in the "informal sector" and is commonly small-scale, requiring low levels of skills, and earning low returns.

In most parts of the developing world, the major benefits of economic growth have failed to reach women. Women have also paid a steep price for the modest glimmerings of modernity that have reached them. In different places around the world, women's labour obligations have multiplied, their independent resources have shrunk, and their autonomy and cultural worth have often diminished as development has unfolded.

Failure to develop women's resources and skills undermines development as a whole. Women's labour, whether paid or unpaid, is essential. Women everywhere are primary care-givers for their families and children. Decisions women make and skills women have materially affect the health, nutrition, attire, cleanliness and emotional equanimity of all family members. With the sharpening recognition that development hinges on the fulfillment of basic human needs and the quality of life, as well as on the transfer of capital and technology, women have at last found their way onto the international development agenda, though the resolution of these problems has barely taken shape (March and Taqqu, 1986).

MANIFESTATION OF WOMEN'S PROBLEMS

Women's special problems manifest themselves across the board but can in large measure be traced to three main areas: the data base for development planning; education and training including extension services; and technological change, not least its social implication.

In the book-keeping system of development plans, women (and girls) have generally been seen as consumers, not as producers. Moreover, women's work in particular rural women's work, is often not counted statistically.

A primary reason for not including women's work in the computation of the gross national product (GNP) is that so much of it is performed in the family setting. Additionally, it is often of a subsistence nature. On both counts such work, when performed by women, tends to be excluded from official statistics. In many countries such work is recorded, in many others it is not fully recorded or omitted entirely. The reason for non-recording is usually that the societal ideal is that women should not perform such work, in particular, not field work. It should be done by men or, in parts of India e.g., by hired lower-caste women (UNDP, 1980).

Because so much of development efforts has been deficient in its attempts to reach the common people, there is now wide spread agreement that the revised development strategies need to be broad-based and people-oriented. For such strategies to succeed, they must combine two basic principles. On the one hand they must provide for a wide distribution of benefits and services like health care, education and training, productive employment, credit, marketing, fuel, water, sanitation and protection against environmental degradation, in particular the loss of cultivable land through erosion. On the other hand, to make such policies a realistic alternative, a greater mobilization of people as productive agents must be achieved. Their labour, capability, motivation and enterprise in bettering their own conditions must be stimulated. In both respects, women's role in development, not least in rural areas, deserves special attention (UN, 1982).

UNDP (1980) summarized its evaluation of the rural women's participation in development reaching the conclusion:

"If the poor are to be given a fair opportunity to participate in the development effort, there is every reason to consider the participation by women as full and equal partners as a major factor in this effort. In other words, as there are two systems of social stratification, there are two problems of integration, that of the poor and, especially within but also beyond this problem, that of women. No strategy is going to succeed within the foreseeable future".

In India, it has been observed that in Kaira district of Gujarat, where the cooperative movement started, women's status has not improved as a result. While in the past, production and marketing were in women's hands, in the new modern dairy industry management its rewards have been taken over by men.

"Of the more than 2000 persons employed in the Amul (Anand Milk Union Limited) complex, there is only one woman veterinarian and a few telephone operators and secretaries. Not even one woman has been given the mastery over the new technology that has taken over the women's traditional tasks of making butter and cheese". (Brandtzaeg, 1979).

With respect to membership in the cooperative, data from 481 societies show that women only constitute from 2 to 15 per cent of the members. Moreover, the majority of woman members are successors to husbands who have died or are dummy members to enable individual families to control a larger number of shares. With the exception of one all-women society, all the other societies are run by men (Brandtzaeg, 1979).

In the less developed countries the labour force is more evenly distributed among the three categories of workers :

employers and own-account workers (self-employed), employees (wage labourers) and unpaid family workers. The distribution of female workers tended to follow this pattern, with the notable variation of a larger proportion of women than of men being employed as unpaid family workers. Indeed, in most cases, including in the more developed countries, females accounted for disproportionate share, often a large majority of the unpaid family workers. Conversely, they accounted for a disproportionately small share of employers and own-account workers. In short, women tend to be under-represented at the higher and over-represented at the lower levels of the labour force (ESCAP, 1989). Let us look at the situation in India as an illustration.

EXPERIENCE OF WOMEN'S PARTICIPATION IN DEVELOPMENT IN INDIA

India's economy and also the status of her women remained stagnant for a long time. They started to change for the better slowly with the advent of the British education system but women are still victims of the basically exploitative mechanism operating against them. In fact, like the resulting development pattern of the Indian economy, the Indian woman has suffered a dualism in status on her way to play effectively her economic and social role (Sen, 1989).

Shyam (1989) in his study of the India framework for Rural Development stated that:

"Women labour force constitutes about half of the unorganized labourers in rural areas. In addition to their 10-12 hours per day engagement in household work, women's role in agriculture, animal husbandry and other allied activities is very important. A large number of women labourers are engaged in marginal occupations to supplement the family income. Their contribution, however, is yet to be quantified in terms of working hours as well as in terms of income generated. The green revolution has aggravated the plight of woman labourers in rural areas".

In the history of the country's planned development, women have remained invisible except for the Sixth Plan in which for the first item, a chapter was devoted to the integration of women into the development process. The main challenge in women's development has been the means of mainstreaming women into the development process.

Indian planners (Planning Commission, 1985) have recognized the fact that:

"The Green Revolution has led to increased demands for casual labour, dispossession of small land holders from their land and consequently, pushing out women from such small land holdings to become wage earners. Though many of the tasks performed by males are mechanized, women continue to toil in labour intensive jobs like rice plantation, cleaning and storage of grain in post-harvest operations, picking of leaves, fruits and hand shelling of groundnut and picking of seeds etc. Women got limited job opportunities in modern occupations / trade as they do not have access to the training required for new technologies. In many areas where multiple crops are grown, the workload of women has increased. In industry, women continue to be employed mostly on unskilled jobs. The average earning of a regular salaried woman worker continues to be less than that of a man".

CONCLUSION

Empowering, enabling and facilitating women to participate in all development programmes is a stupendous task in view of differential freedom and status enjoyed and the roles performed by women and the importance accorded to them across the diverse societies in the world. It is a task so massive and the efforts should also be multi-dimensional and at multi-level wherein the educational institutions, the media, the writers, leaders of all description, the extension personnel and above all the enlightened public should carry on the job of bringing about a change in the value orientations and the psyche of both men and women that the women are not only biological partners in procreation, but equal partners in social and economic development.

REFRENCES

1- Brandtzaeg, B.(1979), "Women, Food and Technology: The Case of India", *Economic and Political Weekly*, Vol.XIV, No.47.

2. ESCAP (1989), *Status of Women in Asia and the Pacific Region*, United Nations Economic and Social Commission for Asia and the Pacific, Bangkok, p.113.

3. March, K.S. and R.L. Taqqu (1986), *Women's Informal Associations in Developing Countries: Catalyst for Change?*, Westview Press, Boulder; p.154.

4. Planning Commission(1985), *Seventh Five Year Plan*, Vol.I and III (1985-90), Government of India, New Delhi.

5. Sen, R.K.,(1989), "The Nature of Women's Role in Economic Development". In Mahajan (ed.) *Women's Contribution to India's Economic and Social Development*, Deep and Deep Publishers, New Delhi; pp.58-73.

6. Setty,E.D.(1985), "People's Participation in Rural Development: A Critical Analysis", *The Indian Journal of Social Work*, Vol.XVI, No.1; pp.73-85.

7. Shahand, A., M.A. Tekie and K.E. Weber (1986), "The Role of Women in Slum Improvement: A comparative Study of the Squatter Settlements at Klong Toey and Wat Yai Sri Suphan in Bangkok, Thailand, *Studies on Human Settlements Development in Asia*, HSD Research Report 10, Asian Institute of Technology, Bangkok; p.161.

8. Shyam, R. (1989), *India's Framework for Rural Development*, Commonwealth Publications, New Delhi, p.112.

9. UNDP (1980), "Rural Women's Participation in Development", *Evaluation Study No.3*, United Nations Development Programme, New York, p.225.

10. United Nations (1982), *Poverty, Productivity and Participation: An Analysis of some Recent Experiences*, Bangkok: UNESCAP.

11

THE PART PLAYED BY NGOs IN RURAL DEVELOPMENT

The rapid increase of state involvement in socio-economic development (loosely referred to as community development) during this century has been accompanied by a gradual consolidation of bureaucratic and technocratic specialization in each of the major development sectors. The result is that particular areas of development such as health, education and housing are now closely identified with government bureaucracies. Most developing countries have functionally specialized ministries which have primary responsibility for the formulation of policies and the implementation of state programmes in different sectors. Many governments have established what are variously known as Ministries or Departments of Social Welfare, Public Welfare, Social Services or Social Affairs. Their programmes are largely remedial in orientation, and are closely associated with the activities of professional social workers.

It is possible to formulate a typology of likely state responses to people's participation in development. This typology suggests that the state may act in several ways when eliciting people's participation. It may, firstly, suppress all attempts at people's participation; secondly, it may actively promote participation seeking to mobilize the whole community for social development and to encourage maximum involvement in decision-making. The state may, thirdly, attempt to use people' participation programmes with ulterior motives and seek to manipulate these programmes for its own ends. Finally, the state may have a vaguely formulated or poorly implemented policy on people's participation; while it does not seek to suppress participatory activities, it fails to provide adequate support. However, it is concluded that state sponsorship of people's participation has been largely incremental and manipulative in character and supports those who believe that state involvement in community participation is a contradiction in terms. It is believed that whether because of bureaucratic inefficiency or a determined effort to exploit particular programmes for ulterior ends, state involvement stifles authentic community responses and defeats the ideals of genuine people's participation in social development. This situation has allowed the proliferation of normative and ideological critiques of the prevalent model of development as perceived and initiated by the state (Hague *et.al.,* 1977).

There are also several new models being advanced at the abstract level of ideological alternatives to the prevalent model. But little or no attention has been paid to the numerous experiments, movements and organizational initiatives that struggle on the ground, to make "development" a relevant concept, a direct experience in the lives of the deprived, the oppressed and the impoverished populations which have either been "untouchables" of development or when touched are affected adversely and have become its victims. It is in these initiatives at the grassroots taking place generally outside the governmental and bureaucratic structure s and away from the normal political processes of parties and elections that another approach to rural development is becoming manifest. These are local actions that are basically initiated, nurtured and taken care by the native population.

Therefore, we observe that though the state assumes a greater share of responsibility for development government alone it is not in a position to build national identity, to institutionalize democracy and to keep up economic productivity. The private sector has an important role in mobilizing resources and in infusing efficiency through the market mechanism. The voluntary sector is an important source of developmental initiatives; in particular, the non-governmental organizations (NGOs) articulate more at the local level than at that of the state or regional level. Hence, the local administration bears a special responsibility as a listening post for incorporating people's views that are made available via NGOs.

NGOs IN ASIA

Depending on how tightly one draws the definition, there are reported to be somewhere one million development oriented NGOs in Asia. They are highly heterogeneous in character, varying considerably in character, geographic scope and sectoral interests. The overwhelming majority of the Asian NGOs are very small, employing generally only one or two staff, rarely more than ten. Frequently, they are the results of the efforts one – often charismatic-individual who draws together others for the purpose of ameliorating some social or economic need. The motivation is commonly charitable and the technical resources available are of a low order. The hope that such groups may make a contribution to development rests on the belief that it may be possible to reinforce them with insight (especially of social dynamics), appropriate intervention techniques and practice.

It is widely believed that non-governmental development organizations (NGDOs, or NGOs as referred to earlier) constitute a potentially important vehicle by which social and economic development can be promoted in developing countries, especially at the micro level. At the same time it is recognized that NGOs too depend largely on people's participation in accomplishing their objectives. Mid-1970s witnessed a revival of voluntary activity, largely attributable to:

(a) The failure of elective local democracy to satisfy the aspirations of the people;

(b) The sense of mission which imbued social workers for the betterment of the underprivileged and neglected classes;

(c) The need for intervention in areas of public life which were suffering from the effects of official apathy and evils associated with the misuse of power.

Since then we observe the birth of a number of praiseworthy voluntary ventures engaged in a variety of activities. A brief analysis of some of them will help in understanding the stimulant forces which gave them birth and the purposes for which they exist. To a casual observer, the strength of the NGOs lie in their ability to effectively motivate people to undertake some development initiatives at the village level, and serve as a intermediary for the government to understand people's needs and priorities.

Generally, the voluntary agencies fulfill several tasks apart from the usual service provision for the needy; these main tasks could be classified into two categories: animation and facilitation. In reality, one cannot clearly be distinguished from each other. Animation means, first of all, conscientisation of the poor. Animators help the poor to regain their self-confidence and self-assertiveness. Only when the poor regard themselves as equal human beings and citizens do they question the reasons behind their poverty, realize their rights, request changes, discover the abilities and capacities at their disposal, have the confidence to change established patterns of behaviour and dare to use their assets to promote their own interests.

Once the poor have been motivated and activated through a process of conscientisation, the animator changes into the role of the facilitator. He/she assists the poor in forming groups, in decision which measures should be taken and in executing the same. He/she acts as an intermediary to get access to governmental or commercial services. He / she, for example, manages to establish first contacts between the poor and the officials (e.g., banking sector) by facilitating to provide the securities banks require (i.e., seed money, incentive deposits or group guarantees), and by helping the banks to change their procedures in such a way that they meet the requirements and abilities of the poor.

NGOs also provide legal aid to the poor and their groups in their disputes with the rich and the government authorities, they encourage them to unite in federations or to take part in support networks in order to promote common interests collectively, and establish themselves as institutions at the service of those of the poor who have no access whatsoever to any services.

Those NGOs which are serious about grassroots development are aware that they themselves could not specifically predict the direction in which the poor will move. They present themselves, therefore, not as teachers and know-alls, but as equal partners and, by skilful questioning, make them conscious of their problems, prompt them to identify the causes and to propose solutions. Such a process provides a code of conduct for the organization rather than hierarchy that is conducive to participation. We can understand this by scrutinizing some movements in Asia.

PEOPLE'S PARTICIPATION, NATURAL RESOURCES AND PROTEST MOVEMENTS

People's participation is not a new concept in the Indian setting. The scope and content of it, of course, have been different at different times of history or in different regions or communities. For traditional communities, it was the management of communal properties and resources which extended to forestland, village land, water harvesting systems and village common cattle, grazing pastures, etc. For religious groups or communities it is a matter of providing and pooling labour and wealth for religious or even social functions. For patriotic groups, it is pooling people in movements such as Dandi March or, Quit India or electoral participation.

In the context of rural development, however, the term participation has a specific meaning. Participation is the introduction of a new set of people into the decision-making process with regard to resource allocation or distribution. By people we mean here those who have been victims of their exclusion from the development process and those who are likely to emerge as the beneficiaries of participation. In view of the complementary relationship between development and preservation of natural resources people's participation should involve the management of natural resources as well. From the history of traditional community organizations in India, people who were by and large concerned with common property resources, one can easily identify three minimal preconditions for such a group to emerge. *Firstly,* the community organizations should be able to reinforce the existing structures of authority as long as tradition and authority are upheld. *Secondly,* the community should feel empowered, and be independent of outsider's(including government) intervention. *Thirdly,* the set of rules and norms of cooperation should be such as to meet the felt-needs of the people.

The above concept and definition of participation in management of natural resources in a way, covers the entire gamut of development activities at the rural/village level. It may, however, operate at different levels of intensity, measured by the kind of activities in which the beneficiaries participate. When these are limited to information sharing and consultation, the level of participation is low. When beneficiaries become decision-makers or start initiating action on developmental activity, it can be surmised that participation has reached a higher level of intensity. All these, *i.e.,* consultation, information-sharing and initiating action on development activity are instances of participation (Bahuguna, 1983).

Though relevant in a wide spectrum of situations, participatory development is becoming growingly pertinent in the management of natural resources. Historically, the ownership and management of these resources always rested with the state, partly due to the failure of the market system and partly due to the eminent domain character of the state. But, due to the public goods nature of these resources, the preservation and policing costs to the government are prohibitively high. Secondly, natural resources qualify not only for preservation but also for their developmental use and as long as the management of the resources is with the government, it is the latter which is being revealed increasingly as the preference of the government. Multipurpose river valley projects such as Narmada, Kali Nadi etc., are only some of the instances. Government's failure to preserve the natural resources together with their excessive exploitation for development purposes has led to serious degradation of the environment and hence its ecological repercussions (Aggarwal, *et.al;* 1985).

It is at this juncture that people's participation can be an alternative to government for providing development with preservation. People on their own may not perceive the preservation objective as a prime one due to their poverty, non-availability of alternative productive opportunities, lack of infrastructural facilities to reap the benefits from preservation, inability to possess private assets which are complementary to preservation of natural resources, lack of arrangements to participate and finally existing legal structures which are non-conducive to people's participation.

A CASE STUDY OF THE CHIPKO AND APPIKO MOVEMENTS

Policies and programmes of land-use as well as forest management, whenever they were put in place without consulting the local communities, have often resulted in "wastelands" and wasted human resources". We have a classic example of the *Chipko* movement in the Himalayan region in India where the people could no longer tolerate the inequity involved in transferring the benefits of the community resources to meet the needs of the people elsewhere. Since late 1970s, however, the people of the region acted together by adopting an unconventional approach and fully incorporating a new institution of people's participation which was totally devoid of bureaucratic and power politics.

The *Chipko*, or "Embrace the Tree", Movement is essentially a Gandhian concept that espoused non-violent resistance to preserve the Himalaya's critical mountain-forest ecosystem. It began in Garhwal in the 1970s when women protected with their own bodies the trees that contractors were trying to remove. This message soon caused the *Chipko* struggle to grow into a national environmental movement. The struggles against limestone quarrying in Doon Valley, in the Haryana and Uttar Pradesh States of northern India, near the Himalayan range, is an extension of the original *Chipko* Movement. For the "last man" in the region, conservation has become a matter of life and death. Environmental destruction undermined the life support system of the poor, and their environmental struggles invite brutal attacks from truckloads of goondas hired by the contractor mafia (Bahuguna, 1983).

Chipko of Uttarakhand in the Himalayas inspired the villagers of the Uttara Kannada district of Karnataka Province in southern India to launch a similar movement to save their forests. In September 1983, men, women and children of Salkani "hugged the trees in Kalase forest (the local term for "hugging in Kannada is *Appiko*). *Appiko Andolan* gave birth to a new awareness all over southern India (Cultural Survival, 1989).

The story of Uttara Kannada region is different. In 1950, Uttara Kannada district's forest covered more than 81 per cent of its geographical area. The government, declaring this forest district a "backward" area, then initiated the process of "development". Three major industries-a pulp and paper mill, a plywood factory and a chain of hydro-electric dams constructed to harness the rivers – sprouted in the area. These industries have overexploited the forest resource, and the dams have submerged huge forest and agricultural area. The forest had shrunk to nearly 25 per cent of the district's area by 1980. The local population, especially the poorest groups, were displaced by the dams. The conversion of the natural mixed forests into teak and eucalyptus plantations dried up the water sources, directly affecting forest dwellers. In a nutshell, the three *p*'s – paper, plywood and power – which were intended for the development of the people, have resulted in a fourth *p*: poverty.

The *Appiko* Movement is trying to save the Western Ghats by spreading its roots all over southern India. The movement's objectives can be classified into three major areas. First, the *Appiko* Movement is struggling to save the remaining tropical forests in the Western Ghats. Second, it is making a modest attempt to restore the greenery to denuded area. Third, it is striving to propagate the idea of rational utilization in order to reduce the pressure on forest resources. To save, to grow and to use rationally – popularly known in Kannada as *Ubsu* (save), *Belesu* (grow) and *Balasu* (rational use) – is the movement's popular slogan.

The *Appiko* Movement used various techniques to raise awareness: foot marches in the interior forest, slide shows, folk dances, street plays and so on. The movement has achieved a fair amount of success: the State government has banned felling of green trees in some forest areas; only dead, dying and dry trees are felled to meet the local requirements. The movement has spread to the four hill districts of Karnataka State, and has the potential to spread to the Eastern Ghats in Tamil Nadu and Goa.

The objective of the *Appiko* Movement's work is to promote afforestation on denuded lands. In the past, *Appiko* activists have successfully motivated villagers to grow saplings. Individual families as well as village youth clubs have taken an active interest in growing decentralized nurseries. An all time record of 1.2 million saplings were grown by people in the Sirsi area in 1984-85. This was possible because the local Forest Department officials were forthcoming in eliciting the support of the people. The villagers initiated a process of regeneration in barren common land. The Youth Club has taken the responsibility for the project and the whole village has united to protect this land from grazing, lopping and fire. The experience shows that in those areas where soil is present, natural regeneration is the most efficient and least expensive method of bringing barren area under tree cover. In the areas in which topsoil is .washed off, tree planting- especially of indigenous, fast-growing species- is done. The irony is that the forest department is resorting to the mechanized planting of exotic species, and also uses huge amounts of fertilizers on these exotic monoculture plantations. This would definitely harm the soil, and eventually the tree cover, in the area. Two obvious techniques of greening are being performed: one, the forest department's method, is capital intensive, and the other, the people's technique of growing through regeneration, is a natural process for sustainable development of the soil.

The other major area of activity in the *Appiko* Movement is related to rational use of the ecosphere through introduction of alternative energy sources to reduce the pressure on the forest. The activists have constructed about 5,000 fuel-efficient *chulas* (hearths) in the area, which save fuel wood consumption by almost 40 per cent. The activists do not wait for government subsidies or assistance, since there is spontaneous demand from the people. Even in towns and other urban areas, these *chulas* are installed in hotels, reducing firewood consumption.

Also, some people deter the regeneration process in the forest area through incorrect lopping practices. The *Appiko* Movement is trying to change people's attitudes so that they realize their mistake and stop this practice.

The thrust of the *Appiko* movement in carrying out its work reveals the constructive phase of the people's participation and movement. Through this constructive phase, depleted natural resources can be rebuilt. This process promotes sharing of resources in an egalitarian way, helping the forest dwellers. The movement's aim is to establish a harmonious relationship between people and nature, to redefine the term development so that ecological movements today form a basis for a sustainable, permanent economy in the future.

In the *Appiko* efforts a persistent leadership (as a catalytic institution) and some support from the government saw to it that what would have been a prisoner's dilemma with repeated non-cooperative game with sustainable development. By 1986, the extent of soil run-off had come down and average crop yield had gone up. Then two important socio-economic questions are raised while analyzing such a case example. *First*, what kinds of links between communal and private property resources are required so as to sustain such a participatory initiative. *Second*, to what extent are the production and distribution mechanisms evolved in such institutions independent of the market, an alternative institution. In Karnataka, increased cattle population, and improved land management are the two major thrust areas in the augmentation of private property resources. Afforestation, soil conservation, irrigation water from the community tanks, access to fodder and *bhabbar* grass on equitable basis etc., are instances of complementary flows of common property resources towards rural transformation on a sustained basis. The strength and nature of the link between these two types of resources is an empirical question, though theoretically there is no unique argument for their unilateral link as a pre-condition for rural development.

Even on the assumption that the market is less relevant in large rural parts of developing economies and the state is favourably inclined to the establishment of participatory institutions, existing property rights shall prevent spontaneous evolution of participation. Property rights emerge to help people to coordinate their productive activities and to avoid wasting time on conflicts, the result of which is purely distributive and not allocative. Since participatory institutions are bound to suggest a changed distribution, the possibility of their organic evolution is constrained by the existing institution of property rights. Such situation was observable in case of "milk revolution" in Gujarat. The group of households who owned land and cattle also monopolized control over the newly started institution of milk production and distribution i.e., AMUL Cooperative. To serve the interests, water from the irrigation tank was sold at a low price even in 1987-88, a year of acute scarcity. A breakthrough could be achieved only when a change in management with a new leadership was brought about in early 1988. It still remains to be seen how lasting the breakthrough will be. Therefore, as a process, participation shall spread only if it is designed so as to be in conformity with the norms that motivate people's social and economic behaviour in that particular society.

The *Chipko* and *Appiko* movements emerged as the consequence of an evolutionary process. People saw the consequences of the "tragedy of the environment" and worked out a set of rules for the management of forests and water from irrigation tanks. Their understanding of the issues involved did change the perception of the outside agencies who moved away from conventional solutions for soil erosion to a participatory approach. By now a large number of villages in the region seem to have followed these models, but with a difference, (UNESCO, 1992).

SUMMARY

We observe that the voluntarism in Asia has passed through a number of stages. The Gandhian (peace loving, silent strugglers) and other types of voluntary agencies that existed prior to the phasing out of Colonialism in the region, on receiving government grants started working closely with and under the broad guidance of the government. They had lost the pioneering independent spirit that they had come to symbolize during the freedom struggle. In the second stage, there came a shift back to constructive work from "progress" or development work, as conceived by the government. The next phase saw a new genre of activist groups came up, ready to struggle on behalf of the poor, landless, *dalits* and other minority groups, against the State and dominant interests. There is a wide variety of such groups working in as different sectors as forestry, migrant labour, women, child labour and so on.

These few examples suggest the richness and diversity of local struggles by people trying to solve problems. The validity of each example, at this stage, resides probably in its specificity, and the fact-finding process has just started. It would be pointless to attempt any generalization. The purpose of this chapter is therefore, only to draw attention to the phenomenon, and endeavour to place it in the proper perspective.

There are various, essentially limited actions taken by groups of concerned men and women having or acquiring some control over their immediate environment and becoming able to define and carry out, in a self-reliant manner, solutions to their social and economic problems while modifying their relations with the State and / or market. They are either spontaneous or stem from encounters of a special kind with outsiders which have resulted in conscientisation. Their two major features are innovation and a certain transformation of social relations within the group and between the group and the larger environment (Guha, 1987).

The immediate result of the successful ones has been that fundamental needs are better met in the material sphere (often the prime mover) as well as in the political sphere, in its widest sense: taking action means self-confidence and reinforcing it; the moment people seize control of their own affairs, they cease to be passive and marginalized. They have started the process of development.

Thus a people-centred approach is not an utopia; it is the way out of poverty and underdevelopment. Already links appear with larger national struggles. One example is that of anti-nuclear popular actions in Asia. Local experiments with soft energies are also linked with a wider social movement which, in the final analysis, is challenging the whole system of values of the consumer society.

Local development action does not take place only in liberal or permissive political conditions. They also happen in the uncontrolled interstices of anti-popular regimes. They will be ignored or tolerated as long as they remain in their immediate locus-as long as they do not challenge the existing order. This is not a reason to remain passive; local actions are important in themselves and in them may be the seeds of larger movements.

REFERENCES

1. Agarwal,A., Narain,S. (editors)(1985), *India: The State of Environment 1984-85. A Citizen Report,* Centre for Science and Environment, New Delhi.

2. Bahuguna,S. (1983), *Walking with the Chipko Message,* Navjivan Ashram (Tehri Garhwal, India).

3. Guha, R. (1987), "Ideological Trends in Indian Environmentalism", *Economic and Political Weekly,* December 3, 1987.

4. W.Haque, N. Mehta, A. Rahaman and P. Wignaraja, (1977), "Towards a Theory of Rural Development", *Development Dialogue,* Vol.2.

5. Regional Unit for Social and Human Sciences, UNESCO (1992), *Forests and Cultures in Asia,* Bangkok.

12

CASTE DYNAMICS IN RURAL DEVELOPMENT

Of several affinities that foster unity, bonds of enduring relationship, solidarity and concerted social action on the part of the people such as territorial, regional, racial, ethnic, political, ideological, religious, sectarian, lingual, occupational and professional, the social institution of caste is a strong and enduring one. The institution of caste is unique in India. It is an unchanging ascribed status and identity for an individual. One may change his political and ideological views and change his religious faith and move from one region to another, but one's caste identity does not change. Caste is both a unifying and divisive force. The forces of caste for and against are apparent in every field. One could witness the caste dynamics operating in the villages creating enmity, cliques, factions, and rivalries, one caste group fighting against another. Caste generates competition, both subtle and vibrant with expression of emotions. Competition by itself is not negative. It promotes improvement and advancement. A healthy competition is a welcome factor in order to make the caste groups in the villages compete with one another and excel and improve their lives.

When it comes to helping people caste promotes favouritism helping the group that belongs to the political leaders and administrators although we have all the rules, regulations and specifications as to whom the help should reach yet caste factors influence the delivery of goods and services to the deserving minority caste groups.

It is well-nigh impossible to eliminate the negative and detrimental caste born attitudes from some caste groups. The problem with caste system is its rigidity in attitude. Caste discriminations are more visible and active in rural areas. One may come across instances wherein numerically dominant and politically influential caste groups are barriers in assistance reaching the lower caste groups or downtrodden ones. One may speak at length about the dynamics and the historical tradition and hereditarily inherited patterns of behaviour associated with different caste groups. As we discuss below there are positive and negative elements in the institution.

In the context of rural development with multiple development and welfare programmes, the development workers at the field level should have some understanding of the caste dynamics. They have to keep in mind the forces that are in operation and manoeuvre over these forces to see that help reaches the deserving and they should also work as effective social change agents to bring about harmony in the rural communities to work towards development of the entire community.

Here, we may mention that it is not only the field workers who are to be sensitive to these forces but the entire administration in the field of rural development should be sensitive and wise-enough to operate in such a way that over a period of time we succeed and gradually reduce the prejudices and stereotypes attributed to different caste groups. In this context, a brief understanding of the emergence operation and slowly declining caste system in India is relevant and interesting.

It is much easier to say what caste is not than what caste is. It is not class, for it consists of rich and poor, literate and illiterate and of high and low mental calibre. It is not colour. An upper-caste man may be black and a Harijan quite fair in complexion. It is not Aryan and non-Aryan, conqueror and conquered. It is not even occupation. Many occupations, mostly of artisans, overwhelmingly identify themselves with particular castes, but the main occupation, agriculture is open to all. Hundreds of castes and sub-castes live on the plough. So occupation alone has not caused caste. Occupational distribution is not now based on caste.

Caste is not exclusively Hindu or exclusively Indian. It obtains elsewhere too in a modified form. Nor does the present caste structure bear much relation to the traditional four *varnas*.

Whatever sets off a group in any way may be sufficient to make it a caste in India. If groups diverge within an established caste they become recognized as sub-castes, perhaps finally to develop into wholly separate castes. Caste is a way of thought that the Hindu has tried to universalize.

CASTES ARE ENDOGAMOUS

All Indian castes are in theory strictly endogamous; intermarriage is intolerable. All possess an intrinsic, unchangeable worth. Thus they automatically rank themselves. Caste embraces one's life activities in their entirety from cradle to grave. Each possesses an occupation, a mode of life and customs, a set of prescribed rituals, inherently peculiar to it. The greater the restriction and prohibition incumbent upon it, the less it relaxes to comfort and indifference, the more spiritual it is, the higher its grade. In consequence it is also more pollutable, and so its restrictions are drawn closer. The wider the gap with the lower classes, the greater becomes its purity.

Life cannot be lived in parts or compartments; it is an integrated whole. So, religion, man's spiritual food, is fused with caste or the other way about.

The *Rig Veda*, the most ancient and sacred of Hindu hymns, does not talk of the caste system. Caste existed during the epic period. Caste is a hierarchy and has no bearing to the original four *varnas* in its content and functions. Hundreds of castes are sub-divided into sub-castes and sub-castes run into thousands. Among Brahmins alone there are over two thousand sub-castes and even among the so-called untouchables, over five hundred. It is the sub-castes which give Hindu society its character. Each caste embodies in itself its rites, taboos, do's and don'ts in food, drink and matrimony.

Caste not only governs one's manner of life, it also fixes the place in society in which one lives. Caste structure, to a larger extent, conditions human relationships and sentiments. "Caste gives its directions for recognition, acceptance, consecration, and sacramental dedication, and *vice versa*, of a human being on his appearance in this world. It has for infancy, pupilage, and manhood, its ordained methods of sucking, sipping, drinking, eating, and voiding; of washing, rinsing, anointing, and smearing; of clothing, dressing and ornamenting; of sitting, rising and reclining; of moving, visiting and traveling; of speaking, reading, listening, and reciting; and of meditating, singing, working, playing, and fighting. It has its laws for social and religious rights, privileges, and occupations; for instructing, training and educating; for obligation, duty, and ceremony; for errors, sins and transgressions; for intercommunication, avoidance, and ex-communication; for defilement, ablution, and purification; for fines, chastisements, imprisonments, mutilations, banishments, and capital executions. It deals with death, burial and burning; and with commemoration, assistance, and injury after death. It interferes, in short, with all the relations, and events of life and with what precedes and follows.......life".

Caste hierarchy was built on inter-caste relationships. It was the elaborate proliferation of the rules governing inter-caste relationships and the meticulous enforcement of them that guaranteed the separateness and integrity of each caste. It was this complete separation of the various social strata which made India's class structure unique.

Caste grew with the sanction of the society. Conditions such as geographical isolation, static society, foreign aggression, rural social structure, influence of the religion, differences of races, and lack of education, have favoured the continued existence of the caste system. However arbitrary it is, it was spontaneous in the growth. It has played a positive cementing role. It has been a unifying force. In the long chequered history of India, it has held together the fabric of Indian society. Caste in unison with Hinduism resisted the onslaught of successive foreign invasions and centuries of alien rule and preserved the content of Hindu culture.

Caste reveals itself most obviously and most rigidly in everyday life, through the concept of pollution, a concept fundamental to the Hindu way of life. Caste which begins with pollution develops into a way of life. The concept of pollution is simply maddening, carried to meaningless, illogical and incomprehensible extremities. How fantastic are its magnitude and ramifications! There is pollution by sight, pollution by approach, pollution by touch, pollution by drink, pollution by food, pollution by matrimony, pollution by travel over sea and so on. The faith or the belief works in this way; God has ordained everything and caste too is His making and so preserve and live the tenets, rituals, taboos and everything that go with each caste.

Caste functions in a multitude of ways, diet regulations for every occasion; ritual bathing, caste deities, the manner of worship, fasts, the colour of one's clothes, the colour of the flowers one wears, the shape of one's ornaments, the pattern of one's rituals, decoration, ancestral worship etc. Further we have the Indian village structure and during festive and ceremonious occasions the distribution of work or division of labour is assigned to each sub-caste and each attends to a specific item of work arranged in gradation underlying prestige and privilege.

CHANGES DESPITE RIGIDITY

Despite the rigidity, conservatism and complexity of caste, changes have been taking place in the system. Many forces opposed the evils of caste system, Jainism, Buddhism, Lingayatism, Sikhism, Christianity and the movements of Arya Samaj and Brahma Samaj and social reformers have proclaimed their opposition to caste. Modern education with its democratic ideals and values, industrialization and urbanization, money power, various movements of social emancipation, increase in the means of communication, political awakening, the emergence of legal machinery, appearance of new social classes and most important the universal adult franchise have tended to weaken the caste system.

Opposition to the caste system works in two ways. People do not believe in either predestined superiority or predestined inferiority. With all these things, the change in the villages is obviously very slow. Caste breathes quite healthily even today in the rural areas.

But, on the other hand, by the very nature and composition of the social structure in towns and cities, caste is ineffective; it does not raise its head, does not make much ado and is fast sinking. Here, no segregation, no discrimination in buses, trains, restaurants and other public places is possible. It is dying a slow and a natural death.

The villager's contact with the town slowly undermines the hold of caste on his thought. As a result of modern education and industrialization, the sanctity of caste has begun to be questioned. The caste hierarchy is slowly crumbling down.

The Constitution forbids the practice of untouchability and does not recognize caste. Though law holds itself against caste and untouchability, yet does not operate by itself but in a social environment. Transformation must take place in the attitude and beliefs of people.

The political parties in their own pursuit for power are reviving the disintegrating caste system. The slow dying embers of casteism are kindled by the politicians at every level during the elections.

The process of democracy is changing the old order; the old structure is being restructured, the functions are changing, power is redistributed, and the whole fabric of the socio-economic order is reconditioned, in a manner unthought of and unheard of before.

Caste differences were accepted as cultural and social norms. So long as it was not challenged, it flourished. Had it been challenged in the earlier centuries, it would have crumbled long ago. Many factors made this institution thrive for a pretty long period. This winding has been going on for centuries and to unwind the whole thing in a matter of few decades would demand a basic change in people's attitudes. For caste lies in the mind of man. Let us hope that at least in the years and decades to come it will become a thing of the past and a primitive institution.

Source: E. Desingu Setty, "Caste Hierarchy : The Crumbling Edifice", Social Welfare, Vol. xxv, No.9, December 1978, New Delhi.

13

DYNAMICS OF DALITS DEVELOPMENT

A large number of programmes under the generic name rural development are meant for the poor and the people below the poverty line (BPL). They are the main target population in terms of ameliorating their living conditions. The intentions are fine, the programmes are appreciable, but the problem always arises in regard to the manner of delivery and extension of services to the target population. The scheduled castes who are now known as Dalits constitute the majority under the BPL. When we are speaking of clinical approach to rural development there is a need to understand the present status and the dire needs of these poor segments of the population. We cannot simply think of the Dalits as a numerical number, but one has to understand their social history and their psychology when attempts are made to better their lives.

Dalits in India numbering around 800 distinguished groups who go by several ethnic names and titles constitute about 15% in India's population. Their lives in millennia have been poignant psycho and social suffocation. The discrimination meted out to them, the humiliation they have suffered for centuries, the hardship they have endured, the servitude they were subjected to and their earlier deep pathos of life runs into volumes. Even today despite constitutional and legislative safeguards and measures providing them some reservations and extending to them incentives exclusively, they have not wriggled out of their psychic social feeling of subordination and sense of inferiority.

Excepting in a few cases, the majority of the so-called higher caste Hindus appear to be reluctant and unwilling to treat the Dalits with equal respect and extend help to them and also see that assistance reaches them. Because of the long discriminatory tradition, a large number of higher caste groups appear not psychologically prepared to accept the Dalits as equals and extend help to them to bring them up to the level of the better off people. On the other hand the Dalits also make hesitant moves. One can find the pattern of behaviour among the elder generation and the younger generation in case of Dalits as well as non-Dalits. One could see today the younger generation among the Dalits, as a retaliatory measure to the past-untold discrimination meted out to their generations of ancestors, is demanding and aggressive in their behaviour. The only analogy to the turmoils undergone by the Dalits is the institution of slavery perpetrated by the white settlers in America.

We bring in the question of Dalits here in the context of clinical approach to rural development. Here it is relevant and interesting to have a comprehensive and yet brief anthropological account of Dalits in India. The statistical data relate to 1981 census.

The details furnished below cover 751 communities and their segments. Many scheduled castes have plural identifies and for an anthropologist the task of listing and studying them poses a dilemma. None of the identities can be ignored, for some of them may be transitory, but a majority is permanent. Indeed the plural identities of these people are largely due to the processes of fission and fusion that plagued the Indian caste system and the reform movements that have changed community names many times over. In retrospect and in the final analysis it is to be believed that every identity has a specificity to itself which is not traceable in another identity. Adi Andhra and Mala are not synonymous, nor Adi Dharmi and Chamar. In some cases, certain communities with similar names and even spelling were treated separately for their distinct cultural features and occupational diversity, such as the Kadaiyan from Kerala and Tamil Nadu, and the Turi from Gujarat and other places. The size of scheduled-caste communities is an important factor. Some of these communities consist of more than a million people, whereas others number fewer than 1000 persons. Out of the total population of the scheduled castes in the country, their largest concentration is in Uttar Pradesh (22.39 %), followed by West Bengal (11.46%), Bihar (9.68 %), Tamil Nadu (8.48 %), Andhra Pradesh (7.60%), Madhya Pradesh (.7.02%), Rajasthan (5.57%), Karnataka (5.34%), Maharashtra (4.28%), Punjab (4.31%), Orissa (3.69%), Haryana (2.35%), Gujarat (2.33%), Delhi (1.07%), and in the remaining states/ union territories their proportion is less. The smallest number of scheduled casts is found in Mizoram (135 persons). The scheduled caste communities perceive themselves mostly as local and regional communities. One hundred and five communities (13.8%) perceive their distribution at national level.

The scheduled caste communities are non-vegetarian except such sections of them as have been influenced by bhakti movements. The number of scheduled castes who are regular non-vegetarians is 404 (53.8%). A number of them consume cow beef – 104 communities (13.8%), whereas 117 communities (15.6%) consume ox beef; others eat pork (358 communities, 47.7%) and carrion (27 communities, 3.6%). Meat is their source of protein. Eighty-nine per cent of the communities reportedly consume milk. In all these communities alcoholic drinks are occasionally consumed; by men in 457 and by women in 284 communities. These alcoholic drinks are purchased mainly from the market, as only 20.8% take home brewed drinks. The transition from non-vegetarian to vegetarian food habits is observed among 101 communities. The incidence of beef-eating has gone down. With the rise in family income there is a marked increase in the consumption of fruits (18.2%), pulses 35.8%) and vegetables (39.9%).

Divisions also exist in terms of sub-castes or subgroups (178 communities) in the case of major scheduled castes. Differentiation among the subgroups is reported at social (428 communities), occupational (125) and religious (63) levels. Stratification has emerged with the rise of elites who have benefited from developmental programmes. Polarization and inequality have increased among various strata of the scheduled castes.

Scholars hold the view that the scheduled castes generally lie outside the chaturvarna system (avarnas). There is the Panchama cluster of communities in Andhra Pradesh who consider themselves the fifth varna. A number of scheduled castes do not recognize or place themselves within the varna system, particularly in Andhra Pradesh, Tamil Nadu, Karnataka, Kerala, Madhya Pradesh and Goa. In Maharashtra and Rajasthan between 25 to 33 per cent do not recognize varna. However, the data also suggest that a substantial number of scheduled caste people (80.2%) are aware of the four-fold varna system and a substantial number of them (70.2%) even place themselves within it. About 70.2 per cent recognize themselves as Sudra, 7.6 per cent as Kshatriyas. This corresponds by and large to the self-perception of scheduled castes. For example, 72.2 percent of the scheduled castes perceive themselves as occupying low, 23.2 per cent as middle, and 4.4 per cent as high positions. Other communities see 91.2 per cent of the scheduled castes as occupying low, 7.9 per cent as middle and 0.3 per cent as high positions. This shows the very long way that the scheduled castes have to go in achieving a measure of equality with others and in getting their equal status recognized. A large number of scheduled castes are endogamous (96.3 %). The incidence of hypergamy and hypogamy is negligible.

The women among the scheduled castes have a role in all economic and income generation activities, as well as in social functions (89.1%) and ritual matters (89.5 %). But they have generally a lower status (73%), and only a few have decision-making powers. The traditional institutions of social control are fairly active in as many as 82 per cent of the communities. The scheduled-caste communities are substantially represented in statutory panchayats which have come into existence. The traditional caste councils decide social maters and imposc punishment for crimes and offences like adultery, elopement, disputes over land and water, disrespect for traditional norms, etc.

The scheduled castes are mainly landless (69.6%), with little control over resources such as land, forest and water. However, the distribution of land among them, besides other factors, has led to an increase in the number of landholders (28.5%). There has been a marked rise in the number of agricultural labourers (49.1%), casual labourers (72 %), industrial labourers (17.3%), plantation (6.1%) and fishing labour (2.5%). Child labour exists in 58.7% of the communities. Unlike the scheduled tribes, the scheduled caste-communities have followed a wide range of traditional occupations, usually more than one. Many of these, however, are rapidly disappearing. Prominent among the traditional occupations are skin and hide work, carrying carcasses, scavenging, drum-beating, playing music and singing. There were also acrobats like the Bazigar, magicians like the Bhanumati, devil dancers and exorcists like the Nalkadaya, the Pambada and the Malayan. The Bangali in Haryana and a few adjoining states, and the Garudi, were snake charmers, while the Baori prepared mohra (seal) and the Sindhuria manufactured vermilions. The Barar and the Kunchi Korava made combs for pit looms and the latter also did fibre-twinning to make ropes for peasants. The Mangan and the Turi are genealogists and bards. Some communities, like the Beda Jangam, the Kuruvan, etc., were soothsayers while the Singhiwala eked out a livelihood with their skills in traditional medicine. The Dhoba in many states of north India and the Velan and the Mannan in the south are wshermen.

Service to the village community was rendered by the women of a few communities, like the Hari, who acted as midwives. Some communities, like the Bhand, earned money by mimicry. The Sindhollu of Andhra Pradesh lived by performing street drams (veedhibhagavatamulu) based on mythologies of the great tradition, and the Sillekyata by performing leather picture shows. The Gandhila were horse and ass traders, while the Sauntia were animal breeders. Communities like the Byagara, the Thoti, etc., were traditionally village servants, and the Kotegar guarded forts in olden days. The Bhoi, the Keot, the Kahar and a few others were palanquin-bearers. The Bindla of Andhra Pradesh had a role in the traditional system of invoking and appeasing village deities. Communities like the Darai and the Patni are traditionally ferrymen. A scheduled caste by name, the Kanda of Tripura supplied flowers to the royal palace (which then existed). An analysis of the occupations among scheduled castes suggests that some occupations like leatherwork, scavenging, etc., were considered degrading. However, in some areas certain groups are considered untouchable, whereas the same occupational groups are not considered so in other areas. If fishing communities are untouchable in eastern India, it is not the case in the western coastal areas or in the south except for the Bharatar of Tamil Nadu. The potters of Madhya Pradesh or Manipur are untouchables, but not in any other area. The washermen in Andhra Pradesh are not untouchable, whereas in many other areas they are, and there they are notified as scheduled castes.

With the degradation of the environment and the depletion of forests there has been a sharp decline in many of the traditional economic activities of the scheduled castes (represented by percentages), such as hunting and gathering (43.86%), the trapping of birds and animals (17.64%) and shifting cultivation (20%). There has been a considerable involvement in modern occupations like horticulture (50%), settled cultivation (31.92%) and terrace cultivation (13.64%). However, there also has been a sharp rise in animal husbandry (32.84%) and wage labour (43.62%). There is increased involvement in activities like business (79.82%), trade (65.84%) and small-scale industry, which is reported from 23 communities. There is a phenomenal rise in white-collar employees (399 communities) and in private service (324) and self-employment (443). There has been a perceptible decline of crafts like dyeing (11.12%), weaving (9.28%), salt making (33.34%), weapon-making (33.35%), and metal work (10%). Specialized categories practising the traditional occupations mentioned above have also suffered. However, a category of skilled labourer has emerged, registering an increase of 64.04 per cent. There is increased involvement in woodwork (51.52 per cent).

Though untouchability has been abolished by law, the study shows the persistence of untouchability, particularly in rural areas,, in relation to the exchange of water and food with communities considered to be higher in the social hierarchy, even though commensal norms have generally weakened. Scheduled castes in every region and area in the country have their own hierarchy which prohibits the acceptance and exchange of water and food. For a Mala, a Madiga is an untouchable, and for both of them a Thoti is an untouchable. For a Meghwal, a Regar and a Bhangi are untouchables, whereas among the later two the Bhangi is an untouchable. Even the subgroups in a larger generic category have these distinctions. Among the Chamars, the Jatav, the Mochi, the Satnami and many others have their own sense of superiority. So, there are a few scheduled castes from whom the other scheduled-caste communities accept neither food nor water. However, the data on the exchange of food and water show that there is a substantial number of communities with whom such exchanges do take place. There are also many scheduled castes, particularly those comprising professionals, who are not considered untouchables and with whom an exchange of food and water takes place. Further, the data also show that 42.3 per cent of the communities have putative kinship relations across communities, and 79.8 per cent of the communities share water sources and crematoria (66.2 %) with other communities. Ninety-one per cent of them visit the same religious shrines. As many as 681 communities (90.7%) participate in the traditional festivals and festivities, and 132 scheduled castes (17.6 %) have a specific role to play in these festivals.

That education has made an impact and promoted mobility is evident from the fact that a class of public servants (250 communities), teachers (364), administrators (155) and entrepreneurs/businessmen (286) has emerged among them. Political leadership has emerged at the village (39.4%), regional (18.5%) and national (4.5%) levels. One of the features of the degraded social status of scheduled-caste people has been the role of myths which explained their lowly origin, and even rationalized it. But there has been a sea change in recent years in the perception by scheduled-caste people of themselves; a new sense of self-respect. Part of this is due to the sanskritization of those sections of these communities which abstained from drinking liquor, eating non-vegetarian food (especially beef and pork)- in fact non-vegetarianism of all kinds. This also involved giving up names which were considered derogatory and assuming names which were considered respectable, e.g., the Chuhras called themselves Balmiki, Lalbegi; the Chandals became Namasudras; the Julaha called themselves Kabirpanthis; the Mala and Madiga named themselves Adi Andhra; the Pallan and Parayan claimed to be Adi Dravida, the Holeyas in Karnataka are now Adi Karnataka; the Chamar and Chuhra, after conversion to Sikhism, called themselves Ramdasia.

A new strand in the self-perception of the scheduled castes are the Neo-Buddhists who stress their identity as members belonging to an order that stands outside the varna system. In fact theirs is a newfound sense of dignity in their identity as members of the scheduled castes *in situ* without associating themselves either with the sanskritization process or various protestant reformist movements. In fact a new sense of self-respect is in the air. The old myths which legitimized degradation are being discarded. Colonial ethnographic surveys were replete with stories of degradation caused by beef-eating and that arising out of functions such as removing carcasses. These are either being ignored now or are referred to very weakly. Instead there is a new sense of dignity and self-assertion symbolized by Dalit literature. The Dalits now not only question the varna system and the ideology underlying it but consider their movement a larger struggle for equality. In this respect they have not only continued with Babasaheb B.R. Ambedkar's struggle for equality and self-respect but have taken it into new areas. The new leadership has articulated a radical counter-ideology, powerfully expressed in a burst of creative writings. The Dalit sahitya is in vibrant form today. The Dalit poetry states the stark truth and calls upon Dalits to act:

As mentioned earlier, the Scheduled Castes are a heterogeneous category. Most of the sections of the scheduled castes have generally lived in symbiosis with other sections of the general population. They have been, and are being, closely integrated with the country's larger society. This fact, and this process, is also reflected in economy, culture and politics.

The Madiga of Andhra Pradesh are also referred to as Arundhatiya, Jambavalu, Jambhavanthulu, Adi-Andhra, etc. There are many legendary accounts of the origin of the Madiga. The Madiga and Mala have common legends that speak of their origins. Many legends say that the divine cow, Kamadhenu, was killed by two watchmen of Eswara and as a consequence they were cursed by him. The descendants of these two watchmen were the Madiga and Mala. Most Madigas live in their own hamlets (Madiga Palle) segregated from the main village. According to the 1981 census, the population of the Madiga in Andhra Pradesh is 3,572,072. They are predominantly found in rural areas. However, a considerable number of them, i.e., 477,596 persons (13.37 per cent of the total population) are returned from urban areas. The Dravidian language, Telugu and the Telugu script are used for both intra-and inter-group communication. The morphometric features of the Madiga in Andhra Pradesh fall between the tribal communities and the agricultural and economically dominant castes and, in general, are similar to the average physical features of the state's population. The Madiga are predominantly round-headed, of below medium to short height and have a broader facial profile. They show a higher occurrence of gene B (27-35 per cent) than gene A (13-14 percent). In the Tirupati area they were found to have an excess of gene O (73 per cent) than in the north-western parts of A.P. (61 per cent). The presence of Sickle cell trait, low levels of Hp^1 allele, relatively low levels of Rh-negative cases (4 %) and low frequency of colour-blind males, indicate their similarity with tribal groups of the area. The Madiga are non-vegetarian and they are in the habit of taking alcoholic drinks frequently. It is stated that their untouchable status was due to their habit of eating beef. Rice is the staple cereal consumed.

Malas are settled in every Andhra village and constitute the backbone of the agricultural labour force. Out of their total population, 49.59% are returned as workers (58.50% males and 40.44 % females). Of them, 67.64 % are returned as agricultural labourers, whereas only 18.41% are cultivators; 1.10% of the workers are engaged in livestock and forestry. The remaining 12.85 % of the workers are engaged in various other services. Intercommunity linkages between the Malas and the other communities are characteristically limited to the economic sphere. Of late, particularly in urban areas, there has been an increasing interaction between the Mala and other caste communities in terms of exchange of food and water. Many changes of greater importance can be witnessed among the Malas in their socio-economic life, mainly due to the government's interventionist and protective developmental programmes. They avail of all the facilities extended to them for the improvement of their quality of life. There has been considerable progress in the field of education. Their literacy rate, according to the 1981 census, is 21.23%. The sexwise literacy rates for male and female, according to the 1981 census, are 29.72 % and 12.51%, respectively.

At present, some Malas are employed as clerks, administrators, doctors, engineers, teachers and defence personnel. They forge and establish intercommunity links at various levels, though only in a limited way. Some of them have improved their economic condition by availing of different developmental programmes. Their literacy rate is only 12.75% (1981 census). The Mala in the Union Territory of Pondicherry call themselves Adi Andhra and are distributed all over Yanam. Their population, including Mala Masti, in Pondicherry, according to the 1981 census, is only 11. It appears that in the 1981 census, they mainly returned themselves as Adi Andhra who numbered 2148. In addition to their mother tongue, Telugu, they are conversant in Tamil.

As Pondicherry was a colony of the French, the elderly people of the community can understand and speak French. The script commonly used for writing is Tamil. In terms of food habits, social division and customs, they do not show much variation.

Neo-Buddhist / Nav Buddhist:- Also referred to as Nav Buddhist, they are the new converts to Buddhism. Baba Saheb Ambedkar initiated these conversions to the Buddhist faith and the first conversion took place in 1956 at Nagpur in Maharashtra. Dr. Ambedkar believed that only by leaving the Hindu fold could the depressed castes free themselves from the burden of untouchability. Conversions have since taken place in different states. A large-scale conversion took place in 1981, the silver jubilee year of the first conversion, when a large number of Jatavs in Uttar Pradesh were converted to Buddhism. Neo-Buddhists are distributed all over the country, but they are largely concentrated in Maharashtra, Uttar Pradesh, Karnataka, Gujarat, Andhra Pradesh and Punjab. In Uttar Pradesh, most of them live in Bareilly, Badaun, Moradabad and Agra districts. The Hindi language and the Devanagari script are used for both inter-group and intra-group communication. They are occasionally non-vegetarians. Of late, there has been a shift to vegetarianism.

Neo-Buddhists use surnames like Gautam, Bodh and Ashok for boys and Gautami for females. Marriages are contracted within the community beyond blood relations. The usual form of marriage is monogamy, and adult marriage is the norm. Glass bangles, the vermilion mark, toe-rings, etc., are the marriage symbols for women. There is no dowry. After marriage, the patrilocal rule of residence is followed. Divorce is not permissible. However, levirate and sororate are permissible. They usually live in nuclear families. Inheritance is in the male line and the eldest son succeeds to the familial authority. Their women share the tasks of bringing potable water, collecting fuel and fodder and assisting their men in agricultural operations. Besides, they are also proficient in embroidery. A pre-delivery ritual known as gabb-mangal is performed, in which panchsheel is adopted and a bhikshu recites the dhammapada and performs the jai managal asthagatha. The bhikshu or bodh acharya names the infants. The first feeding of cereals (annaprasan) is performed at the age of five months. The tonsure ceremony (keshkampan) is initiated by a bhikshu but the Nai is given cash and grains for performing the tonsure. The ear-piercing ceremony (karan vichedan) and initiation to education (vidhya arambh) are performed at the age of five years. The religious course of prabajya is taken by both married and unmarried persons. The jal kriya or samarpan rituals have replaced kanyadan and haldi is performed three days prior to the marriage. The marriage is solemnized at the bride's place. The important marriage rituals are oathtaking, panchsheel, jal kriya and jai mangal asthagatha. Marriages are registered with the Bhartiya Bodh Parishad. On death (parinirvan), the corpse is either cremated or buried. On the fifth day after death, the paaritrana path is performed.

In addition to their traditional occupation of shoe making and leatherwork, they are also engaged in sharecropping as well as wage labour. Nowadays, some of them are employed in government and private services and a few of them are in industry.

The Bharatiya Bodh Parishad to which their community is affiliated takes care of their social disputes. They believe in the original granth, Tripitak. A bhikshu performs their different life-cycle rituals. They observe the general festivals of the Buddhists and also celebrate the birth and death anniversaries of Baba Saheb Ambedkar. They are experts in shoe making and in embroidery on cloth and leather.

Traditional intercommunity linkages with the different untouchable communities are still maintained. They share the same water sources and cremation grounds with other communities. They continue to cultivate the fields of upper caste Hindus as sharecroppers and also work for them as labourers. The scholars, teachers, doctors, engineers and administrators from amongst them promote modern intercommunity linkages. Some of them have emerged as political leaders at the national level.

The Adi Hindu Movement which propounded the theory that the untouchables are the original inhabitants of India did not find favour with the Arya Samaj and its followers like the Jatav, some of whom identify themselves to be Nav Buddhists. In Swami Atma Ram's *Gyan Samudra* it was mentioned that according to Lomash Ramayana found in Nepal, the Jatav race was traced to a gotra of Lord Shiva. Thus, it was stated that the Jatav are Kshatriyas. Now after their conversion to Buddhism in 1956, they have begun to assert that they are indigenes of the soil, who were once Buddhists before they adopted Hinduism after Aryan migration.

Their attitude towards formal education is partly favourable for both boys and girls. For curing their ailments, they use both modern and indigenous medicare systems. Their attitude towards family planning is positive and they have adopted modern methods of family planning. They make use of irrigation and electricity facilities. Their children avail of the midday-meal scheme in schools. Their attitude towards saving is encouraging.

In Karnataka, most of the Neo-Buddhists are converts from Mahar, Chalvadi, Holeya and Madiga communities. They are largely concentrated in Bangalore, Mysore, Tumkur, Bidar, Gulbarga, Dharwad, Belgaum and Kolar districts. The different linguistic groups speak their respective languages at home and use Kannada for inter-group communications. The Kannada script is used. They are non-vegetarians who consume beef and pork. Rice, wheat and jowar are their staple cereals and tur is the main pulse consumed. Their men occasionally consume alcoholic drinks purchased from the market. Smoking beedis and cigarettes and chewing betel leaf are common habits that are encountered amongst them.

They place themselves in the Sudra category of the chaturvarna system. Marriage with one's father's sister's daughter, mother's brother's daughter or elder sister's daughter is permissible. Adult marriage is the norm and marriage is arranged through negotiation. The thali and toe-rings are the marriage symbols for women. Monogamy is the form of marriage. Divorce is not permitted, but widow and widower remarriage is allowed. Vertically extended families are predominant, however there has been a decline in the number of extended families. Their women participate in economic activities like agricultural operations and animal husbandry, besides participating in social, ritual and religious spheres. Birth pollution lasts for eleven days. A few of them observe the initiation ceremony (sila) which is related to the observance of the five principles of Buddhism, i.e., panch sheel (abstention from killing, stealing, adultery, telling lies and drinking of liquor). Puberty rites (pushpavati) are performed on menarche. Marriages are solemnized at the bridegroom's house. The marriage ritual starts with an exchange of garlands followed by the tying of the thali to the bride by the bridegroom. The marriage feast is hosted by the bridegroom's parents. The dead are either buried or cremated and death pollution is observed. On the sixteenth day after death, a mortuary rite known as tithi is performed. Ancestor worship is observed.

In Andhra Pradesh, Dr. Ambedkar's teachings have inspired several communities, which have converted to Buddhism. They are now called Neo-Buddhists and are found in Visakhapatnam, East Godavari and West Godavari districts. They speak Telugu and use the Telugu script. They recite the Panchasheel and Trisaran in the Pali language during the puja. The Neo-Buddhists are non-vegetarian. Their personal names are suffixed with Gautam, Buddha, Vikas, Ashok, etc. Sometimes they are also named after characters in Buddhist literature. They are largely drawn from various scheduled castes like the Mala, Madiga, etc., who, after their conversion, do not strictly follow the earlier caste distinctions. They follow surname (intiperu) exogamy and marry either the mother's brother's daughter or the father's sister's daughter. Sororal polygyny exists among them. Their women wear a thali (mangalasutra), vermilion (kankanam) and toe-rings (Mettelu) as marriage symbols. They follow patrilocal residence after marriage. Divorce is not permissible, but widow and widower remarriage is permissible. The majority of their families are of the nuclear type. All the male children inherit an equal share of the ancestral property. The eldest son succeeds as the head of the family. Women have a role in socio-religious functions and claim to have a secondary status. The tonsure ceremony is performed in the ninth month of the child. Puberty rites (Mangalasnanam) are performed for girls. Marriage rituals take place at the bridegroom's house or at Buddha viharas. A Bhikshu or an Upasak imparts Trisaran and Panchasheel to the bride and the groom before a picture of Lord Buddha. Then their names are registered in the Bharatiya Bodh Parishad. They either cremate or bury the dead. Death pollution is observed for five days. They do not perform ancestor worship.

Agricultural labour is the main occupation of the Neo-Buddhists. Some of them work as daily-wage labourers at construction sites, factories, etc., and a few other are employed as doctors, lawyers, teachers, etc., in government establishments. The Buddhist Sangam settles their disputes. The elderly monks of the Neo-Buddhists follow the Mahayana sect of Buddhism. After their conversion, they started observing Buddha Jayanti or Buddha Poornima, Ambedkar's birth and death anniversaries and Vijaya Dasami (Dussehra). Vijaya Dasami is specially observed because Dr. Ambedkar embraced Buddhism on that day. They have their own Bhikshu to conduct socio-religious functions. A fast is observed on full-moon days, as Buddha was born, received enlightenment and died., i.e., attained Mahaparinirvana on a full-moon day (Poornima). They accept food and water from all Hindu castes. The Brahman, Kshatriya and Vaishya communities accept only sidha food from them. In Andhra Pradesh, the Hindus do not treat them as equals in spite of their conversion to Buddhism. They receive the services of a barber (Mangali) and washerman (Chakali). They have their own viharas where religious teaching is imparted. They share public amenities like cremation/burial grounds and schools with other communities. Their attitude towards the formal education of their boys and girls is positive. Modern methods of family welfare are being adopted. They are also availing of financial assistance from institutions like the Andhra Pradesh State Financial Corporation and from banks. Since 1990, the government has extended the facility of reservation in jobs to the scheduled-caste converts to Buddhism.

Panchama:- The term Panchama means the fifth one, alluding to a non-existent fifth varna. All these groups later came to be called Harijans, scheduled castes and Dalits. It is often pointed out that the Panchama include many other groups. Panchama should be regarded as a varna, because Manu declared that there could never be a fifth varna. Panchama is, in fact, a generic term encompassing different endogamous groups. These are further subdivided by surnames (intiperu). The surnames, besides being exogamous groups, are also meant to indicate descent and ancestry. They also place themselves above the Jambavulu and below the Brahman, Raju, Komati, Kapu, Setti Balija, Gowda and Golla. Some of them consider themselves Sudras in the chaturvarna order. Group endogamy and surname exogamy are the general marriage rules observed. The Panchama are largely landless and only a few own cultivable land ranging from half an acre to five acres. Traditionally, they are agricultural labourers. Toddy-tapping, plucking coconuts, government service, cycle-rickshaw-pulling, etc., are the other occupations tht are pursued. According to the 1981 census, 51.07 per cent of them are workers (62.81% males and 39.13% females). Of them, a majority are agricultural labourers (71.41%) and cultivators (9.57%). The rest (3.32%) are engaged in mining and quarrying, 2.35% in the household industries and 13.35% in other services.

Paraiyan/Parayan: Bishop Caldwell is of the opinion that the name Paraiyan is from the Tamil word parai, a drum, as certain paraiyans act as drummers at marriages, funerals, village festivals and on occasions when government or commercial announcements are proclaimed (Thurston, 1909).

Pulayan, along with the Izhavas and some other high-castes, participated in the Vaikom Satyagraha, which was started in 1924. In 1907, they started the Sadhu Jana Paripalana Sangham (SJPS) and Pulaya Mahasabha. In Perinad in Quilon district, the Pulayan began a movement against the traditional practice of their women wearing bead necklaces, which was considered a sign of degradation. This was strongly resented by the Nairs. Finally, the Pulayan women won the right to throw away the beads.

Santia:- Distributed in Kota and Jhalawar districts of Rajasthan, the Santia are a migrant community from Raipur district in Madhya Pradesh. They are notified as Santia, Satia and their population, according to the 1981 census, is 5372. They are a predominantly rural-based community and more than 91 per cent of their total population is returned from rural areas. They speak the Indo-Aryan language, Gujarati, among themselves and Hindi is spoken with others. The

Devanagari script is sued. Both male and female wear a ceramic bead necklace. They are non-vegetarian and consume beef, pork and carrion. Their staple cereals are jowar and maize. Alcoholic drinks, purchased from the market, are occasionally consumed. There are both Hindu and Muslim segments among them. The former do not practise consanguinity whereas the later does. Village exogamy and monogamy are the marriage rules observed.

Sapela / Sapera:- Known as Sapela, Sapad or sapera, they are snake charmers. The word Sapera is derived from sap, meaning snake. Rose (1919) mentions Sapela, Sapera or Sipada as a snake-catcher, like the Sapela. The Sapela or Sampela claim to be an offshoot of the Jogi. They are distributed all over Haryana and their population, according to the 1981 census, is 4716 (2722 males and 1994 females) and they aro primarily rural-based community. They are also returned from Punjab, Himachal Pradesh, Delhi and Chandigarh. In different parts of Haryana they use the Indo-Aryan language, Haryanvi, for both inter- and intra-group communication. The Devanagari script is used,. Their staple food constitutes pulse (dal), unleavened wheat bread (roti) and vegetable (sabzi). They prefer wheat to rice. They are more or less regular non-vegetarian and occasionally consume alcoholic drinks. The income generating activities are snake-charming, selling of snake venom and rearing mules for sale. To supplement the family income, they play on a gourd-pipe and dance in marriage parties. According to the 1981 census, 15.92 per cent of their total population (25.94% male and 2.26 % female) is returned as workers. Out of them 13.59 per cent are engaged in manufacturing, processing, etc. and 41.41 per cent are in other services which include workers engaged in playing on the gourd-pipe and those who dance in marriage parties. However, a considerable number of them, i.e., 39.28 per cent, are returned as agricultural labourers, 2.53 per cent as cultivators and 3.19 per cent as engaged in various other services.

While the study undertaken by the Anthropological Survey of India has covered the scheduled castes above a population of 10,000 in all the states and union territories of India, it has left twelve communities in a few states and one union territory, whose major components are listed below. These communities along with the state/union territory of their distribution, their population (1981 census) and an explanation for not studying them, are all appended below:

Sl. No	*Community*	*State/UT*	*Explanation*
1.	AD DHARMI	Himachal Pradesh (15,098)	Reported as a synonym for Chamar
2.	ADI ANDHRA	Andhra Pradesh (698,857)	Being a generic group, its constituent communities have been studied.
3.	BARAHAR, BASOD	Madhya Pradesh (60,789)	Studied as Basor in Madhya Pradesh
4.	BHANGI	Delhi (21,752)	Reported as a synonym for Chuhra and Balmiki.
5.	CHAKKILIYAN	Kerala (29,001)	Studied as Arundhatiyar.
6.	HOLAYA, HOLER	Maharashtra (14,927)	Reported as a synonym for Holar
7.	KABIR PANTHI or JULAHA	Haryana (31,503)	Studied as Julaha.
8.	MADARI	Tamil Nadu (346, 899)	Reported as a synonym for Chakkiliyan.
9.	MALA	Maharashtra (11,890)	Reported to be untraceable.
10.	MALLAH	West Bengal (38,101)	Reported as a synonym for Deshwali Majhi.
11.	MOGER	Kerala (19,665)	'Real' Moger are untraceable.
12.	PALLAN	Tamil Nadu (993,070)	Studied as Kudumban.

CONCLUSION

The details of data that are provided above would, it is believed, help the development agencies and the change agents in the field to understand and recognize the way to go about extending help to bring the Dalits to the surface, to the level of other groups who would enjoy respect, recognition and politico-economic advancement. Even though it may take several generations to bridge the gap but genuine attempts are to be pursued to do justice to the Dalits in terms of their overall development.

A list of those unstudied communities, whose population is below 10,000 along with the states and union territories where they were not studied, and their population figures (1981 census or as in the case of Assam, 1971 census) is appended below:

Sl. No.	*Community*	*V. State / Union Territory and Population*
1.	Adi Dharmi	Chandigarh (1431), Haryana (698), Rajasthan (780)
2.	Adi Andhra	Kerala (7353), Pondicherry (2148)
3.	Adi Dravida	Kerala (2458)
4.	Adi Karnataka	Kerala (1087)
5.	Ager	Gujarat (151), Maharashtra (3846)
6.	Agria	Delhi (1139)
7.	Ajila	Karnataka (1301), Kerala (155), Tamil Nadu (35)
8.	Arwa Mala	Karnataka (171), Maharashtra (241)
9.	Arunthathiyar	Karnataka (899)
10.	Audhelia	Orissa (15)
11.	Bagdi	Tripura (239)

(Contd...)

Sl. No.	Community	V. State / Union Territory and Population
12.	Baira	Tamil Nadu (431)
13.	Bakad, Bant	Gujarat (303), Maharashtra (736)
14.	Bakuda	Tamil Nadu (198)
15.	Bandhela	Himachal Pradesh (30)
16.	Bandi	Kerala (24)
17.	Bangali	Chandigarh (49)
18.	Bansphor	Arunachal Pradesh (152), Meghalaya (212), Mizoram (8)
19.	Bantar	West Bengal (2086)
20.	Barar, Burar, Berar Barar, Burar, Berar	Haryana (957), Himachal Pradesh (416) Chandigarh (200)
21.	Basor, Burud Basor, Burud, Bansor, Bansodi, Bansphor, Basar	Orissa (178) Madhya Pradesh
22.	Bathada	Kerala (46)
23.	Batwal	Chndigarh (41), Haryana (524)
24.	Bauria, Bawaria Bauria or Bawaria	Himachal Pradesh (87) Chandigarh (791)
25.	Bavuri	Orissa (50)
26.	Bediya, Beriya	Rajsthan (2361)
27.	Bellara	Kerala (45), Tamil Nadu (44)
28.	Bhangi	Dadra and Nagar Haveli (44)
29.	Bhanjra	Chandigarh (207)
30.	Bharatar	Kerala (1892)
31.	Bhuinmali, Mali Bhinmali or Mali Bhuinmali or Mali	Meghalaya (201), Arunachal Pradesh (36), Mizoram (3)

Sl. No.	*Community*	*V. State / Union Territory and Population*
32.	Bindla	Karnataka (194), Maharashtra (303), Meghalaya (303)
33.	Brittial-Bania or Bania Brittial Bania, Bania	Arunachal Pradesh (102), Mizoram ((2) Meghalaya (115)
34.	Byagara	Maharashtra (356)
35.	Chakkiliyan	Karnataka (2831)
36.	Chalavadi Chalvadi, Channayya	Tamil Nadu (131) Gujarat (58)
37.	Chamar, Muchi	Kerala (298), Tamil Nadu (165)
38.	Chambhar	Andhra Pradesh (520, Daman and Diu (22)
39.	Chanal	Chandigarh (90), Haryana (293), Punjab (139)
40.	Chandal	Rajasthan (1105)
41.	Chandala	Andhra Pradesh (184), Karnataka (175), Kerala (90), Tamil Nadu (37)
42.	Chaupal	West Bengal (37)
43.	Chenna Dasar, Holaya Dasar Chenna Dasar, Holaya Dasar, Holeya Dasari	Gujarat (139) Maharashtra (631)
44.	Chohra (Sweeper)	Delhi (3272)
45.	Dabgar	West Bengal (460)
46.	Dagi	Chandigarh (4), Haryana (50), Punjab (54)
47.	Dakkal, Dokkalwar	Karnataka (141), Maharashtra 342)
48.	Dandasi	Tripura (57)
49.	Darain	Chandigarh (23), Haryana (55), Himachal Pradesh (656)
50.	Dhanak	Himachal Pradesh (34)

(Contd...)

Sl. No.	Community	V. State / Union Territory and Population
51.	Dhaogri, Dhuai	Himachal Pradesh (793)
52.	Dhogri, Dhangri, Siggi	Haryana (438), Punjab (265)
	Dhogri, Dhangri or Siggi	Chandigarh (21)
53.	Dhor	Andhra Pradesh (2443)
54.	Dhor, Kakkayya, Kankayya	Gujarat (877)
55.	Dhupi or Dhobi Dhupi, Dhobi	Arunachal Pradesh (353), Mizoram (33) Meghalaya (313), Manipur (186)
56.	Domban	Tamil Nadu (8482)
57.	Dome, Dom	Rajasthan (3692)
58.	Dum	Tripura (283)
59.	Dumna, Mahasha or Doom	Chandigarh (112)
	Dumna, Mahasha, Doom	Haryana (9248)
60.	Dosadha	Orissa (455)
61.	Dugla or Dholi Dugla, Dholi	Arunachal Pradesh (7), Mizoram (4), Meghalaya (22)
		Assam (4013)
62.	Gagra	Chandigarh (37), Haryana (58), Himachal Pradesh (6)
63.	Gandhila or Gandhil Gondola	Chandigarh (22)
	Gandhila, Gandil Gondola	Himachal Pradesh (6)
64.	Garoda, Garo	Karnataka (1219), Maharashtra (352)
65.	Gharami	Uttar Pradesh (615)
66.	Ghasi	Tripura (443)

(Contd...)

Sl. No.	Community	V. State / Union Territory and Population
67.	Ghasi, Haddi, Relli Chachandi	Andhra Pradesh (1872)
68.	Godagali	Kerala (37), Orissa (24), Tamil Nadu (24)
69.	Godari	Orissa (225)
70.	Godda	Kerala (186)
71.	Gosangi	Karnataka (7474), Kerala (769), Tamil Nadu (157)
72.	Halalkhor	Bihar (5463), West Bengal (1348)
73.	Halleer	Gujarat (28)
74.	Halsar, Haslar, Hulasvar, Halasvar	Gujarat (154), Maharashtra (123)
75.	Hari	Uttar Pradesh (2121)
76.	Hira	Arunachal Pradesh (9), Meghalaya (48), Mizoram(3)
77.	Holar, Valhar	Gujarat (170), Karnataka (1190)
78.	Holaya, Holer	Gujarat (92),
	Holeya	Andhra Pradesh (664)
79.	Holeya Dasari	Andhra Pradesh (620)
80.	Jaggali	Karnataka (229), Tamil Nadu (1248)
81.	Jalkeot	Arunachal Pradesh (34), Meghalaya (8),. Mizoram (2)
82.	Jambuvulu	Karnataka (4082), Pondicherry (237)
83.	Jhalo, Malo, Jhalo-Malo	Meghalaya (1052)
	Jhalo, Malo or Jhalo-Malo	Arunachal Pradesh (75), Mizoram (1)
84.	Jolaha	Jammu and Kashmir (371)

(Contd...)

Sl. No.	Community	V. State / Union Territory and Population
85.	Kabir Panthi	Delhi (4334)
86.	Kadaiyan	Karnatka (172)
87.	Kaibartta or Jaliya	Arunachal Pradesh (764), Mizoram (6)
88.	Kakkalan	Tamil Nadu (66)
89.	Kalladi	Karnataka (511), Tamil Nadu (409)
90.	Kanakkan, Padanna	Tamil Nadu (176)
91.	Kanjar	West Bengal (1067)
92.	Karimpalan	Tamil Nadu (9)
93.	Katia, Patharia	Maharashtra (3207)
94.	Kavara	Tamil Nadu 3711)
95.	Khangar, Kanera, Mirdha	Maharashtra (858)
96.	Koch	West Bengal (9714)
97.	Kooch-Band, Kuchband	Rajasthan (1509)
98.	Koosa	Kerala (268), Tamil Nadu 41)
99.	Kootan, Koodan	Tamil Nadu (147)
100.	Kori or Koli	Chandigarh (1889)
101.	Kotal	Tripura (43)
102.	Kudumban	Karnataka (140), Kerala (3368)
103.	Kurariar	West Bengal (1416)
104.	Lalbegi	Arunachal Pradesh (20), Assam (45), Delhi (134), Meghalaya (30), Mizoram (3)
105.	Madari	Delhi (?), Karnataka (3434)
106.	Madiga	Orissa ((1314)
107.	Mahar Mahar, Taral, hegumegu	Dadra and Nagar Haveli (83) Rajasthan (7635)

(Contd...)

Sl. No.	*Community*	*V. State / Union Territory and Population*
108.	Mahara	Arunachal Pradesh (13), Assam (899), Mizoram (6), Meghalaya (Not available)
109.	Mahayavanshi Mahyavanshi, Dhed Mahyavanshi, Dhed, Dheda, Venkar, Maru Vankar Mahayanvashi, Dhed, Vankar, Maru Vankar	Goa (119) Rajasthan (1868) Dadra and Nagar Haveli (943) Karnataka (719)
110.	Maila	Tamil Nadu (47)
111.	Mazhabi	Himachal Pradesh (221)
112.	Mala, Jhala, Malo, Zala	Orissa (6118)
113.	Mala Dasari	Karnataka (2193)
114.	Mala Dasu	Andhra Pradesh (8384)
115.	Mala Jangam	Karnatakka (291)
116.	Mala Masti	Karnataka (34), Maharashtra (60)
117.	Mala Sale, Netkani	Karnataka (21), Maharashtra (437)
118.	Mang	Goa (686), Daman and Diu (16), Orissa (273)
119.	Mang, Matang, Minimadig	Gujarat (2765), Rajasthan (241)
120.	Mang Garodi, Mang-Garudi Mang Garudi, Mang Garodi Mang Garudi	Rajasthan (177) Karnataka (2339) Gujarat (1184)
121.	Mangan	Orissa (983)
122.	Manne	Karnataka (174), Maharashtra (1752)

(Contd...)

Sl. No.	*Community*	*V. State / Union Territory and Population*
123.	Mavilan	Karnataka (51)
124.	Megh	Chandigarh (338)
125.	Meghwal Meghval, Menghvar	Delhi (1481) Karnataka (22)
126.	Mehtar or Bhangi Mehtar, Bhangi Mehtor	Arunachal Pradesh (209), Mizoram (10) Meghalaya (621), Orissa (2332) Tripura (1279)
127.	Mitha Ayyalvar	Maharashtra (202)
128.	Moger	Tamil Nadu (89)
129.	Muchi, Ravidas Muchi or Rishi Muchi, Rishi	Manipur (193) Arunachal Pradesh (328) Meghalaya (1204)
130.	Mukri	Gujarat (26), Maharashtra (74)
131.	Mundala	Andhra Pradesh (853), Tamil Nadu (26)
132.	Musahar	Orissa (29)
133.	Nadia, Hadi	Karnataka (118), Maharashtra (249)
134.	Nalakeyava	Karnataka (4928), Kerala (269), Tamil Nadu (7)
135.	Namasudra	Arunachal Prdesh (540), Manipur (2423), Meghalaya (1112), Mioram (6)
136.	Nat Nat (Rana)	Chandigarh (21), Himachal Pradesh (232), Uttar Pradesh (?) Delhi (?)
137.	Nayadi	Karnataka (1434), Tamil Nadu (360)
138.	Od	Chandigarh (35)
139.	Padannan	Tamil Nadu (Not available)
140.	Paky	Pondicherry (42)
141.	Pallan	Karnataka (745)

(Contd...)

Sl. No.	*Community*	*V. State / Union Territory and Population*
142.	Palluvan	Tamil Nadu (151)
143.	Pambada Pambada, Pambanda	Tamil Nadu (624) Andhra Pradesh (2333)
144.	Pamidi	Orissa (64)
145.	Panchama	Karnataka (785), Kerala (134), Orissa (269), Tamil Nadu (76)
146.	Panika	Orissa (?)
147.	Panniandi	Karnataka (97)
148.	Paraiyan, Paraya	Karnataka (2307)
149.	Pasi	Chandigarh (928), Gujarat (1164), Himachal Pradesh (226), Rajasthan (943)
150.	Pathiyan	Tamil Nadu (23)
151.	Patni	Arunachal Pradesh (11), Manipur (2293), Meghalaya (54), Mizoram (4)
152.	Perna	Chandigarh (18), Himachal Pradesh (21)
153.	Pherera	Chandigarh (12), Haryana (24)
154.	Pulaya Vettuvan	Kerala (1008)
155.	Puthirai Vannan	Kerala (280)
156.	Raneyar	Kerala (148), Tamil Nadu (4), Andhra Pradesh (1845)
157.	Samagara	Andhra Pradesh (1845), Tamil Nadu (37)
158.	Samban	Karnataka (71), Kerala (2486), Pondicherry (16)
159.	Sanbhai	Chandigarh (89)
160.	Sanhai	Haryana (59), Punjab (73)
161.	Sansi	Maharashtra (531)
162.	Sansoi	Chandigarh (138), Haryana (68), Punjab (32)

(Contd...)

Sl. No.	Community	V. State / Union Territory and Population
163.	Sapela	Chandigarh (138), Himachal Pradesh (23)
164.	Sarbhangi	Rajasthan (613)
165.	Sarera	Chandigarh (215), Haryana (51)
166.	Shenva, Chenva, Sedma, Ravat	Maharashtra (501)
167.	Sidhollu, Chindollu	Karnataka (41), Maharashtra (181)
168.	Sirkiband	Chandigarh (178), Delhi (566), Himachal Pradesh (15)
169.	Sutradhar	Arunachal Pradesh (100), Manipur (11), Meghalaya (270), Mizoram (Not available),
170.	Tamadia	Orissa (238)
171.	Thoti	Karnataka (1184), Kerala (411)
172.	Tirgar, Tirbanda	Karnataka (173), Maharashtra (1154)
173.	Turi	Mahrashtra (275), Rajasthan (2041)
174.	Vallon	Kerala (431), Tamil Nadu (104)
175.	Valluvan	Karnataka (1002)
176.	Velan	Tamil Nadu (318)
177.	Vetan	Pondicherry (307), Tamil Nadu (774)
178.	Vettuvan	Tamil Nadu (143)

Add I, born to be a carrier of carrion, am now
the lowly one to whom the Brahmans come

And lowly bow. They seek
the shelter of my name, Servant of the Sun,
Whose service is the service of the Lord.

- Raidas

(From Sources of Indian Tradition, ed.William T. deBary, trans. J.S. Hawley and M. Juergensmeyer, New York, Columbia University Press, 1982).

The *Brahmin* who flies into a rage at the touch of a *mahar*

- That's no *Brahmin*.

The only absolution for such a *Brahmin*
Is to die for his own sin.

He who refuses to touch a chandal
Has a polluted mind.
Says Tuka, a man is only as chaste
As his own belief.

- Tukaram

(Says Tuka, trans. Dilip Chitre, New Delhi, Penguin Books, 1991).

Source:- The People of India, The Scheduled Castes, National Series, Vol.II, edited by K.S.Singh, Anthropological Survey of India, Oxford University Press, Delhi, 1995.

14

RURAL SANITATION - NEED FOR A PERSPECTIVE PLAN

The sanitation in most of the villages in India presents a dismal picture. It has been a perennial problem, so complex in its character posing a threat to public health. The situation deserves utmost attention and consideration of every individual, local institutions, corporate bodies and the Government at large, for it affects our health and living.

The Japanese are said to be meticulous in their personal and environmental cleanliness. They take as much care of the precincts of their dwellings as they do in the case of their drawing room and bedroom. After a picnic party is over, the Americans do take pretty care to see that they do not leave any litter behind. They leave the place as clean as it was before. What an appreciable civic sense it is! And what do we do here? And what is the environmental sanitary condition in the Indian village?

By sanitary environment we mean a place or village where the residential quarters, cattle sheds, the village precincts, lanes and streets, are regularly swept and kept clean, free from open ditches, pools or slushes, dungheaps or garbage and faecal matter fouling the whole surroundings. A clean village is one free from the above and enjoying drainage facilities and arrangements for regular disposal of refuse. But today most villages in India present a dismal picture. Indiscriminately deposited dung and garbage heaps in various stages of decomposition, ditches and unwanted dirty water pools, ugly looking lanes and streets are some of the characteristic features of the villages. The insanitary conditions pose a constant threat to public health, being the root causes of innumerable diseases and spread of epidemics.

THE MULTIPLE CAUSES

The causes for the bad sanitary conditions in the villages are physical, economic, socio-cultural and psychological. In regard to the patterns of settlement of Indian villages, there are mainly three types – the dispersed or scattered type, the nucleated or the cluster type and linear type i.e., houses built on either side of a road in rows. The nucleated or the cluster type poses many sanitary problems in regard to space for drinking water wells, drainage, bathing and lavatory facilities, disposal of refuse and for sinking of soakage pits. Many of the villages were unplanned houses clustered together with narrow lanes or no lanes at all. Some ancient villages are walled around as a measure of protection from wild animals and thieves. And there will be fields around the village narrowing down the residential quarters. Where the houses are congested and where the villages are situated in low-lying areas, drainage is a problem. So, the very pattern of village settlements, the narrowness and physical or spatial limitations on the expansion of some villages, the topographical features of villages lead to bad sanitary conditions.

In a broad sense, occupation or economic activities of the people also decide the type of environment they live in. India is predominantly an agricultural country. Agriculture in India means use of cattle for draft, milk and manurial purposes which mean housing the cattle in separate sheds and the collection and depositing of dung and other waste materials. Lack of improved cattle-sheds and sheep-pens is a problem in the villages. Either as a matter of convenience or due to socio-cultural and religious attitude of the villagers, the cattle sheds are located near the living quarters and there may not be any wall separating the living quarters and the cattle shed. In many cases the cattle dung and urine are not properly collected. The droppings of cattle, sheep, goats and of poultry strewn all over are usually not taken care of. Even though each household attends to its own immediate surroundings, the village lanes and streets are nobody's responsibility. The villagers also dump indiscriminately cattle dung and all waste material of considerable manurial value around the house and the immediate surroundings of the village. This is due to congestion of space, feeling of difficulty in carrying the matter over a long distance to the fields or outskirts of the village. The indiscriminately dumped dungheaps are seldom covered as a measure to conserve the nitrogenous content in the matter or to prevent foul or stinking smell emanating from them.

Lack of drainage facilities in the villages and the habit of open defaecation on the part of the villagers are other common causes for disgusting sanitary conditions. The open defaecation is a psycho-cultural problem. The villagers are used to it. A change in this habit is long overdue. Either the villagers could use sanitary type of latrines or the centuries old habit of open defaecation persists. The simple fact is that over 90 per cent of the villagers were not used to a flushout latrine in their lives.

Illiteracy, poverty and lack of contract with the outside world contribute to the low civic sense among the villagers.

Another source of insanitation is the drinking water well that lacks raised platforms and causes cesspools making the place dirty.

THE BLEAK BACKGROUND

Illiteracy, poverty and lack of contact with the outside world contribute to the low civic sense among the villagers. Further, the places where shandies and weekly markets are held, when not maintained properly, add to the insanitation of the area. Chewing and indiscriminate spitting is another common social phenomenon.

Having been used to a bad sanitary environment, the villagers do not shudder at anything dirty. The tendency is to take things easy.

There are over 5,80,000 villages in India – just one village per two square miles over the surface of this sub-continent. Now all the villages in India come under the village Panchayat administration. The Panchayats vary in geographical, topographical and economic conditions and cultural practices. Each area in view of its diversity needs a special treatment to solve the problem of environmental sanitation.

In the case of those panchayats which have adequate income, water facilities and have a permanent establishment for sweeping and scavenging, the question of village sanitation is not serious. But the problem becomes acute only with the minor panchayats which cannot or do not have sweeping and other facilities, nor do the villagers in such panachayat areas attend to general sanitation of the village.

Thus we find small villages suffering from (or enduring) a distressing and disease-producing sanitation. Most villagers are aware of the problem, but a remedy is beyond them.

Rural sanitation finds a prominent place of importance in Gandhiji's constructive programme. He often emphasised the magnitude and importance of village sanitation. He practised what he preached. He himself swept the streets and cleaned the latrines. He introduced the ***wardha*** latrine (trench type) which is beneficial in two ways – preservation of night soil (for manurial purposes) and preventing the fouling of village surroundings through indiscriminate defaecation.

LOW PRIORITY

Civil amenities and environmental sanitation are statutory functions of the village panchayat. But apparently the order of priority goes to items like water supply and street lighting and mostly sanitation is not accorded the importance it deserves.

Programmes to improve rural sanitation find a place in the Five Year Plans. Individual and mass sanitary drives were targeted items in the community development extension programmes. These drives in the initial stages were effective and successful and attained a great degree of publicity. The villagers and the school children participated in the drive enthusiastically. Local leaders, officials, men, women and children held brooms in their hands and cleaned the streets. In this, an attempt was made to drive home the dignity of labour and to create among the villagers a new awareness as to the prime importance of the upkeep of the village.

Civil amenities and environmental sanitation are statutory functions of the village panchayat. But apparently the order of priority goes to items like water supply and street lighting and mostly sanitation is not accorded the importance it deserves.

Allied to the sanitation programme are the propagation of sanitary type of latrines, sinking of soakage pits where there are no drainage facilities, construction of *kacha or pucca* drains, improved cattle yards, urinal trenches, scientific methods of compost making, provision of refuse bins, pavement of lanes and streets. This integrated approach is aimed at promoting sanitary conditions in the villages.

Some of the officially sponsored programmes could not make any headway. There were certain inherent shortcomings. Strictly speaking there was no scientific approach on the part of the extension and public health personnel in introducing innovations. The rural workers dictated by a conceptual frame of modern sanitary amenities and accessories as provided by the agencies tried to implant new ideas and habits in the rural communities. For instance, the construction of public lavatories (flushout latrines) in the villages at a considerable public cost was a thorough failure. First, there was no sufficient involvement and commitment of the villagers in this programme. There was the problem of water scarcity. While we discuss the question of rural sanitation water should not be treated as an isolated factor. Above all, the failure in the use of the public latrines was mainly due to the villager's attitude and habits. An attitudinal change is what is desired.

The second factor is limited governmental allocations for programmes connected with village sanitation. Thirdly, poor and inadequate finances of the panchayts and lastly the general apathy of the villagers towards sanitary measures.

As observed earlier, rural sanitation is a complex problem warranting a perspective plan and short-range specific measures to promote better sanitary conditions. The rural Development Agency, the village panchayat, the village school and the voluntary organizations such as youth clubs and mahila mandals could play a significant role in this respect.

The supply of technique, personnel and funds depends on the Government. The programmes towards better sanitary conditions in the villages should be flexible enough so that they could be modified in accordance with the local conditions. A survey of attitudes, felt-needs and specific problems of the villagers should precede on scientific lines before the programmes are formulated. In introducing innovations, the approach should be scientific and institutional. The techniques of group-involvement, group-commitment, propaganda, publicity, demonstration, etc., must be made use of. In other words, the extension methods must be fully employed so as to motivate the villager to use a sanitary latrine and keep the precincts of his house clean. This is a slow, painstaking process. It must be gone through. There is no short cut to it.

In each rural area the vulnerable areas of insanitation and the factors causing unclean conditions are to be located, studied and remedied. The dungheaps should be taken care of. If the villagers are educated on scientific lines of compost making, the ever exposed heaps will not foul the village with stinking odour and become a breeding source for flies and insects. Wherever possible a common compost yard a little away from the village could be established. This could be done by the village panchayat. Drainage depends mainly on two things – the physical feasibility of constructing drains and financial resources. Wherever these two are positive, depending on the size of the village, *kucha or pucca* drains could be constructed as a phased programme. Areas where either of the two is absent, soakage pits are better substitutes. It falls to the lot of the individual householder. Sinking of soakage-pits is cheap and is within the capacity of the commonest man in any village. The only limitations in digging soakage pits are availability of space within the housesite and the composition of the ground soil in the house site. In case of loose soil the soakage pit is not to be located close to the draw-well because of percolation of impure or contaminated water from the soakage pit to the draw-well.

Strictly speaking, the panchayat is responsible for ensuring better sanitary conditions in the panchayat area. In the budgetary allocations of the panchayat enough provision must be made for water supply, drainage, public latrines and refuse bins and recurring expenditure towards sweeping, scavenging, etc. Every panchayat has its annual and Five Year Plans. The panchayats which could not afford full-time sweepers for daily sweeping of the village, could at least appoint either a less number of full-time or more number of part-time sweepers, in order that the villages are kept clean at lest once a week. It is desirable that this minimum programme is carried out by every panchayat.

In regard to the using of sanitary type of latrines by each family, the panchayat should take the initiative and lead in their introduction not only as a civic measure but as a persuasive step creating facilities and favourable public opinion in the use of latrines. In achieving the above-mentioned ends the panchayat can enlist the cooperation of the village school, youth club and mahila mandal and work in unison with them.

The voluntary organizations in the villages could take up village sanitation as one of their main activities and arrange periodical mass sanitary drives. The mass sanitation drives, if carried out sincerely over a period of time, are bound to influence the general public and change their attitude, make them sane to keep their surroundings clean.

The village school as one of the three basic institutions in the viilage could take the lead and function as a pioneer and model in sanitation programmes. It could function as an experimental and demonstration centre for a soakage pit, a lavatory, a compost pit and for environmental sanitation. The school children could be very easily trained to make use of a sanitary latrine, providing one at the school. They carry their ideas and habits to their homes and it may result in a flush-out latrine in their homes. Further, under the guidance of the school teacher the children learn the importance of environmental sanitation and could even participate in the periodical mass sanitary drives organized in the villages.

PUBLIC HEALTH CESS

Some of the corporate bodies at present are engaged in rural developmental programmes. It is a welcome sign that they have assumed this role as partners in rural development. Their role in rural uplift will become more significant and pointed if they could concentrate on rural sanitation. They may take up programmes such as provision of drinking water, sanitation which will include drainage, latrines and gobar gas plants. The Government may also consider income tax relief to the corporate bodies in respect of the amount they spend towards rural sanitation. Further, the nationalized and scheduled banks which have adopted some villages for development may lay emphasis on programmes of rural sanitation. The Government may also bring in legislation towards what may be called public cess. The public health cess as a certain percentage of land revenue will go to the village panchayat and the amount will be utilized exclusively for rural sanitation.

Thus, we see the problems of rural sanitation in India today are deep-rooted, complex and important demanding the attention, cooperation and coordination of the Government, statutory bodies, educational institutions, voluntary organizations and above all the understanding of the general public.

Source: Dr. E. Desingu Setty, 'Rural Sanitation – Need for a Perspective Plan', Social Welfare, April-May, 1981.

15

INTEGRATED APPROACH TO WATER SUPPLY AND SANITATION MANAGEMENT

We may consider water and sanitation as perennial issues. They are the life savers. We have discussed the question of rural sanitation in the previous chapter. In the present one, the focus is on harvesting and conserving rainwater. While discussing conservation of water we also focus on sanitation. Though it may sound a little repetition of what we have already discussed in the previous chapter. The sanitation is brought in here as an organically linked factor with water.

While focusing attention on harvesting and conserving rainwater and going in for various devices for percolation of rainwater in order to have rise of groundwater table, we may have to pay attention to the day-to-day use of water. Further, environmental sanitation is closely associated with the availability and use of water. Conserving water is one thing, utilizing and managing the use is another. The following pages outline an integrated approach to water supply and sanitation management.

I. Water supply and sanitation and their management are an integral part of a rural community and they cannot be isolated from the culture or way of life of a people. An integrated approach to WSS management raises a series of questions before one can think of what the approach should be. Some of the questions are:

i) What are the conditions and problems prevalent in a rural community with respect to WSS?

- the physical nature of the problems, cluster, linear, dispersed type of dwellings
- nature of the soil
- sources, adequacy, distance, and means of supply, storage and use of water
- size of population, its ethnic and class structure and social stratification
- sanitary conditions

ii) What is the present nature and level of WSS in the community?

iii) What is the community's perception of sanitation?

iv) What do they consider as insanitary?

v) The causes they attribute to insanitation?

vi) What is their level of awareness of insanitation?

vii) What have they done to improve sanitary condition?

viii) Assuming that the people are aware of sanitary problems, what are the reasons for their not alleviating the situation?

ix) How does the community organize and manage WSS?

x) What are the physical, economic, social, technological, organizational and managerial requirements to ensure a better/ satisfactory level of WSS?

xi) What are the kinds of resources available within the community?

xii) What are the kinds of resources that need come from outside?

xiii) What are the external agencies that are to provide/ facilitate with the requisite resources?

xiv) In what manner have the WSS activities been carried out by the development agencies thus far?

xv) What is the experience and attitude of the residents of the community vis-à-vis the WSS activities of the development agencies?

xvi) What is the level and nature of integration of WSS activities that obtains now?

xvii) What are the missing links? Where does the lacuna lie?

II. Keeping in view the ensuring of general health and welfare of the community through WSS, what kind of an integrated approach is necessary?

III. The elements in the integrated approach:

i) Physical:- housing, use of the precincts of the house, cattle shed, kitchen, backyard, disposal of waste, the environs, the source, supply, protection, adequacy and use of water, and its disposal.

ii) Technological: improvements/innovations and their maintenance in respect to WSS.

iii) Economic: the cost of improvement, maintenance, the local resources, the anticipated external support, the individual/community affordability

iv) Cultural: values attached to WSS, habits of people in the use of water, defecation and waste disposal, attitude towards environmental sanitation and level of tolerance to insanitary conditions.

v) Organizational: who will organize and manage the WSS activities at the community level? Who from external agencies?

IV. What should be integrated at the community level?

- needs
- interest
- initiative
- activities
- groups
- resources
- leadership

V. What is to be integrated at the external agencies level? How to integrate and the problems of coordination?

- programme planning
- programme implementation
- programme evaluation

VI. The suggested approach is a holistic, integral, composite one linking physical, technological and institutional components: housing – environs – water – sanitation – toilets – waste disposal – the user.

VII. The organization and management of WSS at the community level is dependent upon and influenced by the following aspects of the community:

i) Awareness

ii) Pressure of the need

iii) Resources – material, human

iv) Composition of the group

v) Size of the group

vi) Social structure

vii) Structure of power and authority

viii) Kind and strength of existing organizations / institutions in the community

ix) The kind and strength of local – institutional leadership

x) The degree of influence from outside the community

xi) Channels and pattern of inward and outward communication

xii) Cultural orientations, values, attitudes of people towards sanitation, use of water and maintenance

xiii) Economic level and affordability

xiv) Occupations and professions of the groups

In this context it may be relevant to briefly look into community organization the concept, objectives, benefits and some of the organizations at the rural community level. We may remember that an existing organization may be utilized for a specific new activity. An organized community, in terms of groups, institutions, functions and responsibility is a machinery that may be used for diverse purposes. It does not deny the need for a specific organization or special organizing for a specific activity. The thrust of the question is on organizing the community and revitalizing the existing institutional infrastructure at the rural community level.

I. COMMUNITY ORGANIZATION[1]

It is important for a worker to have a complete understanding about the community with which he works. By making a sociogram of the community, he can work out the pattern of communication and then understand who influences whom and to what extent. The question is often raised as to how best agency workers can assist the people in dealing with recalcitrant individuals and groups whose sole purpose is to block progress. This needs a careful examination and it brings us to the question of skills involved in working with groups and communities. The worker has to understand what exactly is the cause and the real cause may be different from what appears on the surface. The worker may have preconceived notions. He can look for the answer by studying the power structure within the community and the vested interests it upholds. It has also its processes such as decision-making, communication, social and cultural linkage and boundary maintenance. A social compass would provide valuable guidance to the extension worker and if he understands the elements and processes operating in it, he will very easily map out the interrelations of various factors. The components of the social compass comprising of such things as community, governmental structures, education, religion, family, social class, health, communication, etc., can be analyzed in terms of its elements and processes.

Community organization is a method by which an individual is influenced through the group in which he works. This group provides him the "fields" and it is by understanding the "field forces" that affiliations and alignments of individual members are identified and interpreted.

II. COMMUNITY CONCEPTS

The word community signifies different things to different people according to their interpretation. In some places ethnicity and religion may come to the mind whereas in other countries various social communities are mentioned. Community refers to a group of people inhabiting a given geographical area and having some kind of common activities or some degree of common life, irrespective of their social, religious or social differences. It is not confined to any of the various restricted fields of community life on the basis of religion, caste, race, language or profession but one that envelops the whole life of the whole community.

III. DEFINITION

Community organization has been defined as a process initiated to bring about and maintain an adjustment between social welfare needs and social welfare resources in a given geographical area. As a disciplined method "community organization seeks to bring about a social climate in which it is easier to resolve group conflicts and initiate cooperative activity for the common good of the community".

Community organization work concentrates its efforts in narrowing down the areas of conflict and enlarging the areas of cooperation. In short, the negative and destructive aspects of competition is sought to be replaced by the positive and constructive aspects of cooperation.

IV. CENTRAL OBJECTIVE

The objective of "community organization" as a method of social work activity is, one of helping the communities to recognize and realize their needs and aspirations. First, there has to be an awareness about their problems and secondly there must be willingness to work together towards these common objectives.

In any area, there will be problems of some sort and resources both in men and materials and "community organization" seeks to rouse the latter for the solution of the former. There is invariably a gap between what facilities a community has and what it would like to have, in other words, between achievements and aspiration. It is the task of "community organization" to narrow down and bridge this gap between social welfare needs and social welfare resources of a community.

V. SPECIFIC OBJECTIVES

(a) *To obtain consciousness of community:* For harmony and progress of the community, a sense of "we" feeling, a sense of belongingness is to be fostered among the members of a given community. Such a sense of "we" feeling and interrelatedness make the members feel that they constitute a unit by themselves, a social entity as distinct from other communities. Just as self-consciousness is essential for the individual so its importance to the community. The process of integration rests primarily upon definite self-consciousness of the community.

(b) *To Satisfy unmet needs:* Common needs which individuals and groups are unable to satisfy for themselves could be met by the collective action of the community. It may be in any sphere, political, economic, social or cultural. Collective action is the basis for community integration and community mobilization. Determination of the needs of the community is therefore one of the first steps.

(c) *To obtain social participation as a means to socialization:* The ultimate goal of all human association is the development of better personalities by the individuals concerned. A community is composed of various groups in which its people associate. One of the chief handicaps to community action is the number of families and individuals who do not belong to any formal organization, who live a relatively isolated social life associating with their own families and neighbours. The best index of the socialization of the members of a community is the degree of their participation in its organizations.

(d) *To obtain social control:* Community organization is to obtain social control through community spirit and loyalty. Social control becomes possible by the development of community spirit, by loyalty to the community and by symbols which express the common objective of community activity. Sociologists have called these three factors – morale, collective representations and *esprit de corps* (common spirit pervading the group).

(e) *To Coordinate groups and activities:* In a given community there may be several interest groups and their interests and activities may come in conflict. Community organization is necessary in order to prevent conflict and promote efficiency, cooperation and coordination. This is important in a small community. Proper adjustments are necessary. Efficiency may be promoted and ends attained if coordination can be carried out to the point of active cooperation.

(f) *To prevent the community from the introduction of undesirable influences and conditions:* It is not enough to promote community betterment from within, for the community must be able to defend itself from the aggression of undesirable influences. Many a community has found that it can work together for the elimination of a drinking place or any other nuisance to the physical and social health of the community.

(g) *To cooperate with other communities and agencies to obtain common needs:* Frequently, the community is too small a unit to achieve certain desired ends on its own. To obtain them, it is necessary to cooperate with neighbouring communities to obtain a bus line, water facilities, schools, colleges, etc.

(h) *To establish a means of obtaining consensus:* As for having their needs accomplished, it is easily done by coming to a common understanding. In a small rural community, it is obtained by gradual crystallization of public opinion through casual conversation at any shop or public place where people gather usually. Sometimes hearsay, gossiping distort the facts and promote disagreement rather than consensus.

(i) *To develop leadership:* Leadership for any group or collective activity is a must. Potential leaders in the community are to be identified, their talent recognized and developed. Local initiative and local leadership are essential for building up a self-reliant and self-confident community. It is not a question of spoon-feeding, the external agency alone functioning, but creating opportunities so that the local leadership is fully developed and employed for the growth of the community.

BENEFITS OF COMMUNITY ORGANIZATION

(a) Group thinking and common good,

(b) Division of labour and responsibility,

(c) Recognition of individual merit,

(d) Community work, and

(e) Group efforts are more effective than individual efforts.

A MEASURE OF COMMUNITY ORGANIZATION

Community organization should not be conceived as a

relationship which can be set up and which can be abolished. It is rather a process of establishing relationships which will always be in a state of becoming analogous to the growth of personality or character in the individual. One measure of community organization is the degree to which organizations and interests are willing to cooperate in activities or objectives for the betterment of the common welfare, for which they are not primarily responsible and in which others will take the lead.

Another measure is the ability to have competition in politics or business without conflict and the ability to discuss matters with a division of opinion but with tolerance and with united support for the objectives sought.

The degree of socialization of the community is the best measure of its organization. The better a community is organized the more it serves the needs not only of its adult individuals but also of its potential members.

It has been very well summarized that the goal of community organization is enlisting everyone in the community activities so that each individual shall register effectively, that is, shall achieve self-expression and status in community service.

From a behaviouristic standpoint the measure of community organization is the degree to which the members, individuals or groups of the community act collectively for common welfare.

Statutory and non-statutory organizations like Village Panchayats, cooperative societies, special interest groups like DWACRA, Self Help Groups, Vana Samrakshana Samithis, Vidya Committees, Water Users Associations, Water Shed Development Committees etc., constitute some organizations at the rural community level..

FACILITATING COMMUNITY ORGANISATON[2]

A generic description of the process of facilitating community organization in a population group is depicted in Fig.1. Each step in the critical pathway is needed for achieving stated objectives.

- Meeting population leaders: The critical entry point for the worker at which the process of confidence building begins.
- Gathering information (community diagnosis): Demographic, socio-cultural, topographic, and health data may all form a part of the information gathered. Information also serves to broaden dialogue and include women.
- Identifying existing structures: organizations capable of serving as vehicles of community development are identified and the worker seeks to strengthen, mobilize and coordinate them for the subsequent steps. Most communities present several candidate organizations, such as councils of elders, development committees, or saving and loan associations.
- Selecting priority problems: The worker assists the new organized group to agree on a set of problems of greatest importance to the population. Community diagnosis also helps to define these problems.
- Choosing one problem to work on: From the problem set the group selects the one to attach first of all. Usually the problem chosen will be the most pressing to the dominant faction or the most amenable to local solution.
- Informing the people about the problem: By means of explanation, demonstration, and auxiliary materials the workers and others seek to raise the

level of knowledge of, and sensitivity to, the problem and its ramifications.

- Assessing local resources: Money, labour, materials, and technical expertise may all be needed to adequately address the problem selected. The extent to which they can be obtained locally is ascertained.
- Setting staged objectives: The solution to the problem, whatever it may be, can usually be divided into several stages and to each attached a concrete objective, a time for achieving it, and a sense of what it takes in labour, materials, and expertise to reach it.
- Setting responsibilities and time schedules: The staged objectives, attached time frames, and resources requirements, are identified with individuals and groups within the population, to whom are given the responsibilities for execution.
- Implementation
- Evaluation: Achievements are matched against objectives. Problems are identified as well as success and used as platforms for launching a new critical pathway.

It may be noted that "with each successful organized community effort the cooperative and collaborative attitudes and practices of the community are broadened and deepened. Likewise, unsuccessful efforts have profound demoralizing effects".

THE GENERIC PROCESS OF FACILITATING COMMUNITY ORGANIZATON: A CRITICAL PATHWAY

Each step is necessary to achieve objectives

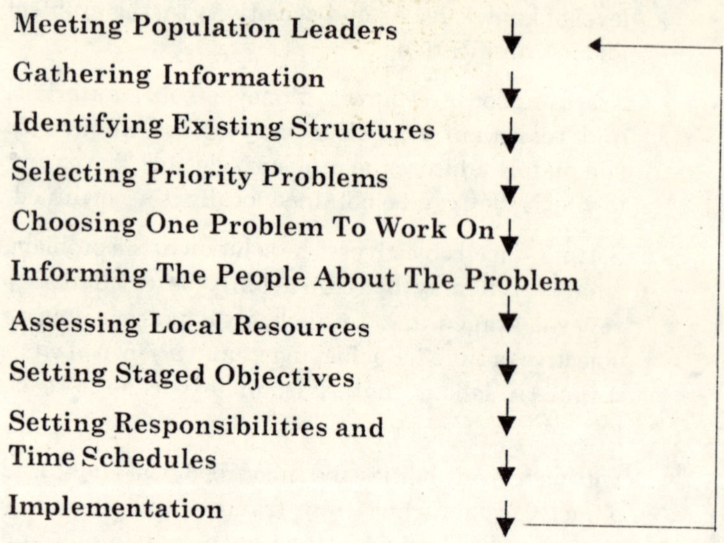

RATIONALE

The appropriateness of the community organization process to water and sanitation programmes resides in two conditions for the success of these programmes:

- If water supply and sanitation facilitates are to function properly they must be maintained and repaired in a timely and correct manner. Maintenance and repair can be assured in most rural communities of developing countries only by an organized and trained constituency.
- If the health and social benefits of improved water supply and sanitation facilities are to be obtained. then the population must participate in an organized way to properly use and protect water, and to incorporate essential personal and domestic hygiene associated with excreta disposal, food handling, and infant and child care.

MAINTENANCE AND REPAIR OF FACILITIES

The appalling rate of breakdown of water supply and sanitation facilities in rural areas of the developing world is well known. Few developing countries are able to provide sufficient numbers of maintenance personnel or the institutional and material support needed to maintain a widespread network of water supply and sanitary installations. Most water supply ministries are seriously hampered by shortages of trained personnel, lack of transport facilities, deficient material supplies and overly centralized organizations. Ministries of Health, the usual repositories of responsibility for sanitation, suffer even more in the usual case from these organizational maladies.

Responsibility must therefore, devolve upon communities themselves at least for the long-term maintenance and repair of facilities. Women must necessarily play important roles in this regard. The success of community maintenance programmes is dependent on how well communities are organized. Community organization is in turn conditioned by a number of other factors.

ACHIEVEMENT OF HEALTH AND SOCIAL BENEFITS

Even if the water supply is safe and in working order, and the excreta disposal facility properly installed, a host of behavioural factors may intervene to mitigate potential health and social benefits.

In the case of water supply, factors associated with water drawing, transport, and storage may bring about contamination of the source or the household supply. Even more importantly, use of excreta disposal facilities needs to be reinforced by personal hygiene: hand-washing, bathing, and washing and protecting food after preparation. A sustained approach to these matters depends on organization of supportive community structures, and networks of peer support for behavioural change.

CONDITIONS FOR SUCCESSFUL FACILITATION OF COMMUNITY ORGANIZATION

Ideally, community organization goes on without the influence of the worker or any other external assistance. In fact, population groups may quite properly be said to have their own intrinsic organization, i.e., the innate ability to deal with defined problems. Yet in practice normal social structures of many communities may have deteriorated and function very poorly at best when challenged with such matters as technological change. Colonial policy, leadership factors, urbanization, disease patterns, and traditional systems of assigning status have been cited among those correlated with variations in adaptive community behaviour.

For water and sanitation the conditions for successful facilitation of community organization need to be made more explicit. Four conditions appear relevant:

(a) Trained personnel

(b) Information about the community (community diagnosis)

(c) Integrated approaches among sectors

(d) Available technology and information

TRAINED PERSONNEL

Personnel need to be armed with skills of three types: diagnostic, supportive, and evaluative. Diagnostic skills relate to the ability to delineate the communities within populations that represent the main social units. Leadership, decision-making and communication patterns, as well as the physical, demographic, economic and health characteristics of the population should be assessed. The worker should be enabled to gather data that will be immediately useful in guiding his/her action without spending undue time or effort in doing so. In essence what a worker needs to know is how he/she can operate within the resources and constraints of a given community to generate optimum participation in the planning, installation, maintenance, and repair of water supply and sanitation facilities. The categories of what information is needed are explained below.

Supportive skills extend from establishing trust to guiding and facilitating group discussion, and providing continuous support and empathy to individuals and social structures until they become independently viable. We may think of a list a number of subsidiary supportive functions:

- Creation of favourable group settings for community leadership to emerge and develop.
- Reconciliation and mediation of conflict or potential conflict, where there is a threat to continuity to community organization.
- Maintaining contact between community structures and their progress on the one hand and external government or agency action on the other.
- Acting as a resource link for village and external resources.
- Knowledge and appropriate use of technical back-up resources.
- Assurance of a continuity of surveillance and monitoring of water and sanitation facilities.

Evaluation skills pertains particularly to understanding the relevance of programme evaluation to continuous programme improvement and effectiveness, and to stimulating the participation of the people of the community in the design and application of evaluative procedures as a means of developing greater commitment on their part to the programme. Community workers should also be able to do simple process evaluation of events, activities, and the characteristics of local participation as well as simple outcome evaluation of change in knowledge and behaviour.

INFORMATION ABOUT THE COMMUNITY

By means of simple observations and selected interviews the community worker should be able to gather a modicum of data sufficient to make the diagnosis of community capacity to participate mentioned earlier. Data items selected from the following categories should be incorporated into a simple instrument feasible for use by community workers.

i). Physical features of the community

   a. Topography

   b. Types of soil

   c. Water table

   d. Types and location of water sources

   e. Meteorological and climatic features

   f. Availability of natural resources

ii). Biologic features

   a. Water quality

   b. Common disease vectors

   c. Prevalent water and excreta-related diseases

iii). Economic features

   a. Assets

   b. Access to resources

   c. Liabilities

d. Economic infrastructure

iv). Demographic features

a. Distributions

b. Ethnic composition

v). Socio-cultural features

a. Beliefs about water and excreta

b. Water use

c. Excretion patterns

d. Local skills

e. Existing local organizations

f. Relationships to outside organization

g. Leadership patterns

h. Communication patterns

i. Decision-making patterns

j. Previous self-help experience

INTEGRATION OF APPROACH AMONG SECTORS

Specific reference to health workers has been deliberately avoided in the discussion above in order to emphasize the intersectoral nature of both water and sanitation programmes and the concern with facilitating community organization. Several sectors depend upon the success of community organization for the achievement of their objectives at the periphery of the population. Among them are agriculture, education, public works, and health. In a sense, facilitating community organization is the primary objective for each, more important in the long run than achieving any specific technical objective. If pumps are installed but break down, whom do they benefit? If latrines are constructed but are not maintained, who will use them? If a primary school is built but teachers refuse to live in the village, how will the children be taught? A feeder road constructed but not maintained may not result in increased access to markets. If one worker undermines or fails to contribute to the success of the community organization others may not be able to achieve their objectives. Workers need to be able to refer "felt-needs" from one organization to another to another and to feel a sense of accomplishment in success achieved outside their particular sector. Figure-2 illustrates these relationships. As depicted, the community organization process is at the centre. Each community level worker contributes to the process while making specific technical inputs.

These inputs need to be made at appropriate points in the process. The figure indicates that the community organization is a dynamic cyclical process. Each successfully completed project in fact enhances the ability of individuals and social structures to work together and strengthens local ability to analyze and solve problems. With each turn of the cycle, as it were, the capacity of the community to absorb new technical inputs and face new adaptive challenges increases.

Thus a community at one point may be able to successfully complete and maintain an open well with a bucket and pulley and though what was learned in both a technical and organizational sense, be able to move on later to the installation and maintenance of a handpump, or even later to the maintenance of a feeder road.

THE COMMUNITY ORGANIZATION PROCESS

CONTRIBUTIONS OF VARIOUS COMMUNITY LEVEL WORKERS

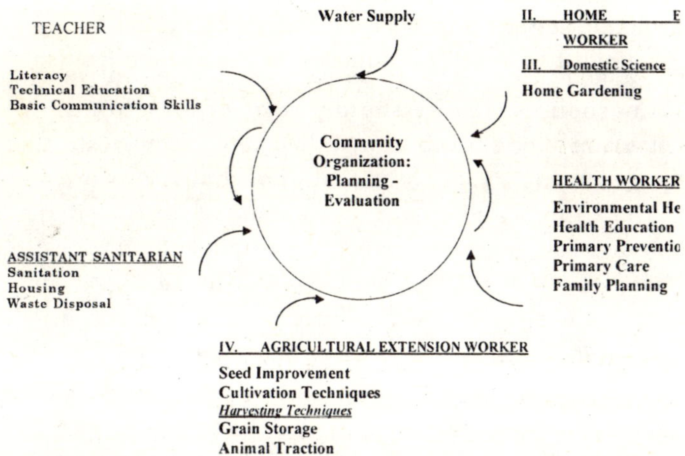

These interrelationships need to be operationalized in joint intersectoral policy-making, joint middle level management, and joint training programmes.

AVAILABLE TECHNOLOGY AND INFORMATION

If community organization is to issue in successfully installed and maintained water supply and sanitation facilities, then community members must have access to adequate and appropriate technology, and information on how to use it. Personnel in public education, public works, health, agricultural, and other services may be the purveyors of both technology and information. The results of community diagnosis should indicate which of available technologies are economically affordable, socially acceptable and technically maintainable for both water supply and sanitation. Careful analysis of previous local experiences of organized problem solving, particularly the most recent experiences will help to determine whether the information and technology introduced at a particular point in the community organization cycle can be absorbed and adapted by the local organization.

A good case in point is that of villages in the South Cameroon, which at the onset of efforts to stimulate community organization installed temporary protection of springs using strictly local materials, but later were able to commit funds and labour to a more permanent protection. The introduction of more sophisticated technology close on the heels of the initial success was a key strategy. An important element in this transfer of technology was the introduction of a technique of splitting rock. The project chauffeur, who had learned the technique on trips to another region of the country, taught the villagers how to pour cold water over a heated rock. This technique facilitated spring box construction.

Information on the use of the many varieties of water supply and sanitation technology is unfortunately in short supply. Most available manuals are written in English and use language and images too technical for practical use by community members. Needed are manuals generously illustrated with non-technical drawings and a minimum of written explanation.

Greater emphasis needs to be placed on the development of demonstration models.

OUTCOMES OF SUCCESSFUL FACILITATION OF COMMUNITY ORGANIZATION

Case histories drawn from Africa illustrate three major benefits of effectively stimulating or facilitating the local community organization process:

1. Reinforcement of local management capacities
2. Enhancement of participation

3. Increased probability of programme success

The first, taken from a village in the South Central Cameroon, illustrates the catalyzing effect or efforts to facilitate community organization on local ability to manage water and sanitation facilities. This village with about 1500 inhabitants in five hamlets, was one of four selected as pilot villages in the AID/OCEAC Public Health Training Project (1972-76). Four years prior to the onset of the project, this village had experienced a remarkable reversal of what had been a deteriorating relationship between the older and younger generations. Through the establishment of dialogue between the generations on a number of important issues, a reconciliation took place which the Project inherited.

A village health committee took shape readily in the central hamlet. Despite having no technical experiences with the protection of springs or the construction of latrines, the committee was able to organize the temporary protection of one spring and the construction of over 40 properly covered pit latrines. Later the spring was protected in a permanent manner, and plans were laid for pumping water from the spring to an elevated reservoir and thence by gravity to a community standpipe. In all, 43 pit latrines were constructed (out of 50 households) and in use. At a later date, the committee had calculated the costs of putting in similar systems in the other hamlets. The health committee had become a community water and sanitation planning board.

A second South Cameroon village presented in 1972 a distressing picture of a predominantly/dependent population (elderly or very young), widespread endemic disease, and virtual absence of water source protection or excreta disposal installations. Leadership was confined to the hands of a few clan leaders surrounding a rather weak elderly traditional chief.

Community leaders agreed to form a health committee, but spring protection and latrine construction progressed little beyond the talking stage, except for a single pit latrine at a clan leader's.

The committee, however, provided a forum in which many others besides village elders participated. Discussions of issues surrounding environmental protection, direct health education presentations, and the baseline medico-social survey, exposed many, including women and youth to new technology and new information. In the second year of the project, with continued efforts to strengthen the committee, other latrines began to appear and protection of four springs moved ahead apace. Facilitation of community organization had a salutary effect on both the characteristics and the extent of participation.

We may think of a framework for analyzing participation as an impact of the community organization process described above. In simplest terms, this framework cossets of two parts: (1) the *dimensions* of participation in terms of what it consists of, who participates and the characteristics (the how) of participation; and (2) the *context* of participation, comprising characteristics of both the *project* and the environment in which the project is implemented.

One could be sure of a steady reduction in the prevalence of intestinal parasites as community leaders took hold of the long-term management of latrine construction and use, albeit and the incentive of periodic vermifuges played an important role. In the same Cameroonian village reported earlier community leaders on the basis of their success with the management of the water supply, took advantage of a change in Cameroonian land tenure laws that allows for optional individual or communal ownership of land, to develop a community-wide landholding. The Malawi enhancement of organization at the community level was prelude to a successful long-term maintenance programme.

Thus whether one is speaking of health or social benefits or simply the proper functioning and use of water and sanitation facilities, improved organization at the community level appears to be an essential ingredient in the mix.

CONCLUSION

Experience to date points, therefore, to community organization and to whatever can be done to stimulate and enhance this process intrinsic to local population groups, as an imperative to the success of water supply and sanitation programmes among most rural populations of developing countries. Organized individuals and social structures appear to be essential for both the proper function of facilities and the achievement of health and social benefits. Certain conditions, however, are needed for facilitation of the process: *personnel* trained in community diagnostic supportive, and evaluative skills, *information* about the community to guide facilitation, integration of approach among services standing to benefit from successful community organization, and *technology and information* the continuous cycle of local development. Finally, successful facilitation of community organization produces in practice certain benefits: improved local management of water and sanitation facilities, enhanced participation by community members, and increased probability of project success in both an operational and an outcome sense.

REFERENCES

1. Setty, E.D. 1970, Community Development and Extension in India", Gandhigram Rural Institute, Gandhigram, South India.

2. WASH Technical Report No. 7, June 1981, WASH Coordination and Information Centre, 1611, N. Kent Street, Room 1002, Arlington, VA 2209, USA.

16

CLINICAL APPROACH TO DEVELOPMENT

In the Clinical Approach to Development, we bring in the analogy of medical treatment, the way the physician tries to know from the patient what his problem is and he on his own tries to diagnose the nature of the ailment or the disease and the cause for it and starts prescribing treatment and follows it up. Here the physician pays individual attention to the patient, sometimes it may be a preventive measure or a curative thing. Similarly in view of the complex and varied development needs in the rural communities what is desirable and pragmatic is clinical approach in understanding the needs and the problems of every segment in the population. Then depending on the resources available at the disposal of the administration and the technology that could be used in development programmes and the resources at the disposal of the people, the areas in which they can mobilize and their readiness for the programme development action may be initiated. In the case of a patient and physician neither the physician tells the patient the formula of his treatment nor seldom the patient asks the physician the chemical content of the medicine he has prescribed. Here the patient is a mute receiver of treatment and largely dependent on the physician but where as in the case of any kind of improvement or development in rural areas, the people have a right to know and need to know the details and advantages and the limitations of any development programme introduced by the development agency. Very often we assume the needs and the problems of people and without taking into account the views and suggestions from the people who move into action. Sometimes the assumed needs or problems of the people may be right but in the psychological sense there is a need to give an opportunity to the people to share their ideas, views, suggestions so that they will have a feeling that they are partners in development.

We find three methods used in development programmes (1) Suggestive, (2) Prescriptive and (3) Directive'. In the suggestive method of development, the change (the villager) has the opportunity to reflect upon the measures suggested, weighs each one and opts or chooses some or all for action. Here you give an opportunity to the changee to reflect over the possible course of action he would choose depending on his interest, his resources and the kind of improvement that he anticipates in him, in his family and the community.

In the Prescriptive Method, the individual or the community may have some alternatives and options for improvement in the case of the individual, family or community. Though prescriptive sounds rather fixed yet one may have some options within the ambit of prescriptive things. But difficulty arises when the development agency gives directives for a particular activity to the people which we may call as Directed Development.

Development cannot be mechanical, it needs human touch. May be the development agency has everything, it could meet all the requirements of the largest population but there is a need to create a sense of achievement on the part of the beneficiary that they have accomplished things. It is not that easy and it depends on the change agents and development administration.

Whether it is a rural community or any larger society, each is a unit target for improvement / development. The emphasis here is on creating in a realistic way an atmosphere or an environment wherein the individuals in the community feel that they have been consulted with, and they had an opportunity of sharing their ideas for the way in which the segments in the community or the whole community are to be developed. Over a period of time, the development agency has to draw people closure and move closure to the people and create a sense among the people that they are the ones who came forward with assistance to the development agency. Development here is not mere physical or material development but it is to be a simultaneous development of the human individuals and the material / physical development. One may lay roads, one may bring in power, one may extend financial assistance, introduce new technology, but in all these endeavours the human individual is not to be neglected and forgotten. The human individual is to be No.1 rest of the things may be either numerals or zeros.

One could observe during the past half a century the multiple development agencies have with all eagerness and intention and commitment initiated a score of rural development programmes embracing a large number of needs and problems assuring the people that they would meet all these needs and solve the problems faced by the people. This kind of continued and periodic assurances by the administration at higher and lower levels has created what is called a 'Cargo Cult". Usually most of the communities have been managing their problems and meeting their needs at their level. With the advent of programmes for rural development, sometimes with over enthusiasm we have increased the expectations on the part of the people. And today, they look toward the government to fulfil the needs or solve the problems which they could solve by themselves.

Here we try to emphasise the psychology of expectations on the part of the people. Though, we have initiated and announced several development programmes, we have not been able to fulfil a large number of them. But there is a need to educate the people at every level that the communities simply cannot totally depend on the government machinery to meet their needs and solve their problems. The administration through the change agents operating at every level may have to remedy this expectation psychology on the part of the people. In this context, close and personalized contact with the people and the leaders appraising them the limitations in meeting most of the expectations of the people which they themselves could have met with and solve is necessary. Here it is to be emphasized that the dependency syndrome is to be gradually reduced, of course, over a period of time. This could happen when the general community needs are met with like water, transport, communication, power, finance. Then the dependency will get reduced over a period of time. The government may have to work towards self-reliance on the part of the community. This self-reliance encompasses local leadership, advanced technology and every element that contributes to the advancement of rural communities. In this context, clinical approach is quite relevant. We will have to get down to the people establishing rapport with them, appraise them the possibilities and the limitations to development.

Keeping this in view that there is a psychological and pragmatic need to adopt clinical approach to development, irrespective of unit of development whether it is the individual, the family, the community or the larger society. The present work details the factors and the approach that matter in the Clinical Approach to Rural Development.

17

FIELD APPRAOCH TO INTEGRATED RURAL DEVELOPMENT

Before, we look into what is called Integrated Rural Development, it is in order to briefly describe as to what constitutes rural development in a comprehensive sense.

Rural development, in general, is a strategy designed to improve the economic and social life of people in a rural settlement and, in particular, it focuses on the rural poor comprising the small-scale farmers, tenants and the landless. Since rural development is intended to reduce poverty, it must be clearly designed to increase production and raise productivity.

Rural development recognizes, however, that improved food supplies and nutrition, together with basic services such as health and education, cannot only directly improve the physical well-being and quality of life of the rural poor, but can also indirectly enhance their productivity and their ability to contribute to the national economy. It is concerned with the modernization and monetization of rural society, and with its transition from traditional isolation to integration with the national economy (World Bank, 1975).

The objectives of rural development, therefore, extend beyond any particular sector. They encompass improved productivity and increased employment, and thus, higher incomes for target groups, as well as minimum acceptable levels of food, shelter, education and health.

Rural development, in a comprehensive sense, is a process of social action in which the people of a community organize themselves for planning and action, define their common and individual needs and problems make group and individual plans to meet their needs and solve their problems, execute these plans with maximum of reliance upon community resources, and supplement these resources, when necessary, with services and material from governmental and non-governmental agencies outside the community. Thus, we see that rural development is focused on the development of the people. It is a dynamic, unified problem-solving approach and the education of the people could be said to be one of the end products of rural development. It is recognized as a social process of directed change.

Further, the essentials of the rural development process are the stimulation of local initiative, location and development of local leadership, and fuller utilization of local resources. In addition to these, self-help and self-reliance, sustained interest and co-operation are other aspects of significance in the concept of rural development. The thrust in rural development is people's participation in the total process and in the entire gamut of rural development, and simultaneous development of people, their conditions and quality of life.

Integrated Rural Development, though connotationally sounds comprehensive, operationally it aims at redressing and alleviating the problems of the poorer segments of the rural population. In the series of approaches, strategies and methods towards rural development during the past five decades, the IRD, is the latest and believed to be a near effective approach in bettering the lot of the rural poor and yet it suffers from some drawbacks and shortcomings at the community-operational level. Also the concept of integrating and mobilizing the material and human resources at the community level is wanting.

The essay looks into the drawbacks in IRD, as it is operated today and focuses on the field forces at the rural community level and recommends what is called a Field Approach towards integrating, mobilizing, harnessing and utilizing the resources within the community for its development.

One of the exciting and serious features in the past five decades in all the developing countries was their concerted efforts towards Rural Community Development ideology, objectives, programmes, organizational structure and methodology of work; and the objective has been singular and specific: to develop rural communities and better the life of rural people. Rural development in developing countries is assuming a new and critical importance as it becomes apparent that the development process to date, impressive though some results may be, has not succeeded in narrowing the gap between the rich and the poor nations. Equally important, it has not narrowed the gap between the rich and the poor within nations. Although millions of fortunate people have been able to leap across this gap, hundreds of millions still remain on the poor side and their numbers are increasing both absolutely and proportionally. Some of the rural development efforts in terms of political tones, economic objectives, organizational process, plan formulation and programme implementation are a new kind of experiences for the people and the development agencies. We are in the process of finding, learning, new and better ways of doing things. There is always a need to look back and take stock of things, so that we can have a clearer perspective of the situation, avoid the pitfalls, overcome the barriers and discover effective approaches and alternatives toward substantial and sustained development in rural areas.

A quick evaluation of programmes towards village development in the developing countries under diverse nomenclature, viz., Rural Development, Community Development, Rural Reconstruction, Rural Welfare, Social Welfare, Tribal Development and the latest label, Integrated Rural Development (IRD), suffer from certain drawbacks. Some programmes are too general, too much diluted, too inadequate in the context of local needs and problems, too narrow, segmental, isolated, more often externally initiated and supported, poorly followed up and sustained. But none can deny, the significant contribution of rural development in terms of planning, formulation and implementation of developmental programmes, organizational set-up, training of personnel, strategies and methods adopted and results achieved. Yet looking at the IRD today and the other related programmes, in the real sense of rural development, we cannot fail to take note of the following limitations:

1. In view of the focus of IRD on the weaker sections of the community, the total community is not actively involved in the developmental process. The IRD is a desirable remedial measure, and in the real spirit of rural development, the total community should be the unit and target of development. All segments in the community should have an opportunity for growth and development.
2. The programme has not fully harnessed and utilized the material and human resources of the community.
3. It has failed relatively speaking, to study and integrate the several sub-systems in the community for a unified social action.
4. It fell short of overcoming the barriers to change and making use of stimulants to development.

5. It aroused great expectations and hopes among people, and lost sight of community mobilization and organization and increased dependency of the people on the development agencies.

6. Though as an ideal, the programme was to be a people's programme with government's participation, it remains largely a government-administered programme with people's participation. Of course, no single agency operating in the field is responsible for this drawback. The complementary role of the people and the government agency has to be realized in the operation of the IRDP. Hence, attempts by all the agencies concerned in changing their approach to their programmes both by governmental agencies on the one hand and the people and their representatives on the other, are necessary.

7. The programme has laid much emphasis on achievements of targets and less in following the right means, methods and process to bring about change in the attitudes of the people.

8. Lack of uniformity in understanding the concept of IRD and the role of personnel at all levels from village to the national level.

9. Lack of integration of segments, interests and needs at the community action-level.

Against the background of experiences gained through success and failure of the IRD programme and based on some of the drawbacks mentioned above, what is ideal and desirable is the Field Approach (total systems approach), wherein the local community or a cluster of communities is the unit and target of action and development.

FIELD APPROACH TO INTEGRATED RURAL DEVELOPMENT

The local community has certain levels of integration and social and territorial affinity. The individual in the community, his network of relationships, his attitudes and group norms are to be reckoned with. It is assumed and it is to a greater extent true, that each community has forces operating in it which thwart or promote change and development. Rural development cannot be thought of in isolation. For effective and enduring development of the community, the whole community as a general system and the several inter-related, mutually inter-dependent and influencing sub-systems within the general system, should constitute the field. The approach to the development of the community is the Field Approach or a total systems approach. It is more germane at the community action-level.

Field Approach does not ignore the individual or selective approach. It is employed to see that all relevant forces, positive and negative, that influence and act on a course of action, a programme, a segment or a social stratum of development are located, thoroughly studied, understood and manipulated successfully. This approach requires an understanding of the clientele community.

ASPECTS OF THE COMMUNITY TO BE STUDIED

In the Field Approach we take the entire community, be it a village, cluster of villages, a mandal, an occupational or a professional group, as a unit of action. We study all aspects of the client system, physical, economic, human resources, cultural patterns, social, political and ecclesiastical structure, local institutions and institutional leadership. The study of the client system precedes the programmes related to community development. The data that are already available in respect to a unit of action will be made use of. The gaps in the aspects of the clientele group will have to be studied afresh.

The major aspects to be studied of a client group are described briefly below.

PHYSICAL CONDITIONS

This includes the physical resources that the area is endowed with, such as rainfall, terrain, quality of soil, the kind of farm activities that are in practice and enterprises that can be undertaken in the locality. This part of the study subsumes the natural resources survey, as to how the people in the area have interacted with the given resources such as agricultural, horticultural, mineral, forest, marine in the past; the resultant economic and industrial activities of the people and related skills the people are proficient in. It will give us an idea of the on-going activities, skills, attitudes, preferences on the part of the people and the kind of economic activities that need modernization and innovative enterprises that could be introduced in the area.

ECONOMIC STRUCTURE OF THE COMMUNITY

In the economic field, we study the types of production within the community; the organization or producing units, capital and labour resources, the ratio in which labour and capital resources are used, occupational structure, the functioning of the local marketing system, farm organization and land tenure. In this area, we also study the network of economic relationships the community has with the outside world.

HUMAN RESOURCES

Usually the local community surveys or techno-economic surveys undertaken by different agencies connected with economic and industrial development pay meager attention to human resources. The requisite emphasis on human resources has not been there. The focus has been on economic resources and the potential thereof, and not on the man and the group behind him. In the Field Approach man or the human resource is in the center. Man is the starting point. Under the human resources, we go in for a census enumeration of literate population, skilled workers, technically qualified people, educated unemployed and various native skills available in the community. Another human resource is the leadership in the client group which is to be studied, promoted and utilized for introducing changes in the community.

CULTURAL PATTERNS

A community or a social group has a history, a value system and a tradition in terms of its occupation and or profession and choices or preferences for economic activities. Individuals in the group when intend to or motivated to take to some new activity, look for sanction and support from within the group. And so, in tho Field Approach we make a historical analysis of the community and the patterns of diffusion and change. We look for the direction and trend of change taking place in the community. This understanding of the cultural patterns of the group lends insight into the group's ethos and it will serve as a lead for further action in the field of rural development.

A study of the cultural patterns of the community takes us to the other intimately associated aspect – its social structure. In the social context of the rural communities, pursuit of economic or entrepreneurial activities cease to be purely an individual's affair. Here it is the group's choice. Hence, the need for understanding the social structure of the group, the network of relationship between various sub-groups and institutions, and the dynamics of the group's influence over the individual and vice-versa.

In the social structure of the community we study the various constituents and the institutions in it. We may begin with the basic constituent of the society – the family, its structure, the decision-making process in the family, functional aspects of the family, and the typology of the families based on occupation and division of functions. Around the family is the kin-group with a set of consanguineous and affinal kin shaping and influencing the individual's decision making and behaviour. We study the kin-group in the client community, its structure and functions; intra-clan, inter-clan, and inter-ethnic relationships and the role of certain kin in kinship circles.

Caste, tribal and ethnic councils are significant and viable social institutions. Despite the influence of Christianity, western styles of life and new politico-administrative institutions among certain tribal groups at the village-community level, the tribal councils still continue to be significant and functional in the life of a tribe. In respect to caste-groups, we find a high incidence of caste councils among the so-called lower castes. These are village or settlement based and community based in a region. Though caste councils are sporadic among middle-ranking and higher castes, we find among some of them, formal caste associations at town, district and regional levels. These caste or religious associations are a kind of foundations to promote the education of the children and other welfare activities of the group. Wherever the caste-tribal councils obtain, whatever may be their strength and influence over the individual and group today, they are to be reckoned with as factors of influence, positive and negative. Further, ethnic groups in a multi-ethnic community maintain or enjoy certain social balance, a particular ethnic group being predominant over the other, a group dependent on another for leadership and guidance or a group blocking changes or progress in the other. In the context of developing countries, in the rural tribal settings, inter-ethnic relationships matter while attempting planned changes among them. This takes us to the study of caste-ethnic council, its constitution and functions, the role and influence of the chief of the council, the council's influence over its members, and the degree of their dependence on the council in matters economic and social. Further, we study the nexus of relationship among different ethnic groups in a community.

The traditional village council (non-statutory) is another ancient social institution still in vogue in most villages. It chiefly deals with village affairs, celebration of local deities, sundry civil and criminal issues and divorce cases. The office of the chief of the traditional village council is either hereditary or elected. Despite the advent of statutory village council, the traditional one still enjoys status and influence over the local community. It is also to be studied and it leadership utilized for community development.

Besides the traditional institutions referred to above, there are the modern associate or feeder organizations viz., Farmers' Forum, Youth Club and Women's Club which do matter as sources of influence, guidance and leadership in the rural development programmes.

While studying the social structure of the client community we may also take into account the sacred institutions in the community – the temple, church, mosque and the sacred specialists or the religious leaders associated with the sacred institutions. Though the sacred specialists' domain is religious/spiritual, they are significant people in the community. The community developer may work through them to clear the way and secure sanction and support for the potential changes to go about their enterprises.

Further, the schoolteacher, considered a friend, guide and philosopher to the local folk, is also a force to be reckoned with and he plays the role of catalyst and his services may be utilized in the programme. The local medical practitioner too sometimes acts as a source of influence for the programme.

Rural development, or introducing of any change in the client group depends on the political leadership, power structure and the politico-administrative institutions at the village, mandal and district levels. In other words, it has a bearing on the initiative, lead and encouragement given by the local leaders. Under the political structure, we study the leadership patterns in the community. At the village level, we can think of five different kinds of leaders. (1). Hereditary leaders such as village officials; (2) Functional leaders who matter in specific areas; (3) Sectional leaders who represent a class, a caste, an ethnic or religious group, a neighbourhood or a locality; (4) Elected leaders of the statutory bodies and co-operative societies and (5) Professional leaders who are from outside the community, officials of different developmental agencies operating at the village level. In the Field Approach one identifies the different kinds of leaders in the community and works through them towards rural development. Whenever the existing leadership is inadequate for promotional activity, new leadership and new organizations are to be developed. It may be noted here that a person with a potential for change in the community may tend to look for some nodding approval and encouragement from the people whom he considers significant in the group.

If the potential changee is convinced of his project or enterprise and if he can venture into action on his own, we need not bother about his environment and referent groups. But, the situation in the rural and tribal areas is not so. Even if he is sure of his project and ready to take the risk and thinks that he could manage his enterprise, he has sometimes an obligation to seek the opinion and secure the approval from the significant members in the group. And so, the community developer enters the client system through the local leaders, exposes to them the idea and prospects of some new activity, tries to convince them so that either they encourage the potential changes to go ahead with their ventures or do not stand in their way of movement. There is every likelihood of the local leaders sometimes playing a negative role.

UTILIZATION OF LOCAL INSTITUTIONS FOR RURAL DEVELOPMENT

One of the several factors that contributes to rural development is the utilization of local institutions. The development here, may relate to improvement or bettering of conditions in the areas of health, education, economic or entrepreneurial development or it may relate to any aspect of community welfare. Until now more emphasis has been laid on finances, planning and implementation mostly from the change agency's side. In developing a given community, we may have to look for the human resources available within the community.

The focus here is on the institutions within a given community – the understanding of the structure and the functions of these institutions and how best the institutions could be utilized for the development of the client community. It is interesting to think for a moment how a society has emerged over a period of time and how it functions at a given point of time. Society is a social unit; it is a web or network of relationships. On one hand society in one sense consists of individuals as aggregate units and on the other hand, it speaks of the network of enduring relationships that exist among these discrete individuals. A society consisting of individuals and a network of relationships has devised certain ways and means for meeting the individual and the collective needs and wants of the group. Institutions in the sociological sense are patterns of behaviour often accumulated over generations. These patterned ways of living or institutionalized ways of behaviour meet the physical, biological, social and psychological needs of people. People in a given society in order to meet the multifarious needs have developed and develop certain ways and means. The norms in the group over a period of time get established as enduring patters of living. These institutions are the guidelines or the patterned ways which facilitate the life of the group. The institutions are lubricants of human collectivity.

The individual is developed by the group and it is the individual who forms the group. Every man is bound into a family and belongs to a family throughout his life. An individual is a member of several groups at a given point of time, member in the family, in the office, in a club, in friendship circle, member in a political party and thus we may find that an individual is a member of several such groups at a given point of time. A man becomes a group member without deliberations or he joins a group by choice or he is forced to be a group member in some situations.

An individual influences and is influenced by several groups. He is held by several institutions and is obligated to several groups or associations. It is the institutions which guide, promote or protect the interests of the individual and the group. In a given community, we may come across different types of institutions and groups. They are: family, race, sex and age-groups, various nationalities, political, economic, occupations, artistic, ethnical, religious, educational, scientific, philosophical, philanthropical, recreational and other groups, cliques, factions and so on. One such resource that could be utilized to introduce and sustain any kind of change is the network of local institutions. Whatever may be the development aspect, the local institutions and the institutional leadership could be utilized for bringing about desirable changes in the client community. We may briefly look into some of the institutions under different heads.

ECONOMIC INSTITUTIONS

Under the economic institutions, we may take into account all organized or institutionalized ways of production, exchange and consumption. When we go down to the rural areas we can think of the village cooperative, the village market, the professional moneylender, banks, labour unions, etc.

SOCIAL INSTITUTIONS

Under social institutions, we may think of the family, the kinship circle, the caste, the tribe and various sects among the castes and tribes. Under religious institutions we may think of the church, the temple, the mosque and other religious organizations which have some enduring influence on the behaviour of people. Similarly, under educational institutions, we may think of school, college or university or any such educational institute. We may likewise think of different associations or organizations which are related to recreational, political and other aspects of life.

Associated with every institute or organization is the leadership behind it. It is these institutions and institutional leadership that regulate or govern the life of people in a given community.

The whole attempt in rural development is to introduce something new in the life of the people or bring about some modification in the ways of people. It amounts to a basic process of introducing change and people accepting the change and the change that is introduced is expected to be sustained and internalized by the individual and the group. An individual as target of the change process may react in two ways. Either he responds to the change proposed or rejects it. The individual or the given local community has learnt to live certain patterns of life over a period of time and has tried to maintain an equilibrium however inadequate it is. Once it is used to a particular pattern of life it will have the tendency to continue the status quo. Anything new that is attempted will be a disturbing or threatening factor to the individual or to the group.

In view of the ways in which an individual has been socialized in group-living as a part of the culture, he is obligated to several individuals in decision-making or in his accepting a new idea or an innovation. Whether it is a question of change in dress, food, a new practice, a school or career, shifting from one area to another, whatever may be the activity, the individual does not always decide for himself and he depends on several individuals within the family, within the kinship circle and within the community. Even when he is convinced of the change suggested to him by the change agency, he seeks the approval or the support of the people within his social sphere. Unless we influence his social environment, secure him the support that he is looking for, it would be difficult for him to accept the change. On the other hand, the power to influence people in decision-making or in modifying their behaviour whether this power is of legitimate authority or power of influence or power through coercion, it is the institutional leaders in a given community who function as gate-keepers and regulators of the group ethos. It is imperative on the part of the change agent to have a clearer understanding of the local institutions and the institutional leadership behind these institutions. He may have to work through these institutions and institutional leaders in order to introduce a change and make the change adopted and sustained by the group.

In sum, it may be observed here, that institutions and organizations in the community may or may not have a direct bearing on or a functional relationship to an economic or social activity in question. The tribal council, the caste/ethnic council, the religious institutions, for example, deal mostly with social aspects of the community, but as traditional and deeply rooted institutions, they influence and control behaviour of people. The change agent tries to make use of these existing institutions and customs to communicate to the people. The leadership in all spheres of communal activity will be utilized to bring about desirable changes in the client community.

BARRIERS AND STIMULANTS TO CHANGE

Rural development sometimes involves a basic complex change. It is met with different kinds of resistance and so it leads us to identify the barriers *(areas of resistance)* and stimulants (*promotional factors*) to change.

Foster, discusses at length the different kinds of barriers and stimulants to change. All societies are constantly in a state of relative tension. Each society can be thought of as a host to two kinds of forces – those that seek to promote change, and those that strike to maintain the status quo. These forces are locked in perpetual combat, the former trying to throw the latter off balance in order to gain ascendancy and the latter trying to prevent this from happening.

It is necessary on the part of the rural development agency to identify the areas of resistance and the factors that contribute to change.

We can think of three kinds of barriers – cultural, social and psychological. These are interrelated in any community. Here, basically we go in for an understanding of the value system of the client community, the factors that inhibit or promote change. On identifying the barriers we work towards loosening their grip over the potential changes, simultaneously using the positive factors available from within the client group.

Despite barriers, changes do take place in all spheres of life – religious, political, ideological, economic and social. When a group is faced with the prospect of change, there exists a balance of forces. On one side of the scale are those forces which are against changes, viz., conservatism, apathy, fear and the like; on the other side are the forces for change such as dissatisfaction with the existing conditions, pride of new occupation, profession, new status or economic and social benefits that are anticipated in the new activity. Successful rural development consists largely of choosing those enterprises where the balance is almost even and then trying to lighten the forces against changes or to increase the factors that promote change.

Some of the positive factors that could be used for inducing change are motivating people to change through education and demonstration of the usefulness of the new activity, working on the desire of clients for economic gain and prestige, making use of a competitive situation obtaining in the client group, using the positive forces of authority, and timing and sequencing the programmes in such a way that the total effort and process results in rural development.

One crucial factor in working with local groups is their value system. The change agent needs to have a knowledge of the dominant values in the culture of the group, and working through these values, gradually bring about desirable changes in the group. The two constants to community wide changes are the groups identity while making changes in their value system. It may be noted here that an important value of a local ethnic group is: "What they want to be"?

Another important factor that is to be taken into account in our approach to bring about development in a community is to know what agencies have worked so far with them, what programmes have been attempted, and with what results. This leads us to an understanding of the community's perception, attitude and experience of the agencies and developmental programmes. For instance, rural development agencies, Christian missionaries and several voluntary organizations have been working with local/ethnic groups for their development for some time now. An understanding of the group's reactions and experiences vis-à-vis the development or change agencies, whatever may be their sphere of activity, will give us an insight into their problems.

This will help us formulate our strategy in a manner that will make the process of change smooth and gradual.

Social change relating to rural development is a complex phenomenon. It requires an integrated approach and a sustained effort on the part of organizations that work towards rural development.

FACTORS CONTRIBUTING TO RURAL DEVELOPMENT :

In the foregoing discussion of Field Approach to IRD, the focus and emphasis has been on the understanding of the client group and using the physical, economic and social resources for its development. But when we look at the entire gamut of rural development in terms of an action programme, we find four factors, significantly contributing to it. They are: (1) Resources – material and human, (2) Organizations concerned with rural development, (3) Infrastructure and (4) the people. We may call them four factors of rural development, which are briefly examined below:

RESOURCES

The resources of a client community are of two kinds: material and human. The material side consists of the natural resources, primary and secondary that the community is endowed with viz., agricultural, horticultural, mineral, forest, marine, textile, animal, etc. Here we examine how a given community living in a region has interacted with the resources it is endowed with and the kind of economic and industrial activities and the associated skills that are generated as a result of people's interaction with the resources. This will give us an idea of the enterprises that the people in the area carry on with, and which have become a part of their culture. Based on the on-going economic activities we can demarcate the enterprises that need modernization and the areas in which innovations can be introduced based on the available resources. Here we move from the familiar (to the people) to the unfamiliar but associated entrepreneurial activities. The usual techno-economic surveys or industrial potential surveys take care of this aspect of the resource.

The human resources chiefly consist of the literacy among the clients, the technically qualified and skilled people, the kind of leadership available in the group and the economic and social institutions that could be utilized to bring about a marriage between the material and human resources. What is envisaged here is that the rural development agency should examine the potentialities of the material resources, in what manner they could be developed, both traditional and innovative, making use of the human material available in the target community.

Speaking of natural resources we may think of a particular resource, how it is being utilized in a given area, in how many ways and how the same resource is utilized or processed in another area or what kind of industries are based on a particular resource. Let us take for example coconut. It is cultivated in abundance in Assam, but is chiefly used as a food article as it is, and for ritual, ceremonial purposes, whereas the same coconut is used in over hundred different ways in Kerala. Coconut constitutes a base in Kerala's economy. Similarly, bamboo is used in multiple ways for handicrafts in Tripura but its economic and industrial use elsewhere is limited to a couple of utilities. Another example is the abundant cultivation of ginger in Mizoram but a total absence of any industry based on this product in the state.

It may be mentioned here that it is the responsibility of the rural development agency to assess the resources available in the area, the possible industrial uses they could be exploited for and the kind of technology and infrastructure required for the newer uses of a resource and thus guide the potential entrepreneur and his group.

ORGANIZATIONS

Several organizations or institutions figure in the realm of rural development. These are governmental, quasi-governmental and voluntary organizations. Based on the way the organizations are related to rural development, the degree of functional responsibility held by them and their closeness to the rural development activities, they may be categorized into three groups.

The first group of organizations have a primary function and a direct responsibility in rural development. They are chiefly organizations or departments connected with agriculture, animal husbandry, forestry, horticulture, sericulture, pisciculture, small and cottage industrial development, minor irrigation, health, sanitation and medical care, primary and adult education and local self-government. The primary set of organizations are basic and are supposed to carry on stimulatory, supportive and sustaining kind of activities in respect to rural development. They are to do the primary job of bringing in changes and enrichment in their respective fields. More of emphasis is needed on the stimulatory activity in generating awareness and a climate for change.

The second group of organizations which may be called secondary comprises different corporations or agencies of finance, marketing, infrastructure and raw materials and banking institutions which mostly carry on supportive and sustaining kind of activities in RD. These secondary set of organizations are partly connected with rural development activities.

We may call the third group of organizations as tertiary which are indirectly or remotely connected with rural development – departments of public works, highways, transport, communications, power, etc. Though these departments or agencies are not directly connected with rural development, any improvement or expansion in them contributes to rural development. The secondary and tertiary agencies are the sources, feeder and supportive agencies which generate the potential and scope for rural development.

The categorization of organizations into three groups is rather arbitrary and the situation may differ from country to country. There is an imperative need to build up functional linkages amongst these three sets of organizations at the state, district, mandal and down to the village level which should facilitate rapid rural development.

INFRASTRUCTURE

We mostly relate infrastructure to physical facilities such as land, site, building, power, water, transport and communication for starting any farm or non-farm activity. But we may think of two kinds of infrastructure for developing communities. They are: (1) Physical and economic infrastructure and (2) The social infrastructure. The first one comprises the items noted above plus finance and marketing facilities. The social infrastructure consists of the positive attitudes, values and preferences of people and a climate for change and development. One could see that the provision of physical and economic infrastructure is in the hands of and under the purview of several governmental agencies. Most of theses agencies fall under the secondary and tertiary organizations discussed above. The State governs and regulates the provision of these facilities. Again in a relative sense, the physical and economic infrastructure could be provided by the State with comparative ease. But the question arises; whose responsibility is it to educate the community and generate a climate for change. It falls primarily on the primary set of organizations and especially the department of rural development wherever it exists as a separate unified department. It has the primary task of creating a conducive climate in the communities. The role of other agencies in building up or providing social infrastructure for rural development is rather marginal and peripheral.

It is here that the primary rural development agency which on studying the client community in all its aspects appraises it, what its resources and potentials are, in what direction and in what ways it could harness and develop its material and human resources, and the ways and the extent to which the agency could extend its help to the community in its development.

The approach here envisages an intimate and continuous dialogue between the clientele group and the agency. It is obvious that some of the material resources (*finance, power, transport*) are scare and they are to be allocated judiciously for rural development but the most scarce material is the potential changee. How to identify him, how to motivate, encourage and assure him so that he takes initiative and ventures into some entrepreneurial activity. What may be called the human end product in rural development is the function of social infrastructure or the socio-cultural climate. This leads us to the people now.

THE PEOPLE

The people in a community are the basic or primary resource in rural development. What happens when you have the required resources, promotional organizations, physical and economic infrastructure and lack the people to respond to the resources and facilities and make use of them? To a considerable extent we find ourselves in this situation today. We are looking for the right kind of people. They are not born as such, but they could be made as such.

As we have mentioned under resources, a comprehensive survey, taking family as a unit, is to be made. The survey would comprise the special skills in the population, their capabilities, their ideas and plans of development, an inventory of significant individuals and socio-economic institutions in the community, what they look for from development agencies, the divisive forces or barriers, and stimulants to change, the kind of enterprises that are feasible in the community, the internal resources available, material and human, the external resources and assistance required to start and carry on the enterprises; the on-going enterprises, the kind of improvement they require, the unemployed, the source and means of generating employment within the community and the kinds of training required. The community surveys would form the base for further course of action.

CONCLUSION

The field approach against the background of integrated rural development in developing countries envisages gradual and fuller utilization of local material and human resources manipulating the key elements in the total system simultaneously. It emphasizes examining, developing and establishing organizational and functional linkages among the four factors of rural development: resources, organizations, infrastructure and the people. Further, the approach focuses on the utilization of local institutions and institutional leadership to guide and educate the community towards development. This will generate an awareness, an entrepreneurial climate, an enthusiasm for change from within the community itself and make change more acceptable to the community.

REFERENCES

1. Setty, E. Desingu, A Study of Leadership in Two Valaya Communities in Tamil Nadu, *The Indian Journal of Social Work*, Vol.XLII, No.4, June 1982, Bombay, TATA Institute of Social Sciences.
2. Foster, George M., *Traditional Societies and Technological Changes*, New York, Harper & Row Publishers, 1973.

3. Setty, E. Desingu, Field Approach to Entrepreneurial Development in *'The Communications of Ideas'*, L.P. Vidyarthi, (Ed.), New Delhi, Concept Publishing Co., 1980.

Source: Setty, E. Desingu, *Field Approach to Integrated Rural Development*, Vol.7(6), pp.675-688 (1988), NIRD, Hyderabad, India.

18

MODEL FOR SECURING PEOPLE'S PARTICIPATION IN RURAL DEVELOPMENT

INTRODUCTION

People's participation is a central feature of present thinking about rural development. There appears to be an increasing consensus that participation is essential for any effective development. From this pre-supposition arise the attendant questions of how best it can be operationalized on the assumed grounds that more of it is beneficial. In what activities, in what manner and shape, can the participation be maximized? Can participation be perceived in this way, as an ingredient to be injected into target groups as though they were ill and, as though, this was somehow the panacea? Can participation even be institutionalized? Or legalized? Or must be perhaps be forever on the margins of official policy prescriptions and in that way provide a vehicle for countervailing explanations and organizations that are so necessary in the struggle against entrenched orthodoxy.

In these latter terms, participation provides a potentially powerful tool, together with communication, education and conscientisation. Present concerns with participation are rooted in a complex historical context. People's participation has been a constant theme since the beginning of rural development in all the Asian and African countries that have emerged free from the colonial powers.

Further, we need to ask ourselves a few basic questions and lay emphasis on some aspects of people's participation in rural development. They are:

1. What constitutes rural development?
2. What is people's participation?
3. Objectives of people's participation.
4. Why should people participate? (the philosophy and assumptions behind people's participation)
5. The range and variety of participation
6. Why people fail to participate?
7. Magnitude of people's participation.
8. The mockery of people's participation.
9. Enabling and facilitating people's participation in multiple ways in organizing the community and through decentralization, extension educational process and statutory measures.

In the analysis that follows, the terms "rural" and "community" are used in the same sense, denoting a rural settlement as distinct from towns and urban centres with large population and diversity in social structure and social and economic interactions.

Before we look into the various aspects of people's participation in rural development, there is a need for a definition of what constitutes rural development which would indicate the scope, the limitations and the manner in which people could participate in their development.

Rural development, in general, is a strategy designed to improve the economic and social life of people in a rural settlement and, in particular, it focuses on the rural poor comprising the small-scale farmers, tenants and the landless. Since rural development is intended to reduce poverty, it must be clearly designed to increase production and raise productivity.

Rural development recognizes, however, that improved food supplies and nutrition, together with basic services such as health and education, cannot only directly improve the physical well-being and quality of life of the rural poor, but can also indirectly enhance their productivity and their ability to contribute to the national economy. It is concerned with the modernization and monetization of rural society, and with its transition from traditional isolation to integration with the national economy (World Bank, 1975).

The objectives of rural development, therefore, extend beyond any particular sector. They encompass improved productivity and increased employment, and thus, higher incomes for target groups, as well as minimum acceptable levels of food, shelter, education and health.

Rural development, in a comprehensive sense, is a process of social action in which the people of a community organize themselves for planning and action, define their common and individual needs and problems make group and individual plans to meet their needs and solve their problems, execute these plans with maximum of reliance upon community resources, and supplement these resources, when necessary, with services and material from governmental and non-governmental agencies outside the community. Thus, we see that rural development is focused on the development of the people. It is a dynamic, unified problem-solving approach and the education of the people could be said to be one of the end products of rural development. It is recognized as a social process of directed change.

Further, the essentials of the rural development process are the stimulation of local initiative, location and development of local leadership, and fuller utilization of local resources. In addition to these, self-help and self-reliance, sustained interest and co-operation are other aspects of significance in the concept of rural development. The thrust in rural development is people's participation in the total process and in the entire gamut of rural development, and simultaneous development of people, their conditions and quality of life.

WHAT IS PEOPLE'S PARTICIPATION?

People and their participation. Who are the people? The people in general comprise the target population, the clientele, the beneficiaries, the men and women, the old and the young, the formal and informal leaders in the community, people of different segments and strata of the community, depending upon the specific development programmes and activities.

Rural development programmes comprise: agriculture, animal husbandry, cooperation, rural industries, rural engineering consisting of minor irrigation, roads, buildings, health and sanitation including family welfare, family planning, women's welfare, child care and nutrition, education including adult education/social education and adult literacy, youth welfare and community organization. In each of these areas of development, there are several programmes, schemes and activities which are additive, expanding and tapering off, covering the total community, some segments, or specific target populations such as small and marginal farmers, artisans, women and, in general, people designated as weaker sections – the people living below the poverty line.

The programmes or the activities, by their nature, determine or limit the scope, shape and manner of people's participation. The development programmes could be classified into three broad categories: 1. individual-based wherein the target or the beneficiary is the individual and the participation is restricted to the individual (e.g. agriculture, livestock, poultry, family planning, nutrition, adult literacy); 2. community-based, the projects or programmes that cover the total community or some segments of the community (e.g., irrigation, plant protection, contour bunding, roads, buildings, schools, community centres, mid-day meal programmes, environmental sanitation and activities of community-wide nature; and 3. individual-cum-community based programmes. Some of the programmes mentioned above, fall both under individual and community categories. Such programmes cannot be successfully initiated and accomplished without the response and support from the individuals and the community at large.

The question that arises at the outset is who participates with whom? And for what purpose? All development plans and all strategies for assisting the poor and the needy necessarily should have the community as its central focus and starting point. All other resources, techniques and expertise are of relative importance compared to the community. Begin with the community and build with them. In the context of development programmes, the agencies and institutions cannot be the prime factors in the dynamics of participation. If community's growth and development is the vital and ultimate concern then the community necessarily assumes the prime status in the relationship between community and agency. The healthier and meaningful approach would then be not people's participation in agency's programmes but agency's participation in people's programmes. It has to be remembered that agencies, programmes, expertise are all secondary resources restricted to the role of assisting the community, they do not form in any way the major content in the development process.

The ultimate goal of providing for people's participation in the programmes is imparting the community with skills, strategies, opportunities and support to enhance its own functioning towards self-sufficiency and self-development. In concrete terms, the goal of people's participation in programmes could be helping people to build their own organization and institutions equipped with and capable of accelerating their own development. This implies that the community which is continuously being provided with opportunities for participation in the programmes will one day take on itself the role hitherto played by the agency of enhancing its own capacities to meet its needs. Further, it follows that all agencies and their programmes have a time-bound role in their intervention for the development of the vulnerable sections.

People's participation is a challenging concept; a review of its understanding, use and practice by numerous agencies often betrays a superficial commitment to it. The agencies and development workers who are seriously concerned about the development of the community need to do a thorough heart searching to find out whether there is a feeling of insecurity preventing them from expressing and demonstrating their real concern for people's participation. It could be like a leader who enjoys leading, though expressing concern for the development and progress of his followers, frequently experiences insecurity of being overtaken by the ones whom he leads. People's participation, if it achieves its desired goal, would necessarily make the patron agency obsolete beyond a given point of time. Of course, the agency can still renew its relevance and role if it identifies new areas to continue in its helping intervention. An attempt is made in this chapter to critically look into the various facets of people's participation in development activities not as an embellishment but as a functionally necessary component to build a healthy, egalitarian, democratic society.

CONCEPT AND OBJECTIVES OF PEOPLE'S PARTICIPATION

People's participation, in a broader sense, means their total involvement with development agencies in deciding the programmes and activities, fixing up of priorities, taking initiative and carrying out the projects as partners by the contributing of their ideas, interest, material, labour and time. The scope of people's participation depends upon the nature of the activity, the duration of its execution, its technical nature, the clientele it covers, whether it is an individual project or concerns the total or some segments of the community, its location, the amount of funds it involves and, above all, what the development agency stipulates about the kind of participation at different stages of activity and the quantity and quality of participation it expects from the people.

Of late, several terms have come into development terminology in respect to involving people for their betterment. Terms like people's participation, popular participation, community participation, target group participation, public community participation, citizen's participation and so on are in current use meaning almost the same thing that people as partners in their development. Participation is a comprehensive concept embracing all the facets and phases of development beginning with people's initiative and unto their sustaining the activity.

In view of the nature of rural development programmes, most of them initiated by the development agencies, the participation of people could be as diverse as follows:

1. Responding to the programme, accepting the process and adopting technology and innovations;
2. Extending moral support;

3. Participation in decision-making, cooperating in implementation;
4. Contribution of money, material and labour;
5. Taking initiative, mobilizing people and resources; and
6. Assuming leadership and ownership of projects.

People's physical and monetary contributions also irrespective of the nature and degree of people's involvement in the development programmes are recognized as people's participation. This kind of contribution of material, money and labour, rather modest in quantitative and qualitative terms depends on the affordability on the part of the people. In other words, people's economic participation depends upon their affordability.

People's participation is a question of values, giving importance and recognizing individuals and groups in communities as equally important and significant in the overall development and welfare of the total community. People's participation is not just complementary to what the development agency does, allocates, spends, but it is more than that. Social participation in terms of policy support in decision-making, adoption of strategies and implementation of development programmes depends on the social structure, social status, traditional role expectations and role boundaries of members in a rural community.

Participation is a process and it could be viewed as a means to an end and in one sense as an end in itself. In a broader sense, people's participation is beyond rural or urban development. It is organizing, building responsive, active and democratic communities. Participation is a learning process. It is transferring knowledge and skills to the people while they participate in development activities. It is a non-formal education and education through activity. Participation is a democratic process and it provides equal opportunities and strengthens democracy.

Participation of the clientele in the development activities throughout the life of a project will prepare people knowledge-wise and skill-wise to sustain the activity after the development agency withdrew from the scene of action. Participation is people's response, a matching support from the people and their local institutions. It is activating dormant groups, enabling them discover their talent, potential, capabilities, resources and strengths. It is participative planning, development and management of development activities. Rural development is instrumental to people's participation. Community organization is a means and a measure to facilitate and secure people's participation. Participation is a contributing and stabilizing factor to community organization and its strength.

People's participation in activities that concern them, is providing them equal opportunity to share their ideas, views, plans and other material and non-material resources. Most of the developing societies are ridden with economic and social disparities, racial, ethnic and religious. They stand stratified with graded inequalities and suffer from social and cultural communication and restrictions. Some of these graded social structures with privileges and denial of these privileges are centuries and decades old. In such a social structure wherein economic and social inequalities operate in varied degrees, people of all segments participating in the individual and community promotional activities would work against social and ethnic barriers and rigidity gradually breaking down the graded compartmentalized sanctions for and against participation.

Enabling and encouraging the disadvantaged and the poor people to participate in the programmes that affect them and the local community at large is one way of empowering them. It is legitimizing the diverse roles that may be played by different groups standing at different distances in respect to social positions and interactions. People's participation is bringing people together functionally. It is physical, psychic and emotional involvement of the clientele with the development activities. It is training and organizing the community for self-reliance, responsiveness and leadership. Process-wise, people's participation is drawing people from periphery to the center of action, widening their sphere of thinking, contacts and contributions. It is bringing people from relative to total isolation to mutual interaction.

OBJECTIVES OF PEOPLE'S PARTICIPATION

As mentioned earlier, people's participation in rural development is an educational process. It is a training for development involving people in the projects, making them their own. It is to create a sense of awareness, a sense of participation, a sense of belonging, a sense of possession and ownership. It is to develop self-reliance, self-confidence, competence and managerial capacity. It is to train people to take initiative, accomplish and sustain their activities. It is to build up and reinvigorate communities and generate social action. It is to enable people to discover their strength, increase their aspiration level, mobilize and channelize their resources for productive purposes. Participation is bringing people to the core from the periphery, to activeness from passiveness, and to be thinkers, decision makers, doers and implementers from acceptors.

Further, participation facilitates discovery, promotion and encouragement and utilization of new ideas, views, talents and new resources. It is sensitizing the people. Participation creates a sense of individual and group worth, creating awareness of rights, duties and obligations on the part of the members in a community. In a larger sense, society with its culture and civilization is a product of people's social, economic and political participation.

People's participation is not restricted to rural development but it has far greater implications. It is building a new social order, wherein every individual and group will be active participant in community-wide activities, and thus contributing to a certain degree of minimization in social distinctions and differences. Paradoxically, though caste differences and social distance are apparent in the Hindu society, there is to a larger extent smooth running of family and community affairs at the village level.

One could go at length speaking of the objectives and effects of people's participation. It creates *esprit de corps* and ensures dignity of labour when it is labour contribution by the people. It is a means to foster social responsibility and community ownership among the people, and it is organizing and reorganizing groups and community. As a human resource development, people's participation facilitates utilizing and adopting indigenous knowledge system for new programmes. It is a measure to understand people's interests their nexus of relationship with other groups in the community and it also functions as an aperture to understand the ethos, the strengths and limitations on the part of the clientele community. Involving people in development activities is a kind of political education.

To participate is to identify with a cause, purpose, self-interest and interest in the good of the larger community. It is to legitimize, he or she being a member of a group, to make one's presence felt, his or her contribution recognized. It is common interest and common concern that bring people together fostering collective social action especially at the grassroots level. In people's participation, in several of the development activities, new grouping and new alignment emerge and the participants are to learn new ways of adjustment, contribution and coordination which may be termed as re-socialization or neo-socialization.

Some of the development projects on their completion are to be taken over and sustained by the people and so there is a need to involve them in the project activity all through or at crucial stages, so that there is a smooth change over of management of such projects to the people from the development agency (e.g., roads, school buildings, community toilets, minor irrigation projects).

In the ultimate sense, the whole purpose and process of people's participation is Human Resource Development (HRD) – the development of human and inner material resources, with stimulus and support external to the community. Unless we create this culture of people's participation, democracy will not grow.

PHILOSOPHY AND PSYCHOLOGY OF PARTICIPATION

WHY SHOULD PEOPLE PARTICIPATE?

There is no controversy as to whether there should be people's participation in the development programmes designed to meet the basic needs of the people. In fact, governments and development agencies have learnt at a great price as to what happens when programmes have overlooked this important factor of "People's Participation" in their planning and implementation. The *postmortem* of many unsuccessful programmes has shown that they have invariably failed when they failed to provide an adequate place and importance to people's/ target group's role at various stages of implementation.

We are all aware today that there are no plans which do not allot a role to people's participation. In fact, all agencies involved in the field take great care to speak about people's participation repeatedly in all their project plans, annual reports and periodic meetings. It is an all too frequent fact that this term has received abundant lip service rather than convinced practitioners.

There is a body of philosophy and a set of assumptions behind people's participation in rural development. We may briefly look into them.

1. The whole philosophy of rural development is based on one very simple and apparent assumption that the government machinery, however big and efficient it might be, is grossly inadequate by itself to achieve the economic and social revolution needed for ensuring a better and richer life for the vast masses of humanity living in the rural areas. The rural development personnel were to function merely as "catalytic agents". The idea was that a programme started as a government programme with people's participation should gradually and eventually shape itself into people's programme with government's participation.

2. Communities can develop their own capacity to deal with their problems (we assume that people do want and can change).

3. People participate in giving direction to social change in their communities. Change which is brought about by sharing of an effort and social participation, possesses democratic vitality and is also realistic. Self-imposed changes have permanence as compared to those imposed from outside and above.

4. Holistic approach is better than fragmented approach, because the life of a community is itself a whole and any attempt to tackle one aspect of the whole is bound to affect others.

5. People must learn participative skills in democracy because, unless they themselves share responsibilities and participate in fulfilling them, they do not strengthen the democratic structure of their society.

Democracy will weaken, if not perish, unless the supporting institutions are created. The basic plank of community development is the growth of the democratic idea. Democracy does not function unless there is a decentralization of power to be shared very widely at various levels of the social strata.

6. People need help in solving their new problems. External help provides stimulus to inner resources of the community. Communities are like infants who need a prop while they learn to walk. This is rationale for agency functioning and agency support.
7. The tendency of sub-groups, developing themselves as separate entities inside a community, produces social tension and has, therefore, to be channelized and their energies to be diverted to common initiatives.
8. The barriers that prevent active participation by individuals in the direction of social change inhibit personal development. The process of community development is, therefore, to be so organized that the community functions for the good of the individual and the growth of the community. The communities have to be so organized that they promote the growth of individuals.
9. The process of urbanization has destroyed the feeling of belonging to a community and it is necessary to revive this feeling in rural area where the masses of agricultural populations of the developing nations dwell. The contractual relations of an urban society do not work well in a rural society. The problem of developing and maintaining common and shared values, which form the basis of cohesion in a community, is made vastly more difficult by industrialization (Setty, 1970).

10. Beneficiary or target community consists of people who are adults and thinking human beings. They are also intelligent and pragmatic in their own way just as the patron or the helping agency.

11. If given the opportunity, people can organize and draw out solutions to the problems.

12. The community is in the best position to understand its own problems in all their dimensions and complexity.

13. The best resources for their progress and development are they themselves who, if assisted and supported, could be the vital and effective inputs for their own growth and development.

14. Outside assistance, support and expertise are only secondary though important resources provided within time-bound frame.

15. The role of the community cannot be substituted or taken away, however great the vulnerability of the community may be.

16. The apparently most helpless community can be an active factor in helping itself.

17. People always have their own wisdom of meeting their basic needs, however antique and tedious the mechanism of doing so appears to be.

The above assumptions need to be convictions of all those agencies and people who believe in people's participation in development programmes, lacking which no agency can meaningfully provide for the participation of people in any venture (Pinto, 1982).

Further, in a historical perspective, in ancient times, the primary face-to-face group of the communities were knit in a close everyday relationship of togetherness with one another. The "we" feeling was dominant. In the social structure of the rural communities of ancient times, depending upon the value systems of those days, the individual sub-served the needs of the community and the community, in turn, gave him services, environmental freedom, and congeniality to grow to his maximum stature. It was out of this concept of mutual interdependence of the community, the individual and the state, that the welfare of the subject was considered as a primary function of the state. Like two halves of an arch the citizens and the state were supported by and supported each other. The ancient village communities, relatively speaking, had more harmony and community cohesiveness.

By passage of time, the village communities tended to become closed, isolated and limited in functioning, having little intercommunication among them. For instance in India, in medieval times, the Moguls developed a system of feudalism, which increased the distance and tended to diminish the close contact between the ruler and the ruled. The intermediaries acquired symbols of authority in their status and roles, and applied sanctions according to the delegations of authority operating in the system.

In the colonial regimes which most developing nations have passed through, the emphasis shifted to urban centres of trade and it suited the colonial powers to evolve a system of administration which bestowed patronage on certain classes. This naturally ignored a bulk of the villagers and their participation in the administration and their development.

A witness to this fact is the colonial past, the civilizing efforts of the colonizers, the dependency psychology they have created and the legacy they have left behind. The self-centred, urban and elite-oriented administration and development created a sense of alienation among the rural communities. They tended to withdraw. Sometimes, the natives were bewildered, frightened, awestruck, unwilling, uninvolved spectators of the civilizing efforts, and schemes of the colonial administration and the so-called development. In the name of humanitarian work and to serve his purpose, the master did attempt to improve the imagined facilities and needs of his subjects. But the subjects were seldom involved. It was not their programme. They did not and could not appreciate the purpose behind them and so they were not involved and were not participants in the programmes meant for them. This tendency of uninvolvement in government initiated and sponsored programmes continued even after the people became free. The sense of alienation and un-involvement, looking to the government initiative and action, and a tendency to underestimate their abilities, capacities and inner resources, grew over the centuries and decades. These trends had to be remedied, reversed, and a need arose to make people enlightened and full-fledged participants in their development.

In a large sense, the whole civilization and culture of a society, its social organization and institutional apparatus are the product of people's participation. When the people are convinced that a project or a programme is beneficial to them, they are likely to participate and involve themselves in the activity. People more often look for immediate material/ tangible benefits. The gestation period for the programmes to yield results tangible or intangible varies depending upon the nature of the programme. The onus of carrying conviction to the people for their involvement depends on the development personnel and the local leadership, and the way people's participation is facilitated and received. Motivation is a factor in participation.

Participation may sometimes decide your social status – high, middle or low – or your status or rank will influence the nature of participation. Asking for participation is recognizing one's (individual or group) existence and importance. One gets recognition by participation. For instance, when we approach marginal people in the economic and social sense, and women in some communities who are seldom consulted for their ideas, views and opinions, for their participation in planning and implementing any development activity, there would be a gradual transformation in their behaviour. They feel important. It is according recognition and dignity to them. On the other hand, you cannot ignore the elite in the community, who normally (in some programmes which would benefit them and enhance in their eyes their prestige and status) expect the development agency invite them to participate in the programme. Their participation, as we shall discuss further, may be in terms of policy decisions and monetary support.

People tend to participate (take part) as a social conformity, not to stand excluded from community activity. Prestige is a factor both for participation and non-participation. Participation in a group comprising general, social and economic strata, engaged in a development activity reduces individual and group prejudices. In a philosophical and psychological sense, people's participation in development programmes, meant for the people, is endowed with several virtues, economic development, optimal utilization of human resources, healthy environment and social harmony.

FAILURE, ABUSE AND MOCKERY OF PEOPLE'S PARTICIPATION

WHY PEOPLE FAIL TO PARTICIPATE?

People's participation, as we have observed earlier, depends upon the social and class structure of the rural community, the patterns and traditions of decision-making and carrying out communal and individual activities, the way people perceive the programmes and projects initiated by the development agencies, and people's own ability. Further, and importantly it depends upon what the development agencies expect from the people with respect to participation, the stipulations they make and the manner in which the agencies mobilize, motivate, encourage and facilitate people's participation.

People's participation sounds like begging the question. When programmes are meant for people, for their benefit, welfare and advantage, the paradox is why people fail to participate. Ignorance and lack of motivation is a factor of non-or negligible participation. When matters are of technical nature beyond the understanding and outside the experience of the people, participation is less. People look for immediate and tangible benefits. For instance, the problem of population explosion and, consequently, the need for the family to participate in family planning programmes, is a distant cry for the individual or the family. The individual does not feel the urgency of it, its immediacy, and he or she does not visualize the magnitude of the problem, does not see the population explosion within the family and so does not respond. The tendency is to accept a situation as given and live with it.

Sometimes, group rivalry, cliques, conflicts within the community, vested interests, conflict in values, opposition to the programmes, resistance to change and poor local leadership are factors as to why people fail to participate. We just cannot blame the people for their poor response or their failure to participate in rural development activities. The responsibility lies equally on the part of the personnel of the development agencies. Centralization of authority weakens popular participation. Effective implementation of rural development programmes could not be achieved so long as decision on matters concerning them are taken by a super agency. A decentralized system, which allows participatory development from below, is necessary for a healthy society.

Sometimes, you have to sacrifice the quality in the works (e.g., roads or buildings) that are accomplished through people's participation, mostly in terms of labour and unskilled work.

We do not question the enthusiasm and good intentions of the planners, administrators and field personnel in rural development but, at the same time, we have to appreciate the fact that people are not ready to tune in to our development programmes, our expectations, and targets in terms of their participation. Often, participation sounds like a rare material, ethereal in nature, difficult to grasp to have a strong grip on, or to secure enough of it and blend it with government initiated programmes. Despite limitations, and though poor in quality and quantity, instances of people's participation abound in number. It provided the impetus to popular enthusiasm, channeled their ideas and energies and brought in an element of sense of integration in rural development activities.

When it comes to participatory planning and development, people are to be placed first. It is not as a political slogan, but as an indispensable factor of real, acceptable and sustainable development. People for whom all the development is meant may not be all wise but they are important. Sarvodaya leader Vinobha Bhave likened the people to numeral '1' (one) while the government is '0' (zero). The values of zeros, he said, placed after 1 increases but no value for the zeros without numeral '1'. Vinobha stressed the importance of people through this analogy.

When it comes to the poor in community for their participating when the programmes affect them or the programmes are of general nature covering the entire local community, they lack affordability for economic participation and at the same time do suffer in the social sphere, since they are marginalized socially and hence not invited and involved in participation. Another paradoxical and unfortunate situation often is, even in areas where the poor could decide for themselves they leave the decision-making to the elite in the community, ethnically and economically so-called superior and dominant groups. Though the poor are the beneficiaries, sometimes, the choices and decisions for them are made by the development personnel or the local elite or the two groups together. In such instances, the poor out of respect or fear or being uninformed or unaccustomed to such decision-making and exercising their freedom of choice, give the decision-making unto the elite and the development personnel or the latter arrogate to themselves what the poor should be doing at their end.

Often we come across situations in the rural communities where the elite's stand runs as follows:

"We take decisions on our behalf and on behalf of the poor in our community. We expect and let the poor to be silent and just contribute labour to projects where it is required. The poor are an ignorant lot; they have no ideas. We have to think and act for them".

Similarly, if the development agency is more bureaucratic in its style of functioning, there is likely to be less involvement of the people and their participation, especially of non-material nature will be less. The "after all" attitude and notion on the part of the development personnel in respect to the villagers, meaning that people do not matter much, is highly regrettable. We are to seriously ponder over questions like: What prevents people from participation? Who prevents people from participation? What are the issues to participate? What are the opportunities to participate?

The responses to these questions would aid in mobilizing and motivating people to participate. One has to look into the poor or negligible participation and the problems and barriers thereof and whether the poor participation is an internal problem or related to the way development agency has operated the project. Participation should not only be a nexus of relationship between the target population and the development agency, but it should be the responsibility of the client system (target population plus the larger community) in securing and ensuring people's participation. It should become an internal affair and responsibility of the clientele. Such a response and responsibility on the part of the clientele would be an hallmark of real people's participation.

People's participation in terms of their giving ideas, opinions, methods and solutions to certain problems may indicate their status, rank and intellectual capacity; material and monetary contributions, their economic status and affordability and mere physical labour contribution, people's economic poverty. It is a rough kind of categorizing the people based on the type of their participation. It is a common phenomenon to observe in rural communities that factions, cliques, rivalry and group hostility are the factors obstructing participation. Interestingly, pride and status both operate as barriers and stimulants to participation. When people sense that they are brushed aside by the development agency and / or the elite in the community; when their material and non-material contributions are treated as inconsequential, when they had negative experience at the hands of the development agency, when they have not been accorded any recognition by the development agency, when people's requests for help were not properly responded to, there is all likelihood of people not coming forward to participate.

In the name of "participation" often the rich and the powerful in the local rural communities exploit the poor in labour contribution. There have been instances wherein contractors of roads, culverts, school buildings, and other kinds of earthwork exploit the local community in the name and guise of people's contribution, make profit, showing on records, that they have spent money on those parts of the work which were accomplished by people's contribution, in terms of labour and material.

It is not sometimes, the poverty of ideas that prevents the poor from participation, but it is the social distance, isolation from decision-making, and a notion that their ideas, views may not be worthy of consideration, the poor holding a low image of themselves and their ideas, the decay and death of initiative among the people, in general, especially among the weaker section. No attempt is made here to generalize the situation. The upsurge of initiative and action for progress among the poor on the other hand, is quite evident. The presence or absence of initiative and action, the degree to which it obtains, depends on the social composition and economic levels of the people in the rural communities.

Another social phenomenon of interest is the old and the youth playing leadership and influence roles. In a group where old age is respected, experience and wisdom associated with or attributed to the old, the old dominate and the youth are deprived of participation in discussions pertaining to development issues and on the other hand, during recent times, in some communities, as a result of education, urbanization, change in the values, the youth dominate and the old are relegated to the background. Whether it is the old or young, men or women, the barriers to participation are cultural, social, psychological, religious and political. There are many genuine reasons why a lot of agencies and people do not actually provide for people's participation in their programmes.

a) Some development workers, agencies, planners and experts do not seriously believe that the beneficiaries of the programmes have anything important to contribute. They think that the clientele are people who need to be helped but cannot help themselves.

Thus being ignorant and incapable how can they contribute to or participate in plans aimed at helping themselves?

b) Some believe that programmes that are minutely drawn up by experts and planners cannot be exposed to the risk of being messed up by the beneficiaries. They feel that the agencies know best what their beneficiaries need.

c) Others feel that once access is left open to the beneficiary community to participate in planning and implementation of the programmes, then results will take too long to come. It is very tedious to work with unqualified people. Agencies want to see material results in the quickest possible time.

d) Allowing for people's participation necessarily implies complex dynamics and a readiness to be very flexible. It also implies getting down to the beneficiaries' level and following their pace to develop. Agencies often experience a cross-culture conflict in this regard and ultimately circumvent involvement of the beneficiaries.

Some organizations and workers who claim their belief in people's participation have their own way of expressing it in practice. It is obvious that in spite of their supposed motivation and efforts, their kind of expression of people's participation is far from what it should be. There are reasons why agencies and people shy away from the genuine practice of people's participation. If one understands the dynamics which controls the operation and functioning of these agencies, it could possibly point out to the reasons why people's participation in its true sense is not within the capacity of these agencies.

People's participation is differently understood and implemented in as many different ways. It is also a fact that all those who claim to value people's participation in programmes and services do not always mean it seriously. Fortunately however, there are numerous agencies who are genuine believers in the need for emphasizing people's participation in programmes and are as serious to give scope to this in their actual operations.

THE MOCKERY OF PEOPLE'S PARTICIPATION

Since it was stipulated and emphasized as a necessary component (on the material and monetary side), people's participation led to blowing and boosting up of figures under people's contribution to community projects. In cases such as approach roads, culverts, irrigation works, school buildings, and community centres, the people were expected to contribute to the extent of 25 percent of the estimated cost of the project. In the absence of such a contribution or when it was only a part of the stipulated amount, the personnel at the mandal and district level had the works executed within the 75 per cent of the government grant, and the local contractors who were entrusted with these works managed to have their profit too. In realistic terms, the works were executed within fifty to sixty per cent of the estimated cost. In such cases, the quality of work suffered. The roads, culverts and tank bunds were washed away and the buildings collapsed. It was not only a physical loss and damage but it created a bad image among the rural people and it became increasingly difficult to get their involvement in newer projects.

The tendency to manipulate and blow up figures under people's contribution (as symbolic of people's participation) in order to show achievement of the targets, and to satisfy the higher-ups in the hierarchy, corrupted the people. The morale of the officials was affected and the people's participation was not taken seriously. With a nod, it was accepted, it was taken for granted. It became nominal. It lost its significance.

In some instances, people's participation meant and was taken to be the physical kind such as labour, and monetary contribution while the people's involvement in the choices, decision-making and programme planning was lost sight of by the development agencies. It became a mockery. There were several instances wherein the community toilets and bathrooms constructed were a total failure, for, in these cases, the local people were not involved, they were not consulted, their habits were not taken into account, the availability and supply of water was not given any thought, and the people were not educated and motivated to use the toilets and bathrooms. The whole project was unimaginative and was carried out in a mechanical way. We took the needs of the people for granted. We never bothered to know the people's views, and the way they would like to have things. We were under the pressure of heavy and unrealistic targets; we were in a hurry to accomplish the targets. The casualty in this hasty process (pursued, of course, with all good intentions) was people's involvement and their participation.

THE RANGE AND VARIETY OF PARTICIPATION

A village community consisting of men, women and children of the village, is the best agency for organizing people's participation, on a systematic basis, for working on projects of common benefit. As mentioned earlier, participation is at various levels and it is of various kinds and modes. It is at the people's level at the grassroots, and it is through people's representative leaders from the village council to the parliament, and through voluntary organizations, advisory bodies, consultative committees, seminars, workshops, conferences held at various levels. The formal and informal organizations at various levels that function as machinery and instruments of rural development, are expected to facilitate and increase people's participation.

Participation at the village level depends upon the social structure of the community, the class composition, social stratification and status hierarchy of groups, the distribution of power and authority, and traditionally determined decision-making patterns and participation. In some groups, women and children are excluded. In some decisions, that concern the total community (community projects), the weaker sections and the less influential are ignored or left out. When participation is voluntary, it depends upon self-interest, obligations to the community and socio-economic conditions of the family. Sometimes, the participation, mostly in terms of labour, material or money, is compulsory or is done under social pressure. In such cases, the individuals have no choice and they have to meet the social expectations or the obligations. Outwardly there will be participation but without the psychological and emotional involvement. It may happen when a programme is not apparently of interest to some individuals and groups, or if the programme does not show any immediate benefit, or meet their needs, or solve their problems.

When we look at people's participation at the rural community level, the following common pattern emergences (refer Fig. 1.1.). The pattern of participation shown in Fig. 1.1 is illustrative of the kind that generally obtains in rural communities.

Participation of the people in the programmes could be right from the formative stage or at some point in the course of the life of an activity. The question is how important or significant is that stage in the life of the project wherein the people participate. Participation depends on the nature of the activity, and the areas, activities, issues and problems that are of common interest and concern of the larger community and interest groups within the community. Further, there could be variations and fluctuations in the people's participation overtime. In terms of typology of participation it could be voluntary, obligatory, induced, mandatory, under coercion, occasional, once-in-life time, recurring, continual and what may be called supportive participation.

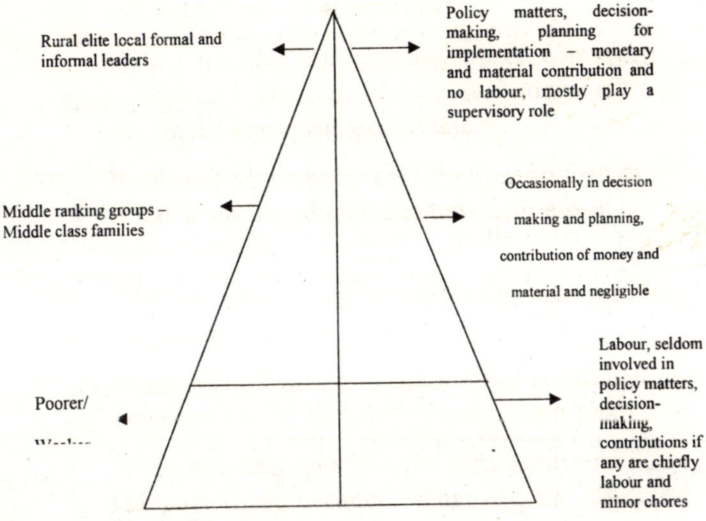

PATTERN OF PARTICIPATION

There could be in the initial stages of an activity almost nil and negligible participation of the people, and over a period, it may have gradual increase and depending on multiple factors, especially when people think that the activity is beneficial to them and it is in their long-term interest, their participation would be stable and enduring. On the other hand, people in the initial stages of an activity imbued with exuberance and euphoria may participate in large numbers with intensity, and the participation may decrease as the initial enthusiasm dies out. Further, the other kind of phenomenon is very little participation in the beginning, its significant increase for some time and then its tapering off. These fluctuations in participation could be in terms of number of people participating at a particular stage of the project and the kind and intensity of their participation. You may call them as tides of participation with ebb and flow.

The motivating factors for participation could be self-interest, concern for others, concern for environment and a sense of common cause and public good. The participation further is of two kinds: participation in the programmes initiated by the people within the community and in the ones introduced by the external development agencies. People to people participation and people to development personnel. In terms of activities, people's participation could range from sanitation to disaster management, from irrigation to immunization and from pest-control to poultry rearing. This is just illustrative.

MAGNITUDE OF PEOPLE'S PARTICIPATION

In many instances (related to India) the people's participation in terms of cash, kind and *shramadan* (gift or contribution of labour) has exceeded the share of the government. While there is no limit to people's maximum contribution, a rough scale has been prescribed, the scale being flexible in exceptional cases e.g., in its application to the scheduled and tribal groups. In over fifty years of rural development in India, hundreds of miles of roads, and a number of school buildings, community centres, parks, drinking water wells, water sheds and several other community projects, or assets, have been accomplished, in full and part, by the villagers by dint of their labour and contribution in cash and kind.

The other aspect is people's direct participation at the operational level and the participation of people's representative leaders at various levels in the hierarchy of rural development set-up, in formulating policies, in decision-making and in the implementation of the programmes. Above all, people's participation, as a necessary component of rural development, has created an awareness, provided an opportunity and made people think, realize that they have ideas, they can mobilize themselves, mobilize their scarce material resources, and can build their homes and communities. The real measure of people's participation is their involvement in development activities, which has not been in a desired measure earlier. While we should give credit to the personnel of the rural development agencies for their accomplishment in securing people's participation, we cannot ignore the negative side of it.

In a broader sense, there is no realm in the life of the community wherein people's participation does not arise. It is energy and technique with massive potential to build healthy societies.

ENABLING AND FACILITATING PEOPLE'S PARTICIPATION

People's participation in rural development has short-term and long-term goals. The former deals with the involvement of people in the current programmes and development activities, and the utilization of local material and human resources, while the latter aims at building self-initiating, self-reliant and self-managing rural communities. It is a continuous process of democratization. In this process, two basic things draw our attention : community mobilization and group formation. At the rural community level, two human groups that are universal in all societies and which have been and still are the generators and preservers of primary group, are families and the local communities themselves.

We need to have trust and faith in the ability of the people in rural communities, provide them with the opportunity for participation, however humble and insignificant it may be, respect their ideas and views; channelize and integrate their energies and resources for improving the quality of their life.

Even at the cost of repetition, it may be mentioned that the process of working with people demands understanding, appreciation, respect, patience and, above all, wisdom. One effective methodology for channelizing people's participation is through community organization and, cooperative development. Participation shows the ethos and the pattern of behaviour on the part of the people. We may think of several core and marginal factors in a contextual sense either facilitating or inhibiting participation.

FACTORS INFLUENCING PARTICIPATION

1. Awareness on the part of the individual as to the nature and details of the activity and his own abilities to take part in the activity.
2. Self-interest.
3. Motivation to participate.
4. Encouragement provided by the people, leaders in the community and personnel in the development.
5. Authority vested in the individual and exercised by the individual and individual's response to authority within and outside the community.
6. Knowledge and skills on the part of the individual or group which are relevant to the activity.
7. Attitude on the part of the individual or group vis-à-vis the activity and the sponsors of the activity.
8. Ideas that people think which would enrich or improve the activity.
9. Availability of time, money and materials.
10. A felt-need.
11. Interest in the welfare of the community.

12. The cost of participation i.e., how much does the participation cost people.
13. The monetary and non-monetary value of participation.
14. The extent to which individuals and small groups are answerable to the community than to external development agencies.
15. The extent to which the client community is cohesive and organized.
16. The nature and quality of the client community.
17. Internal nexus of relationship and social structure of the community.
18. Easy implementability of the programme.
19. Uniformity.
20. Absence of social, cultural, physical and psychological barriers.
21. Easy to monitor.
22. Within the economic, social and cultural framework and capabilities of the target population.
23. The programme having a good demonstrative effect.
24. Quick results.
25. People could easily understand, respond and adopt.
26. Effective local leadership and leadership on the part of the development agency.
27. The kind of approach made by the development agency.
28. When people are recognized.

29. When you have started the programmes from where people are.
30. Individual/family/ethnic status and prestige.
31. Sex and age.
32. Division of labour in various functions in the community.
33. Hereditarily and traditionally assigned roles to individuals and social groups in the community.
34. Traditionally ascribed/expected participation in social, religious and secular activities.
35. Primary group values.
36. Role of functional specialists in the community.
37. Pattern of local internal communication.
38. Influence of culture and religion.

The above list of factors and situations in a community either facilitating or inhibiting people's participation is only illustrative but not exhaustive.

AN OPERATIONAL MODEL FOR SECURING AND ENRICHING PEOPLE'S PARTICIPATION IN DEVELOPMENT ACTIVITIES

Participation as such is not new in any community. There is always certain kind and degree of participation at certain levels in certain activities. Participation takes place as an economic, social, cultural and psychological functional necessity but participating in activities introduced by development agencies is new. Principally, this was because the government and the bureaucracy have distanced themselves from the people and so the emphasis on encouraging and securing people's participation in the activities that are meant for their welfare and progress. The model that is presented here is a series of methods, measures and approaches based on physico-economic and socio-psycho-cultural factors and characteristics of the client community.

1. Identify the target population and their views on the project.
2. Appraise them of: the nature and details of the project, the benefits they would have from the project, the role of development agency in the project, the kind of participation expected from the client group.
3. Assess what the people could contribute towards the project.
4. Motivate, encourage and facilitate and utilize people's participation (material and non-material).
5. Provide space for participation.
6. See at what stage and in what manner the people can participate in the project now and in the future.
7. Identify the leadership behind the target groups.
8. Assign the responsibility to the groups/leaders.
9. Gradually institutionalize people's participation.
10. Develop channels and channelize people's participation.
11. Gradually delegate and transfer the management of the project to the people/their local institutions.
12. Organize people into groups, assign roles and responsibilities to the existing groups. Organize new groups based on knowledge, skills, affordability and capability and based on residential locality and interests and prepare them to be active participants in the project. Build up a sense of responsibility and accountability on the part of the client community.

13. Let the people come up with their ideas, solutions and strategies.
14. Allow people to work initially on their own and having accomplished that, come up with your improved ways and methods and throw them up as a challenge to the people.
15. Make people's participation their responsibility.
16. Start with initially responsive individuals and/ or groups however small and modest their participation may be. Later, people including the recalcitrant individuals and groups will come to know why they should participate and the manner in which they could do it.
17. Create a sense of pride and competition among the individuals and groups in their participation and contribution to and accomplishment of projects. This could be among various age groups, residential groups and even between men and women.
18. Demarcate the respective functional jurisdictions of individuals/groups for them to play their respective roles.
19. Draw in and legitimize the participation of non-participating and seldom participating groups such as women and weaker sections.
20. Encourage participation in the programmes and issues that arise from within the community so that it may become easy and set a pattern for people to take part and contribute to the programmes initiated by the external development agencies.
21. Make people literate so that you can increase their participation.

ROLE OF A DEVELOPMENT AGENCY

The onus of providing space, encouraging and facilitating people's participation lies on the part of development agency. The development agency (multiple agencies in the field for that matter) may have to indicate, open up, solicit and encourage people to participate in large number of programmes at different stages in the process of development activity. It may be a school lunch programme, adult literacy, an approach road or provision of drinking water facilities.

The right attitude and orientation is required on the part of the development personnel, people's elected and informal leaders and the dominant groups in the community. There are some programmes which are pre-determined and in such cases, there is no question of people participating in policy or decision-making and so the programme by its nature and the type of clientele determine the quantity and quality of participation. Sometimes sacrifices are to be made in terms of time and quality of people's participation, especially in terms of skilled labour and material contribution. Getting labour, money and material symbolizing people's participation towards a project is one thing, but involving people in the process of identifying, formulating and implementing a project is another. The material contribution is for a specific project, but the non-material participation is of far more great significance.

WORKING WITH THE PEOPLE

In order to involve people, we should work with the people. It is the field level functionaries in the filed of rural development, agriculture, livestock, public health and medicare, education etc., who are supposed to have more close and frequent contact with the community. People's participation depends to a large degree on how the field level personnel manage the involvement of the people in the development activities. Involving people and securing their participation depends on the attitude, patience, skills, wisdom, commitment and leadership on the part of the development personnel. Working with people is an art and it is human relations and it is an essential part of human development.

In order to maximize people's participation in rural development and build strong, viable rural communities, the following ten questions may be borne in mind:

1. How can the maximum number of villagers be mobilized for undertaking both village and national improvement projects?
2. How can village communities be helped to develop into self-perpetuative units of social action, many of which will become permanent units of local governments?
3. How can solidarity of, and loyalty to, local groups and local communities be developed without developing resistance to outside guidance and possible resistance to outside assistance?
4. How can old established local groups be used to further the prescribed objectives of national development?
5. How can the levels of aspiration (the standard of living) of both individuals and local groups be raised?
6. How can the local group participation of traditionally low-status persons be increased in undertaking local improvement?
7. How to dissolve, or in some way make constructive use of, local factions or other divisive local community groups?
8. How to develop hundreds of thousands of local small groups and leaders who can help develop local responsibility and initiative?

9. How can overhead (Center and State) governments make maximum contributions of money and personnel to local group undertakings without diluting local group initiative and responsibility?

10. To what extent, and by what means and methods, can the highest degree of traditional "village culture" be preserved, and at the same time, a concern on the part of the villagers be developed for problems and issues which, in the past, have been beyond their social and mental horizons (Taylor).

The knowledge about group and community processes cannot be passed down to others in terms of gadgets, which they can use like material tools. The only common denominators to various and varying types of groups are the social processes of group formation and group functioning. In the use of technical, sociological knowledge, each person, who attempts to catalyze and guide group behaviour, must understand these processes. Elton Mayo, a great production efficiency expert, describes the capacity to apply sociological knowledge as a "social skill". Each director of a programme who works with and through human groups, should possess this skill. He cannot, as is done with scientific material knowledge, depend on engineers. He must himself be a social engineer.

The use of these social skills is needed in all societies, because in no country is it the solution to the problem of preserving community values to let, or help, local communities to revert to their old isolated local community self-sufficiency. The solution is to understand and use the known methods by which people who live and work in small communities can, by organized effort, exercise responsibility for the improvement of every aspect of personal and community living. If encouraged and assisted to do so, local leaders will emerge effective; purposeful regrouping of local residents will occur; and communities will grow rather than stagnate or be completely lost in secular organizations and interests. In this process of working with people, organizing, encouraging and enabling them to participate in their development, their participation occupies a place of pride in rural development.

CONCLUSION

People's participation is a necessary component in rural development. Its essence lies in the proper coordination of individual and group efforts, in fully utilizing the potential of the local institutions, the higher level statutory bodies, the village cooperatives, the village school and other associate organizations such as farmers' forums, youth clubs, women's clubs, and in proper harmonization of individual needs with group needs and group needs with national needs.

REFERENCES

1. Pinto, Gerry, 1982: "People's Participation: The Spurious and Genuine Concern", Social Welfare, New Delhi; Central Social Welfare Board.
2. Setty, Desingu E, 1970: "Community Development and Extension in India", Gandhigram, Gandhigram Rural Institute, pp.7-9.
3. Taylor, Carl C., "Community Mobilization and Group Formation", New Delhi; Ministry of Community Development and Cooperation (n.d.) p.42.
4. World Bank, 1975: "Rural Development Sector Policy Paper", Washington, D.C., World Bank.

APPENDIX

THE STUDY OF A RURAL COMMUNITY : ASPECTS TO BE COVERED

The study of a rural community may be divided into three broad parts:

Part I : The historical background of the community – its physical setting – social composition – socio-economic system – the resources and the ongoing economic and industrial activities.

Part II : Recent development and promotional activities: economic, industrial, social, educational, health, recreational, transport and communication – organizations working with the community – recent changes – direction of change – developmental response from the community – impact of change on the life of the community.

Part III : Harnessable resources – material and human potential and prospects of social and economic development – existing infrastructure, required infrastructure for development – a plan of action for development comprising resources, resource mobilization, programmes that may be implemented in a stipulated time perspective.

1. A Brief History of the Rural Community

- When did the community come into existence?
- Under what circumstances?
- What groups were the earliest inhabitants of the community?

- What groups followed?
- What groups moved away?
- Why? With what effects on the community?
- Can the history of the community be divided into periods? If so, what are the characteristics of each period? What is the influence of each period?
- What are the present trends?
- What are the factors underlying change?
- What are the turning points in the life of the groups?
- Any legends in respect to the rural community?

2. The Physical Setting of the Community

- Its location – boundaries
- Transport and communication facilities and their influence on the community.

3. Social Contacts of the Community

- What contacts does the community maintain with surrounding communities?
- What outside influences are most pronounced?
- What is the degree of influence on the old and young?
- What is the effect of social contacts upon group solidarity? Upon the entire culture of the group?
- To what extent are the outside contacts breaking up the social cohesion of the community?
- What social and personal problems are created by social contacts?

- To what extent do outside contacts enrich the cultural life of the community? To what extent do they bridge or widen social distances?
- To what extent do contacts with the outside world promote personal initiative, ambition, individualization of conduct?
- What are the manifestations of community solidarity? Are there any evidences of over solidarity and exaggerated unity?
- How does community sentiment manifest itself? What is its bearing on the development of social responsibility?
- To what extent does it tend to eliminate pursuits for personal gains?
- What is the bearing of community sentiment on development of "distinct" community types?
- What new contacts has the community made in the past three decades? What are the effects of such contacts?

4. Social Isolation of the Community

- To what extent is the community socially isolated from surrounding communities?
- What are the bases of social isolation: physical barriers, religious, racial, cultural differences, occupational differences, different economic levels, different social levels?
- What is the effect of social isolation on the culture of the group? On its life organization? On the younger generation?
- To what extent does social isolation within the

community result in social conflicts?

- What are the manifestations of differences in the community?
- Do these differences ever threaten to destroy the community? To weaken it?
- Under what circumstances do they tend to support the unity and solidarity of the community?
- Among what classes, groups, generations, and institutions do these differences arise? What course do they run? Do they assume the form of Conflict? Of competition?
- What social problems do these differences tend to create?

5. Demographic Characteristics

- What is the population of the community? Sex-wise? Age-grade-wise? Educational attainment-wise?
- To what races, ethnic and occupational and religious groups do the people of the community belong?
- What groups predominate?
- Which are increasing or decreasing? Why?
- What is the influence of the population composition on the social life of the community? On the economic life?
- What proportion of the people own their homes? What proportion rent?
- What types of dwellings do they occupy? What is the proportion of new buildings?

- What kinds of material are used for building the houses?
- Are there housing problems?
- What is the pattern of village settlement – class, occupational, professional, ethnic, religious?
- What is the level of environmental sanitation?
- What are the sources of water for drinking and domestic purposes?
- Is water adequate?
- What is the significance of the stability of the people?
- Of their migrations? What are the causes and effects of migrations?
- What is the proportion of votes in the community? How do they vote? What are their political affiliations? What is the significance of such affiliations? What problems are created because of such affiliations?
- What religious affiliations do the people in the community maintain? What is the significance of such affiliations?
- What is the role of women and the aged (over 60) in the economy of the community?

6. The Natural Resources that the Community is endowed with the Economic System

- Physical conditions: rainfall, terrain, quality of soil, and enterprises that can be undertaken in the locality
- What are the natural resources that the

community is endowed with? (such as soil, water, agricultural, livestock, forest, horticultural, marine, mineral etc.,)

- Occupational and professional distribution of the population
- The types of production within the community
- The organization of the producing units
- Capital and labour resources
- Land tenure
- Farm organization
- The functioning of the local market-system
- The kind of non-farm activities, business, trade and enterprises that are carried on in the community.
- Human resources: literates, skilled workers, technically qualified people.

7. The Social Structure of the Community

- Social organization of the community
- The family – the kin groups – the ethnic groups
- Inter – group relations : cooperation – conflicts, common interests
- How the community is organized around individual, group and community interests?
- Social/class stratification of the community.

8. Local Social Institutions

- What are the social, economic, political, educational, recreational, religious institutions in the community?

- What is their structure? How are they organized?
- What are their functions?
- How are they inter-related?
- What are the kinds of change taking place in these institutions?
- What are the factors causing such change?

9. The Political Structure of the Community

- What are the patterns of decision – making in the community?
- Which is the dominant group in the community? Why?
- What is the pattern of local leadership? Sources of leadership? Types of leaders? Functions of leaders?
- What kinds of change are taking place in the local leadership?
- What is the role of local leadership in the development of the community?

10. Social and Economic Problems

- What are the social and economic problems of the community?
- Related to:
- Land, irrigation, credit
- Housing
- Health and medical treatment
- Education
- Marketing (buying and selling of goods and services)

- Transport
- Communication
- Indicate instances, if any, how the community has been able to solve some of the problems
- What are the felt-needs of the community?

11. Recent Development Activities in the Community and their Impact on Social and Economic Life

- What are the important development agencies working with and through the community?
- What are the programmes that are being attempted and with what success?
- What are the barriers to change and development in the community?
- What are the strengths of the community – positive factors that would contribute to development?
- What is the role-played by the youth and the women in the development activities?

12. The Potential and Prospects of Development in the Community

- What are the material and human resources that have the potential for development?
- What kind of development is feasible? In what sector-area?
- What kind of infrastructure and support are required to promote/develop the suggested enterprises/activities?
- Indicate plan of action for developing the community in the next five years.

INDEX

Q

R

■■■

AKANSHA
IW: 21/7/08

TRP